Game AI Pro 360

Game AI Pro 360
Guide to Tactics and Strategy

Edited by
Steve Rabin

CRC Press
Taylor & Francis Group
Boca Raton London New York

CRC Press is an imprint of the
Taylor & Francis Group, an **informa** business

CRC Press
Taylor & Francis Group
6000 Broken Sound Parkway NW, Suite 300
Boca Raton, FL 33487-2742

© 2020 by Taylor & Francis Group, LLC
CRC Press is an imprint of Taylor & Francis Group, an Informa business

No claim to original U.S. Government works

Printed on acid-free paper

International Standard Book Number-13: 978-0-367-15088-4 (paperback)
International Standard Book Number-13: 978-0-367-15094-5 (hardback)

Visit the Taylor & Francis Web site at
http://www.taylorandfrancis.com

and the CRC Press Web site at
http://www.crcpress.com

Contents

About the Editor

Steve Rabin has been a key figure in the game AI community for more than a decade and is currently a principal software engineer at Nintendo Technology Development. After initially working as an AI engineer at several Seattle startups, he managed and edited seven game AI books in the "Game AI Pro" series and the "AI Game Programming Wisdom" series. He also edited the book *Introduction to Game Development* and has more than two dozen articles published in the "Game Programming Gems" series. He has been an invited keynote speaker at several AI conferences, founded the AI Game Programmers Guild in 2008, and founded the GDC AI Summit where he has been a summit adviser since 2009. Steve is a principal lecturer at the DigiPen Institute of Technology, Redmond, Washington, where he has taught game AI since 2006. He earned a BS in computer engineering and an MS in computer science, both at the University of Washington, Seattle, Washington.

About the Contributors

Kyle Anderson has written games for everything from cell phones and PCs to low-level hardware controllers for motion-activated exergaming equipment. He is currently interested in all things VR. Kyle is the lead programmer at Shikigami Games.

Nicolas A. Barriga is a PhD candidate at the University of Alberta, Edmonton, Canada. He earned BSc (engineering) and MSc degrees in informatics engineering at Universidad Técnica Federico Santa María, Valparaíso, Chile. After a few years working as a software engineer for Gemini and ALMA astronomical observatories, he came back to graduate school and is currently working on state and action abstraction mechanisms for RTS games.

Daniel Brewer graduated from University of Natal Durban, South Africa, in 2000 with a BSc (engineering) in electronic engineering focusing on artificial intelligence, control systems, and data communications. He worked at Cathexis Technologies for six years, as a software engineer writing software for digital surveillance systems, where he was responsible for operating system drivers for PCI video capture cards, image capture scheduling, video compression, and image processing algorithms such as motion detection, people counting, and visual camera tamper detection. He moved to Digital Extremes in 2007 where he is the lead AI programmer and has worked on several titles including *Dark Sector* (March 2008), *BioShock 2* multiplayer (February 2010), and *The Darkness II* (February 2012), *Halo 4* multiplayer DLC packages (2012), and *Warframe* (2013).

Michael Buro is a professor in the computing science department at the University of Alberta, Edmonton, Canada. He received his PhD in 1994 for his work on *Logistello*—an Othello program that defeated the reigning human World champion 6-0. His current research interests include heuristic search, pathfinding, abstraction, state inference, and opponent modeling applied to video games and card games. In these areas, Michael and his students have made numerous contributions, culminating in developing fast geometric pathfinding algorithms and creating the World's best Skat playing program and one of the strongest *StarCraft: Brood War* bots.

Alex Champandard is the founder of AiGameDev.com, the largest online hub for artificial intelligence in games. He has worked in industry as a senior AI programmer for many years, most notably for Rockstar Games where he also worked on the animation technology of *Max Payne 3*. He regularly consults with leading studios in Europe, most notably at Guerrilla Games on the multiplayer bots for *KillZone 2 & 3*. Alex is also the event director for the Game/AI Conference, the largest independent event dedicated to AI in games.

David Churchill is the lead AI programmer for Lunarch Studios on the online strategy game, *Prismata*. He completed his PhD in computing science at the University of Alberta, Edmonton, Canada, in the area of artificial intelligence for video games, specifically in real-time heuristic search techniques for *StarCraft*. Since 2011, he has been the organizer of the AIIDE *Starcraft* AI Competition, and won the competition in 2013 with his entry UAlbertaBot.

Michael Dawe has been solving AI and gameplay problems in games since 2007, working on games such as *Kingdoms of Amalur: Reckoning, Dance Central Spotlight*, and *Grand Theft Auto 5*. He is a frequent speaker for the AI Summit at the Game Developers Conference, is a founding member of the AI Game Programmers Guild, and has written previously for the Game Programming Gems and Game AI Pro series. Michael holds an MS in computer science from DigiPen Institute of Technology, Redmond, Washington, as well as a BSc in computer science and philosophy from Rensselaer Polytechnic Institute, Troy, New York.

Kevin Dill is a member of the senior technical staff at Lockheed Martin Rotary & Missions Systems and the chief architect of the Game AI Architecture. He is a veteran of the game and military simulation industries with more than 15 years' experience, and has worked on AI for everything from games (including several major hits, such as *Red Dead Redemption, Iron Man*, and *Zoo Tycoon 2*) to military training to emotive avatars. His professional interests include improved techniques for behavior specification, tactical and strategic AI, spatial reasoning, and believable characters. He was the technical editor for *Introduction to Game AI* and *Behavioral Mathematics for Game AI*, and a section editor for "AI Game Programming Wisdom 4" and the "Game AI Pro" series. He is a prolific author and speaker, and has taught at Harvard University, Cambridge, Massachusetts, Boston University, Boston, Massachusetts, and Northeastern University, Boston, Massachusetts.

Matthew Jack founded Moon Collider (www.mooncollider.com) in 2010, where he consults on AI for companies in the US and Europe and builds bespoke AI systems. He specializes in *CryEngine 3* and *Recast/Detour*. He developed AI at Crytek for many years in a senior R&D role, including work on *Crysis* and *Crysis 2*. He has since worked for Microsoft and AiGameDev.com, and consulted for games and serious games companies. Clients include Xaviant LLC and Enodo, with products delivered to companies such as BMW. He has written for *Games Programming Gems* and presented at the GDC, Paris Game AI Conference, Develop and at Google.

Eric Johnson is a senior AI engineer in the Advanced Technology Division of SQUARE ENIX, developing the AI systems for *KINGDOM HEARTS III*. Before joining the industry in 2008, Eric received his master's degree in artificial intelligence from the Georgia Institute of Technology, Atlanta, Georgia, focusing on case-based reasoning for real-time strategy games. In addition to SQUARE ENIX, Eric has developed AI systems at CCP, KIXEYE, and LucasArts.

Kevin A. Kirst has specialized in artificial intelligence in the gaming and simulation industries since 2008. His previous work with companies including Crytek and Ubisoft has blessed him with the opportunity to be credited on two released titles (*Crysis 2* and *Tom Clancy's Splinter Cell: Blacklist*) as well as two unreleased titles. He is a graduate of Full Sail University in Orlando, Florida, The City Beautiful, where he once again resides. His current employment with RealTime Immersive, Inc., a subsidiary of Crytek, allows him the freedom and resources to continue growing, researching, and solving problems concerning AI development in the entertainment gaming, serious gaming, and simulation market spaces. Programming is his love; AI is his passion.

Hylke Kleve (hylke.kleve@guerrilla-games.com) is principal AI programmer at Guerrilla Games, where he has worked on *Killzone 2* and *Killzone 3*. He developed planning and pathfinding technology. Hylke Kleve holds an MS in computer science (2003) from the University of Groningen, the Netherlands.

Mike Lewis entered the game industry as a programmer in early 2002, and has spent most of the intervening years focusing on game AI and surrounding technologies. He has lectured at the Game Developers Conference and published articles in previous volumes of *Game AI Pro*. Currently, Mike calls ArenaNet, LLC, home, where he tirelessly schemes to bring better AI to the world of massively multiplayer online gaming.

Dave Mark is the president and lead designer of Intrinsic Algorithm, an independent game development studio in Omaha, Nebraska. He does consulting on AI, game design, and mathematical modeling for clients ranging from small indie game studios to AAA companies including EA, Sony Online Entertainment, and ArenaNet. Dave is the author of the book *Behavioral Mathematics for Game AI* and is a contributor to the *AI Game Programming Wisdom* and *Game Programming Gems* book series from Charles River Media and the first
Game AI Pro book from CRC Press. He has also spoken at numerous game conferences and universities around the world on the subjects of AI, game theory, and psychology. He is a founding member of the AI Game Programmers Guild and has been a coadvisor of the Game Developers Conference AI Summits. Dave continues to further his education by attending the University of Life. He has no plans to graduate anytime soon.

Robert Morcus is a senior AI developer at Guerrilla Games. There, he has helped build the tools and technology for most titles released by Guerrilla Games: *ShellShock:Nam'67*, *Killzone, Killzone 2*, and *Killzone 3*. His field of interest before starting game development was in electronics and audio synthesis/signal processing.

Sergio Ocio Barriales has been working in the game industry since 2005. He received his PhD in 2010 from the University of Oviedo, Asturias, Spain, with his thesis about hinted-execution behavior trees. He has worked on the AI for numerous major titles, such as *Driver San Francisco, Splinter Cell: Blacklist, DOOM*, and *Watch_Dogs 2*. He joined the team at Hangar 13 as a lead AI engineer in 2016, where he continues pushing character AI forward.

Michael Robbins is a gameplay engineer with Gas Powered Games working on everything from UI to AI. He has been working in the industry since 2009, after being a long time member of the Gas Powered Games modeling community. His most notable work is featured in the AI of *Supreme Commander 2*, released in March 2010.

Gijs-Jan Roelofs is the AI and lead programmer at Goldhawk Interactive where he has, among other projects, worked on the "Xenonauts" series. He is also the founder of CodePoKE, an independent game development company aimed at innovative applications of AI in games that cooperates with the Department of Knowledge Engineering at Maastricht University, Maastricht, the Netherlands. His passion for AI was ignited by Professor Mark Winands and the emergence of MCTS during his time in Maastricht. He is currently working on techniques for procedural generation of narratives, and tactical AI using MCTS.

Marius Stanescu is a PhD candidate at the University of Alberta, Edmonton, Canada. He completed his MSc in artificial intelligence at University of Edinburgh, Edinburgh, the United Kingdom, in 2011, and became a researcher at the Center of Nanosciences for Renewable & Alternative Energy Sources of University of Bucharest, Bucharest, Romania, in 2012. Since 2013, he has been helping organize the AIIDE StarCraft Competition. Marius' main areas of research include machine learning, AI, and RTS games.

Remco Straatman for 10 years led the AI coding team at Guerrilla, and developed AI for *ShellShock:Nam67, Killzone, Killzone:Liberation, Killzone 2*, and *Killzone 3*. Currently, Remco is feature architect and leads a game code team at Guerrilla. Before joining Guerrilla, Remco worked as a researcher in the field of expert systems and machine learning, and as developer of multimedia software. He holds an MS in computer science (1991) from the University of Amsterdam.

Tim Johan Verweij is a senior AI programmer at Guerrilla, Amsterdam, The Netherlands. The past six years he has worked on AI technology and AI behaviors for *Killzone 2* and *Killzone 3*, both first-person shooters for the Playstation 3. He studied AI at VU University, Amsterdam. For his master's thesis he did a research project on multiplayer bot AI at Guerrilla.

Martin Walsh has been in the industry for 10 years. In that time, he worked on *Rainbow Six: Lockdown* and then on *Splinter Cell: Conviction* as AI technical lead. On *Splinter Cell: Conviction*, he created a dynamic navmesh system that became a middleware at Ubisoft (used in titles such as *Assassin's Creed* and *ZombiU*) and was the subject of a Game

Developers Conference (GDC) presentation in 2010. After leading the middleware team, Martin rejoined production to work as AI lead on *Splinter Cell: Blacklist*.

Rich Welsh graduated from Durham University, Durham, United Kingdom, in 2007 and went immediately into the game industry. From humble beginnings at a studio in his hometown of Newcastle, he has gone from strength to strength working on both gameplay and AI for the *Crackdown* and the *Crysis* series of games, as well as being part of the AI system development team for *CRYENGINE*. Presently, he is a senior gameplay programmer working at Ubisoft Massive on *Tom Clancy's The Division*.

Baylor Wetzel has degrees in psychology and computer science and until recently taught artificial intelligence and English at a major university. When not making NPCs behave properly for others, he enjoys designing and writing dialog for his own story-rich indie games. Baylor currently works as a game designer at indie game studio Shikigami Games.

Mieszko Zieliński has worked in the game industry throughout his professional life—that is close to 13 years at the time of writing—most of which focused on game AI. For the past eight years, he has been with Epic Games, with the past five spent on leading the AI system development in Unreal Engine 4. He has recently been micromanaging Paragon bots, which he found a very refreshing activity after the time spent on working for generic AI systems.

Introduction

Steve Rabin's *Game AI Pro 360: Guide to Tactics and Strategy* gathers all the cutting-edge information from his previous three *Game AI Pro* volumes into a convenient single source anthology that covers game AI strategy and tactics.

This volume is complete with articles by leading game AI programmers that focus largely on combat decisions made in wide variety of genres such as RTS, RPG, MOBA, strategy and tower defense games.

This book, as well as each volume in the *Game AI Pro* series, is a testament to the generous community of game AI developers as well as the larger game development community. Everyone involved in this effort believes that sharing information is the single best way to rapidly innovate, grow and develop. Right now, the game AI community is larger than ever and we invite you to discover all the wonderful resources that are available.

In addition to reading about new game AI techniques in the *Game AI Pro* series, there are annual conferences, which are academic and developer-centric, all over the globe. Organized by developers, there is the Game AI summit at GDC in San Francisco each year and the game/AI conference in Europe. Organized by academia, there is the AAAI conference on Artificial Intelligence and Interactive Digital Entertainment (AIIDE) and the IEEE Conference on Computational Intelligence and Games. Outside of events, there are two communities that have also sprung up to help developers. The game AI Programmers Guild is a free professional group with more than 500 worldwide members (www.gameai.com) and there is a wonderful community of hobbyists and professionals at www.AIgameDev.com. We warmly welcome you to come and hang out with us at any one of these conferences or participate in one of the online communities.

Web Materials

Example programs and source code to accompany some of the chapters are available at http://www.gameaipro.com.

General System Requirements

The following is required to compile and execute the example programs:

- The DirectX August 2009 SDK
- DirectX 9.0 compatible or newer graphics card
- Windows 7 or newer
- Visual C++ .NET 2008 or newer

Updates of the example programs and source code will be updated as needed.

Tactical Position Selection

An Architecture and Query Language

Matthew Jack

1.1 Introduction

Agent movement is arguably the most visible aspect of AI in any game, and this is particularly true of shooters. Choosing between positions—and generating those positions to consider in the first place—is critical to the success of these games. Not only is it key to an agent's effectiveness in combat, but it also visibly communicates his role and status in that combat. More generally in games, an agent's movement helps define his personality and often much of the core gameplay.

In this article, we describe a complete architecture for choosing movement positions as part of sophisticated AI behavior. We outline a query language for specifying those positions, consider how position selection integrates with our behaviors, and give some specific building blocks and best practices that will allow us to develop queries quickly and to the best effect. Performance is given special attention, both to ensure our results reach the final game and to allow us to employ more powerful query criteria. We also discuss techniques for handling group movement behavior and the tools required for effective development.

Techniques developed for the Tactical Position Selection (TPS) system, a CryEngine component used in *Crysis 2* and other upcoming titles, provide the core of this chapter [Crytek 11]. We supplement this with a number of approaches seen in other games, as well as promising directions for future work.

1.2 Motivation

Any system used for choosing movement locations faces design pressures from many directions. It must be flexible and expressive, as it will define the movement possible for our agents. It must be capable of rapid, iterative development, and it must include powerful tools, as these will limit the quality of our final behaviors. Finally, since it is used frequently and in reaction to the player, it must be a fast and efficient workhorse, delivering results within a few frames while always remaining within CPU budgets.

The core problem of tactical position selection comes down to the question that designers will ask you when they are working with your behaviors: "Why did he move here, when it's just common sense that he should move there instead?" It's a question you should be asking yourself as you test your AI, because it's the question that players will ask themselves too.

Modeling that "common sense" is what makes this such a tough problem. Indeed, many shooters decide to use triggers and scripting to orchestrate the movements of their AI, leaving it to designers to provide that human judgment in each and every case—and this can be highly effective. However, this is a time-consuming process not suited to all development cycles, inherently limited to linear gameplay, and unsuitable for open sandbox games.

With the right abstractions and efficient processing, we can describe that human intuition for the range of contexts that our agent will encounter, and strike a powerful balance between specification and improvisation. In the process, we greatly speed up our behavior prototyping and development and gain a versatile tool for a wide range of gameplay applications.

1.3 Fundamentals

At their core, systems of this kind typically take a utility-based approach [Mark 09, Graham 13], evaluating the fitness of a set of points with respect to the requirements of a particular agent in order to identify the best candidate. Sources for these points are discussed in the Generation section, but they may be placed by designers, generated automatically, or some combination of the two. Usually we will collect or generate points within a specified radius of our agent's current position before beginning evaluation.

Evaluation will first filter out unsuitable points based on criteria such as the minimum distance from a threat and the direction(s) from which they provide cover. It will then score the remaining points based on desirability criteria such as how close they are to a goal point or how exposed they are to a number of threats.

We then choose the highest-scoring valid point as the result and use this as a movement target for our agent. By combining various criteria in different ways and weighting their effect on the score, we can produce effective queries for different agent types, environments, and behaviors. We can also use the same system for other applications, such as targets to shoot at or spawn locations. Good examples of tactical position selection have been given in previous work [Sterren 01, Straatman et al. 06] and in this book [Zielinski 13].

1.4 Architecture

Our tactical position selection system comprises a number of subsystems, and it must also integrate with the rest of the AI framework. Figure 1.1 shows the overall structure of the architecture.

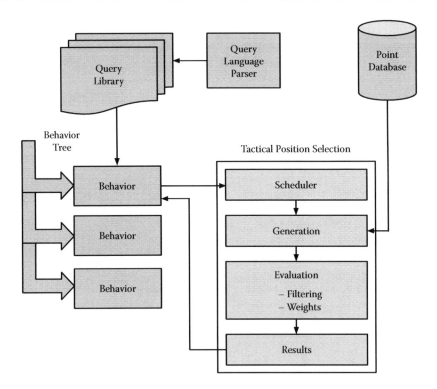

Figure 1.1

An architecture for tactical position selection.

The specification of individual queries can be thought of as the first step in the process of position selection, and a powerful *specification language* forms the first component in our architecture. We use this to build a *library* of context-specific queries to express each of our agent's behaviors in each of the environments it will encounter.

We employ a high-level AI framework, such as a behavior tree or finite-state machine, to provide the current *context*, which is the combination of the agent's current behavior and its current environment. We then use the context to select the appropriate query from the library. Should a query fail to find a valid location, this can serve as an input to the high-level framework, allowing it to respond should circumstances change.

We use a *database* of points, which may be manually placed or procedurally generated, to form the main input data for the evaluation process. A *scheduler* will often be required to help manage asynchronous queries and to amortize their cost.

Evaluation itself begins with *generation*, where points are collected from the database or generated on the fly, as required by the query specification, to form the set of candidate points for each query. We then *filter* those candidates with conditions, and apply *weights* to those that remain, as described above. In practice these two tasks may be interleaved for more efficient evaluation and spread over multiple frames by the scheduler. Finally, the full *results* of that evaluation may be displayed in the world graphically and summarized in the log for debugging before being reduced to the one or more points required by the query. In addition, each of these stages may be monitored by profiling systems.

1.4.1 A Query Specification Language

Expressing common-sense spatial reasoning is not something C++ or any common scripting language was designed for. The case for Domain-Specific Languages (DSLs) has been eloquently argued at the Game Developer's Conference [Evans 11] and here a powerful means of expression allows us to focus on the intrinsic problem and achieve rapid iteration. The key attributes of a successful query language for position selection are:

- *Abstraction*—We gain a lot of power if we can reapply existing criteria (keywords) in new ways.
- *Readability*—The intent of a query should be understood as easily as possible by developers.
- *Extensibility*—It should be easy to add new criteria to the language.
- *Efficiency*—The language itself should not add overhead to the evaluation process.

Many DSLs are built on top of existing languages. When developing the query language for tactical position selection within Crytek, we exploited Lua tables to provide the basic structure, but then parsed the content into a bytecode-like format so that no Lua was used by the system at runtime. The following is a simple example in that syntax.

Listing 1.1 shows a query that is made up of two subqueries, called "options." The first option is preferred but, should it fail, subsequent options will be tried in the order that they are specified before failure is reported. In this example, the first option will collect hidespots effective against the current attack target within a radius of 15 m around the agent, discarding any that are less than 5 m from the agent and discard any point closer to the attack target than the agent himself. Of the points that remain, it will prefer any hard cover that is available to any soft cover and prefer the closest point. The second option

---

Listing 1.1. A simple example in the Crytek query language syntax.

```
Query_CoverCompromised_FindNearby =
{-- Chiefly for use when our current spot has been compromised
    {    -- Option 1
        -- Find hidespot from our target a short distance from us
        Generation = {hidespots_from_target_around_puppet = 15},
        Conditions = {min_distance_from_puppet = 5,
                        canReachBefore_the_target = true},
        Weights = {softCover = -10, distance_from_puppet = -1.0},
    },
    {    -- Option 2 (fallback)
        -- Move away from target, taking a position in the open
        -- but preferring any that blocks line-of-sight
        Generation = {grid_around_puppet = 10},
        Conditions = {min_distance_from_puppet = 5,
                        max_directness_from_target = 0.1},
        Weights =   {visible_from_target = -10,
                        distance_from_puppet = -1.0}
    }
}
```

(the fallback) generates a grid of points to move sideways or away from the target and prefers to block Line-of-Sight (LOS). Both options share the goal of moving to a new, safe location at least 5 m away. Thus, this query might be used in reaction to a grenade landing at the agent's feet.

The Generation section of each option specifies the source of our candidate points. The Conditions section contains the filters that should be applied during evaluation, which must all pass if a point is to be valid. The Weights section tells the AI how to score the fitness of those valid points.

Each line in those sections is a Lua table entry comprising a string and a value. The string, in the syntax of our DSL, is formed from a sequence of keywords joined by underscores, which is trivially parsed back into the keywords themselves. Usually the most important keyword comes first—for example, `hidespots` or `distance`—and specifies the evaluation or generation method that we are going to apply. This can be referred to as the *criterion*.

Criteria often take an object, which allows the same method to be applied in different ways. For example, rather than having a `distanceFromTarget` keyword, we allow the same keyword to be used with many different objects, such as `puppet` (the requesting agent), `referencePoint` (general-purpose position), `player` (in single-player contexts), `leader` etc., and in particular `target` (the agent we are attacking if any). Objects are key to turning a set of parameters into a versatile query language. Some criteria do not take any objects—e.g., `softCover`, which is simply a property of the point.

The `min` and `max` keywords may prefix a criterion string, such as `distance`, that represents a float value. This changes the way the criterion is applied and also where it is used. Without the `min` or `max` keyword, it would simply be applied as a weight, but with these keywords we instead produce a Boolean result, depending on whether the actual value is above or below the specified limit. This allows us to use the same criteria in either the Weights or the Conditions section, as needed. In the example above, for instance, `min_distance_from_puppet = 5` is used to specify that points must be at least 5 m from the requesting agent.

There is also a set of "glue" keywords such as `from`, `to`, `at`, and `the`, which must be put between the criterion and its object, serving only to produce a more human-readable sentence—such as `distance_from_puppet`. The user is free to pick the word that forms the most natural expression in each case; the glue word is simply discarded during parsing.

Each keyword is registered with type markers as to where it can be employed. This allows us to detect and reject invalid queries during the parsing process, and to provide useful debug output.

While Lua was the most natural choice in the Crytek codebase, JSON, XML, or a simple custom format would also be reasonable vehicles for this kind of language. Queries can, of course, be changed while the game is running, in this case by editing and reloading the appropriate script files. A similar language has been implemented with a Kismet-style graphical interface under *Unreal 3* [Zielinski 13].

Documentation of the Crytek TPS system can be found online [Crytek 11] and it is available for use in the *CryEngine Free SDK* [Crytek 12]. Should you try any queries from the article, note that the common keyword `target` is shortened here; the correct keyword is `attentionTarget`.

1.4.2 Contexts and Query Library

As we discussed in the Motivation section, our agents face a complex and dynamic world, and players expect the agents to consistently make judgments similar to the ones that they themselves would make. One approach to achieving believable, reactive movement behavior across the range of environments in our game is to build a very complex "über-query." However, the problem becomes much more tractable if we break it down into bite-size chunks, each consisting of a specific behavior (such as flanking, retreating, or providing covering fire) that we wish to perform in a specific environment (such as a dense forest or a postapocalyptic New York street). We refer to each combination of behavior and environment as a context, and we can form a library of such queries.

It is much easier to describe exactly where to move if we make assumptions about our environment. For example, while we might be able to tweak a query until it allows us to advance effectively both between trees in a dense forest and from car to car in a city street, if we consider them separately, then our separate queries become much simpler. In fact, with the right criteria available, query construction becomes very predictable to the developer, and with some thought good results can be achieved without spending a lot of time tuning the queries. We discuss this further in the Best Practices and Specific Criteria section.

1.4.3 Integrating with Behavior Selection

To make use of a library of queries specific to context—the combination of behavior and environment—we must be able to choose the appropriate context at any given time. This can be achieved by viewing each behavior as having a core movement query and incorporating the current environment type as part of our behavior selection framework. This maps well onto a "first-generation" behavior tree, such as that used at Crytek [Martins 11], consisting essentially of a decision tree with behaviors as the leaves; different environments can form branches of the tree. Alternatively, the same behavior might use different queries in different environments; which is best will depend how much behavior is shared between environments. In *Bulletstorm*, a FPS game from People Can Fly, a similar system was used with a more sophisticated behavior tree [Zielinksi 13], and it could also be done with other architectures.

Basic knowledge of our current environment can be based on simple high-level cues, such as a per-level setting, or designer volumes or triggers. However, the behavior selection framework can also receive feedback from the queries we run and use this both to guide the selection of behavior and to inform us reactively about our environment. This feedback takes the form of failed queries—queries that return no valid results—which can occur for a couple of different reasons.

One way failure could occur is that we have designed our query for a common case, and this is an unusual example. For instance, our behavior and thus our queries might be designed for a dense forest, but obstacles or a path could mean there are very few trees in the local area. This might be a level design problem, but we may choose to provide a fallback for such cases—a second "option" in the query.

The fallback might often relax the filters and/or extend the query radius, especially if we used that smaller radius simply for performance reasons. It might also use different generation criteria: perhaps generating some points without cover around us and looking for one that at least has blocked line-of-sight to our target. The fallback essentially hides the failure from behavior selection and lowers our quality bar on this occasion, to get us smoothly past this tricky spot.

However, there is a more informative case: our context isn't as we thought, and what we are trying to do is wrong for this situation. If we have designed our query correctly, it has not simply ranked all the points in order of preference, but also eliminated all the points that were not appropriate. If, for example, we are flanking left around a target in a forest, failure indicates that there is no suitable location to our left—we have run out of cover or our way is blocked. We can acknowledge this—for instance, by flagging this state in our blackboard—in order to choose a different behavior or indeed, in a squad context, to inform allies that a group action may have to be aborted. In the Crytek system, a query specification can include a specific signal to send or blackboard state to set in the event of failure.

1.4.4 Forming a Database of Input Points

Most games will form a static database of hidespots for consideration, and these form a mainstay of the candidate points for evaluation. These may have been placed by designers—for instance, the oriented "hide anchors" of *Far Cry* and *Crysis*, which indicated a position for the point as well as having a directional cone from which cover was provided. They may be automatically embedded in certain objects, such as trees; manually embedded in static or dynamic objects, such as vehicles; or generated automatically around complex objects. All of these have been combined in Crytek titles—with *Crysis 2* introducing automatic generation based on designer hints [Martins 11]. Notably, *Killzone 3* pregenerated its hidespots with an automatic process [Mononen 11], while *Brink* had no such static database and relied entirely on dynamically generated points [Nelson 11].

In general, such a database allows more time to be put into offline processing or designer work and provides a cheap resource of reliable points as input to a TPS system. Of course, the database can contain other types of positions in addition to (or instead of) hiding locations. Locations representing choke points, doorways, sniper spots, vantage points, respawn points, etc. may also be used as candidates, using specific criteria to generate a particular type or to distinguish between them. This represents a rich source of designer hints about the environment.

1.4.5 Collection and Generation

The first part of evaluating any query is to form a set of candidate points, whether by collecting them from a database or generating them at runtime. Typically, our primary source is to collect them from the static database described above, using a criterion such as that in our example:

```
Generation = {hidespots_from_target_around_puppet = 15}
```

This finds hidespots from a target and illustrates three parameters that are key to this phase: the center of the query—here, the `puppet` object, the agent itself; a radius for collection/generation—15 m; and an object, which for this criterion represents the primary target from which we wish to hide—in this case, the `target` object.

The best basis for an efficient query is to generate points in the specific location or locations we're actually interested in and within as small a distance as possible; the choice of center and radius should be made with this in mind. Centering on the requesting agent is not always the best choice: for instance, when entering close combat we might center it on our target or the center of our squad (as we will discuss in the Group Techniques section). A common technique for designer control is to restrict agent movement to an area—for example, to defend, patrol, or advance upon. We can provide generation criteria for this based on an associated point or polygon, rather than relying upon conditions.

If we provide a primary hide-target (in this case `target`, the current attack target), this enables a range of powerful and efficient generation criteria. In *Far Cry* and *Crysis*, hide-spots around trees were neatly handled by generating a hidespot on the opposite side from the hide-target. These omnidirectional hidespots are also useful in that they were refreshed on each hide request, moving an agent around the obstacles as its hide-target moved. The hide-target also allows us to use directional hidespots effectively—immediately rejecting cover points that are not correctly oriented for this hide-target using a dot-product test.

As well as collecting from our database, we may generate points on demand—for example, as we do in our fallback option in the query above:

```
Generation = {grid_around_puppet = 10}
```

In this case, we generate the candidate positions in a 10 m square grid around the agent. These arbitrary points can then be analyzed for their potential as cover or other properties. For example, if there is no explicit cover nearby, we may still try to block line-of-sight to our target; we may simply want to escape an overriding threat, such as a grenade, or specifically to move out into the open.

Brink generated points in concentric rings to find all of its cover dynamically [Nelson 11]. We could simulate something similar with a query such as the following (which would find the nearest point to the agent which blocks LOS to the target):

```
Generation = {circles_around_puppet = 10},
Conditions = {visible_from_target = false},
Weights =    {distance_from_puppet = -1.0},
```

Cover rails, as used in *Crysis 2*, are a relatively recent development that avoids representing cover as discrete points and instead stores a path, anywhere along which an agent may take cover or move in cover. On demand, we generate locations on the rail for tactical position selection. This allows us to, for instance, generate at least one location at the closest point on the rail to the agent or to generate locations at an optimal spacing from other agents using the rail.

Given the benefits of these different kinds of points, the role of this phase is to collect or generate relevant candidates from all these possible sources and to present them in a uniform manner to the rest of the process. While explicit hidespots may come with properties such as flags for high or low cover, cover quality or direction, grid points will have none of these, but ideally we will otherwise be able to treat them just the same in our conditions and weights.

1.4.6 Filters

Filters (or conditions) are criteria that will check the validity of a point and may then reject it. We can think of them as logically forming a second phase of the process, but in practice it can make sense to interleave them with weights for performance reasons (as we will discuss in the Performance section).

Filters may simply be a property of a point, such as whether it provides high or low cover, soft cover, or hard. They may also involve some kind of evaluation against an object or position, such as raycasts to check whether, from relevant firing stances, we would be able to shoot our target. We can require these criteria to be either true or false—it can be useful, for instance, to find points that are visible from a target or to find those that are not.

When points have been generated from multiple sources, some filters may not make sense on some points. For instance, the condition `providesHighCover` simply looks up a Boolean flag in a collected hidespot, while a point generated in the open has no concept of direct cover at all. The Crytek system handles this by criteria returning the value that makes the most intuitive sense—for instance, a non-cover point returning false for `providesHighCover`—but a system might also be structured to skip over criteria that are irrelevant to a given point.

1.4.7 Weights

Weights are criteria that make a contribution to the score of a point. In most such systems the value returned by the evaluation itself is multiplied by a user-defined weight, allowing the contribution to be balanced against other weights. In the Crytek system, the values returned by all such criteria are first normalized to the 0–1 range, which makes balancing more intuitive. The user-specified weights we multiply those values by are over any range and can be either positive or negative. The results are summed and the best point is that with the highest, or least negative, score.

Most commonly, criteria that return a continuous value, for instance representing distance, will be used as weights but Boolean criteria may also be employed, returning simply 0 or 1. This allows us to give a fixed advantage or disadvantage to points in an easily balanced manner, for instance based on high or low cover.

Many weights are based on distances, and here clamping to known limits makes an enormous difference to the ease of specifying a query. If we simply return the raw distance, say, from a goal point or the closest enemy, then the maximum value is simply unknown, and while we may tweak for a common case of, say, 0–20 meters, when less common cases occur, our scores may be quite unbalanced. We can avoid this problem by choosing an appropriate maximum useful range for our game—say, 30 meters—and clamping to this, normalizing all distance criteria within that range. This means that we can then confidently predict the range of values when choosing our multiplier and comparing those to the expected effect of other weights in the query.

To achieve this, each criterion that returns a continuous value has declared limits for its output, so that when used as weights all such criteria are normalized in output to the [0–1] range. This also facilitates some of the optimizations we will discuss in the Performance section. When `min` or `max` are applied to make it a condition, we do not apply these limits; instead, we use the original, unnormalized value.

1.4.8 Returning Results

We have considered our context and chosen the relevant query, generated the appropriate candidate points for that query, applied conditions to filter them down to those that are acceptable, and evaluated their weights to score their fitness. We can now take the top points and return them as the result of the query.

In the ideal case, we are only interested in one point: the point that our agent will now move to. However, there can be good reasons to return multiple results, such as to help with hidespot contention, as we will discuss later. In general we should not need to return a set of points for a subsequent system to choose between; if our API or query language is flexible enough, we should be able to do this within our system. Further, each point returned forces us to fully evaluate its criteria and lose the potential optimizations that we will discuss in the Performance section.

We can widen the applicability of the system by returning more than just a position vector. For example, we might return the type of point (i.e., cover point, point generated in the open, etc.), and any type-specific metadata. If the point is a hidespot from a database, we can specify this and give its unique ID, useful when marking the hidespot as occupied. In the Crytek system, points can be generated at the position of all entities of a specific type, and with these we return the original entity ID. Regarding results as objects in the world, rather than just points, allows us to consider reusing the architecture for a host of other AI and gameplay applications: from choosing which of our squad mates to signal for assistance, to prioritizing between opponents in target selection, to finding nearby objects to interact with.

1.5 Best Practices and Specific Criteria

For great results from your tactical positioning system, you don't just need a good architecture, you also need powerful criteria that fit the task at hand, and you need to use those criteria effectively. Here, we discuss some criteria and approaches that have proven effective in the development of games at Crytek or elsewhere.

1.5.1 Weights and Balancing

Queries can be built by using a large number of weights and tweaking and tuning them until your desired results are seen. However, more rapid and robust development can be achieved by preferring to use criteria as conditions rather than weights, by making use of fallbacks, and by further breaking down our queries to be more context-specific.

For example: when we want to flank left, rather than weighting all points according to "leftness," just invalidate any point that is not left of your current position; rather than tweaking a tradeoff between hard/soft cover and distance, write an option that only considers hard cover, then a fallback that only considers soft.

Keeping the number of weights down—ideally to one or two—results in queries with predictable results for given contexts and saves a lot of tuning time.

Effective criteria will also help you keep your queries simple—we examine some examples now.

1.5.2 Directness

When approaching a goal, an obvious basis for our query would be a weight based on inverse distance to the goal:

```
Weights = {distance_from_referencePoint = -1.0}
```

However, in many cases we do not wish to reach the goal directly, but to approach it in a series of hops—for example, ducking from cover to cover along the way. When this is the case, pure distance to the goal quickly becomes hard to work with and to balance other weights against. It is encouraging us to get as close to the goal as possible, when what we're really looking for is a succession of carefully selected waypoints. In other words, what we really need is a measure of progress towards the goal, with distances to be specified separately.

Directness is a measure of how much closer a point will get us to a goal for the distance traveled.

$$directness = \frac{\text{distance from agent to goal} - \text{distance from point to goal}}{\text{distance from agent to point}} \qquad (1.1)$$

Using Equation 1.1, if we are 50 m from our goal, a point that is 10 m away from us and 45 m from the goal will score 0.5 on directness. This measure is very predictable: the closer to a straight line to our goal, the higher the score, regardless of distance. We can ignore distance and simply request the point closest to a straight line to the goal:

```
Weights = {directness_to_referencePoint = 1.0}
```

Even simpler, rather than using it as a weight, we can make it a condition by specifying that it should just be positive, so we will always make progress towards our goal, however small, or that it should be at least 0.5, so that for every 10 m we move, we will get at least 5 m closer to our target. These are easy to reason about and orthogonal to other criteria we might introduce, so we can apply it to existing queries without long sessions of retweaking.

```
Conditions = {min_directness_to_referencePoint = 0.5}
```

Further, this simple measure of directness actually offers a lot of power beyond goal-seeking. We can, of course, retreat from a goal in the same way by using a negative weight or requiring a negative directness:

```
Conditions = {max_directness_to_referencePoint = -0.5}
```

However, we can also get quite different behavior from the same criterion. By making a condition that the weight must fall in a set range around zero—for instance [–0.1, 0.1]—we specify locations where, by moving to them, we will have made no real progress towards or away from the target. This is a great basis for flanking, which we might specify as the following (note that this query does not imply any particular direction—which we can easily add):

```
Generation = {hidespots_from_target_around_puppet = 15},
Conditions = {min_directness_to_target = -0.1,
              max_directness_to_target = 0.1},
Weights =    {distance_from_puppet = -1.0}
```

Directness can also bring out zigzagging. In one case, core to gameplay on a Crytek project, designers desired agents to approach the player rapidly through forests, dashing from cover to cover, often without stopping. If they approached directly, their movements would be very predictable and offer too easy a target. Here, we can specify directness both as conditions with a maximum value and as a negative weight:

```
Generation = {hidespots_from_target_around_puppet = 15},
Conditions = {min_directness_to_target = 0.5},
Weights =    {directness_to_target = -1.0}
```

Thus we take a route that is as indirect as it can be, while always making minimum progress of 1 m towards the player for every 2 m traveled, with irregularly placed trees and player movement providing a "random" factor. The result is zigzagging movement converging rapidly on the player.

1.5.3 CanReachBefore

If an agent runs towards a hidespot only to have an opponent occupy it before him, it can hurt us twice: first by the agent appearing to lack any anticipation of his opponent, and second by leaving him stranded in the open and abruptly changing direction towards other cover.

This is easy to prevent with a couple of provisions. The simplest is to focus on our current primary opponent and discard any point closer to our enemy than to us, effectively assuming that both agents will move with the same speed. We can implement this as a simple condition, such as:

```
Conditions = {canReachBefore_the_target = true}
```

This rule of thumb is so pervasive to good behavior that in the *Crysis 1* hiding system it was not optional; you might make it a default in all queries.

This focuses on just one opponent. *Far Cry* and *Crysis* also exploited perfect knowledge of which hidespots all agents are moving towards, never picking a hidespot that another agent had already claimed. Here prominent visual debugging is advised, since queries from one behavior or agent will have non-obvious interactions with others.

1.5.4 CurrentHidepoint

Often, it can be useful to generate just the point that we have already chosen, either to adjust it or to verify that it is still good enough.

Sometimes the exact position of a point will be determined on demand—for instance, the hidespots for trees in *Crysis*, mentioned earlier, that would always be generated on the opposite side from the hide-target. If we are using cover rails, we might just want to adjust our position on the rail, to reflect the movement of our target or to maintain separation from a nearby squadmate who is sharing the rail.

Once we have started to move towards a point, we usually want to show a certain amount of inertia behind that decision: changing direction if it becomes slightly less desirable, or, as a slightly better spot becomes available, will often look artificial to players. However, if circumstances change considerably—perhaps as a grenade lands or an enemy movement leaves a position clearly exposed—we do need to react.

Hence, once we have chosen a point, we can periodically check it with a simplified query that generates just that single point, where weights are irrelevant and just the critical conditions are employed—making it cheaper, simpler, and more tolerant than the original query. This query is verifying that the point is still "good enough." When this does fail, we may fall back to the full version of the query to pick a new point with the same criteria, or go back to our behavior tree to reevaluate our context. Should the situation change dramatically—for instance, due to the presence of a grenade—we rely upon the behavior tree to switch us to a different behavior and thus a different query.

Bulletstorm used a similar validation of chosen hidespots, but implemented it as a specific type of criteria within a single query, rather than separate versions [Zielinksi 13].

1.6 Group Techniques

So far we have discussed individual agents making the best decisions about their own movement. When we start to consider agents as members of groups or squads, or indeed companions, then new criteria can help us build their behaviors while coping with this added complexity.

1.6.1 Spatial Coherency—A Squad Center

In considering a squad, our most fundamental property is spatial coherency—that is, keeping the squad together. We can do this by defining a center for the squad—for instance, its current average position—so that each member's queries can specify they should stay close to that point. We can implement this by reapplying our existing criteria with a new object, squadCenter.

Perhaps the most obvious approach is to weight our queries to prefer points inversely proportional to their distance from the center.

```
Weights = {distance_to_squadCenter = -1.0}
```

This is very useful when our squad needs to converge (perhaps reacting to being surrounded) or, conversely, to spread out (perhaps under threat of mortars). However, as a building block, it has the problem of being a weight that must be balanced against any others in our query. Coherency is not a behavior in itself, but a property of all the other behaviors we would like to show—hence, ideally we would specify this in a manner orthogonal to other criteria.

A simple way to achieve that is to simply limit the maximum distance. Our members are then entirely free to move within that radius of the squad center, which will travel with the squad as its members progress [Champandard et al. 11]. Note that we can achieve this very efficiently by centering our collection/generation on the squad center and setting the radius appropriately.

```
Generation = {hidespots_from_target_around_squadCenter = 10}
```

The results have some very nice properties. If some of our squad is trailing behind while moving towards a goal—for instance due to a scattered starting configuration or some members taking long paths around obstacles—then those at the front will find their queries return no new valid points, as the only ones that progress towards the goal are outside of range of the squad center. In this case they should handle this "failure" by waiting, until those at the rear catch up and the squad center moves forward. This gives rise to a loose leapfrogging behavior without any explicit consideration of the relative position of squad members.

Here, we generally assume that the goal we are progressing towards is a common one across the squad—and by choosing that goal's location appropriately we can present that as the squad advancing or retreating, or even give designers direct control of the goal, allowing them to direct the squad according to scripted events.

However, individuals can also choose a completely different behavior and move independently for a time without disrupting the group. If, for example, an individual is avoiding a grenade, or collecting nearby ammo, he may well ignore the group coherency criteria in that query. While he may appear to leave the group, he still contributes to the squad center and so they will not proceed too far without him, allowing him to catch back up.

1.6.2 Hidespot Contention

Whenever we operate within a group while maintaining spatial cohesion, there will be more contention for available hidespots. This can present both behavioral and architectural problems.

Whenever individuals are responsible for the choice of location, they can only optimize choices, given their own preference and the points currently available. Hence, the rifleman who occupies the ideal location for a grenadier, or the agent who takes the nearest available cover for himself, leaving his squadmate to run awkwardly around him to reach any at all.

This can be resolved by performing queries at the squad level rather than the individual level, maintaining a central set of points that are assigned to squad members with the whole squad in mind. This approach was used effectively for the group behaviors in *Crysis*. However, this can lead to tightly coupled behaviors that are hard to extend.

There is also the problem that if we have queries in progress on multiple agents at the same time—for instance, running in parallel on multiple threads—they may both try to take the same point, which we must somehow resolve. One way to do this is to return multiple results for each query, so there are other points to fall back to. As we will note in the Performance section, returning the full list of results would mean we cannot take advantage of some important optimizations—but one or two extra results will usually be sufficient and can be generated with only an incremental increase to the cost of the query.

1.6.3 Companions and Squadmates

An NPC designed to interact closely with the player is one of the biggest challenges in game AI. When the NPC shares movement locations such as hidespots with the player, their movement choices must become like cogs in a machine, meshing closely with the unpredictable movements of the player if we are to avoid a painful clash of gears.

In first-person and third-person games, the problem is especially acute as we face the conflicting demands of remaining in the player's field of view to keep her aware of our movements and activity, while trying to avoid getting in the way or stealing a location from the player; in shooters, we also have to keep out of the player's Line-of-Fire (LOF) ... the list goes on. There are some specific criteria that can help us in finding solutions:

`cameraCenter` returns a value indicating where this point is in the players' view frustum. It interpolates from 1 for the dead center to 0 at the edges and negative values off-screen, allowing us the control to specify positions towards the edge of our view or just off-screen. Variations on this can specifically prefer positions to the left or right.

`crossesLineOfFire` takes an object to specify whose LOF to consider, usually the local player. Our implementation uses a simple 2D line intersection test, comparing the line from the specified object to the candidate position against the forward vector of the player, although more complex implementations are certainly possible.

Using these two criteria we can form a simple squadmate query:

```
Generation = {hidespots_from_target_around_player = 15},
Conditions = {crossesLineOfFire_from_player = false
              min_cameraCenter = 0},
Weights =    {distance_from_player = -1.0,
              cameraCenter = -1.0}
```

This query is for a context where we already have a target we are attacking and try to find a cover point from that target, insisting that it must not cross the player's LOF to get there and that it must be on-screen, but as close to the edge of the player's view as possible and balancing that against staying as close to the player as possible.

Of course, this is just a starting point in a long process of design and development. For instance, the player's view changes constantly as he looks around and our companions should not run back and forth to remain in view; nor does the player's forward vector at any given moment always represent his likely line-of-fire. We can begin to address these by averaging these vectors over time, by considering a "golden path" representing likely movement flow through the level and by considering the targets the player is likely to fire at.

As we try these new ideas, we can add them as new criteria, exploiting the rapid prototyping capabilities of our query system to help us try out all their permutations quickly and effectively.

1.7 Performance

In developing a system of this kind, work on its performance must go hand-in-hand with the expansion of its capabilities and its use. The more efficient the system and the more sophisticated its handling of expensive criteria, the more freely we will be able to use the system and the more powerful criteria we will be able to add to our toolset. Tactical position selection is one of the most productive uses to which we may put our AI cycles, but unless we have performance under control, our ideas will not make it into a shipped product. Here, we discuss ways to reduce and manage the cost of our queries.

1.7.1 Collection and Generation Costs

When collecting points from your database, an efficient lookup structure designed for cache coherency is essential on consoles. Without this, it is quite possible for the cost of collecting the points to exceed the cost of their evaluation. Crytek games have used various schemes for storing points and hidespots, including storing them in the navigation graph, using spatial hashes, and separating them by type. We could also maintain only the set of points relevant to this section of the game, swapping them out as we might an unused part of the navigation graph.

In generating points dynamically or verifying the cover of collected points, prefer to generate the candidates as cheaply as possible and defer any expensive tests—for instance, for occlusion from a target, for later in the evaluation process where we may be able to avoid their cost altogether.

1.7.2 Minimizing Raycasts

Raycasts are commonly used for a host of purposes, including establishing that you are hidden from a particular target, or establishing whether you could shoot at a particular target using a particular stance. In many games, they are the dominant cost of position selection or of the whole AI system, and as such deserve special consideration.

A physics raycast operation is always expensive and will generally traverse a large number of memory locations. Should it be performed synchronously, this will be painful in terms of cache misses, cache trashing, and possibly synchronization costs with any physics thread; on consoles this is quite prohibitive. Asynchronous operations allow batching and smooth offloading of the work to other cores such as PS3's SPUs. TPS systems thus should prefer an asynchronous API, even if only for the efficient handling of raycast-based criteria.

We may be able to form points in our database such that we can assume occlusion from some directions and avoid raycasts completely. In a static environment we can use a very simple approach of implied direction for every hidespot, such as the "hide anchors" in *Crysis*. We can then simply test if a target falls within a cone from the hidespot's direction. In a dynamic environment we may also need to periodically check that the cover object is still valid. Taking this a step further, *Crysis 2*'s cover generation system actually maps the silhouette of associated cover objects and is able to remap them upon destruction [Martins 11]. This allows us to test occlusion from a point against this nearby geometry without raycasts.

When minimizing an agent's exposure from multiple targets we will need to be able to consider cover from a number of angles and also consider what other geometry might be blocking line-of-sight, which means that we are likely to require raycasts. However, in many games such attention to exposure is not required, and in many contexts, in terms of believability, digital acting, and gameplay, it can be more effective to focus on hiding well from the single opponent we are actively engaged with, rather than attempting to hide from several.

One source of raycasts that is very hard to avoid is those which verify we can shoot at the target effectively from a location, usually by aiming over or around our cover geometry. After all, when we request a place to hide, what we usually really mean is a firing position with cover; we must verify that we can shoot at, or near, our target if gameplay is going to be interesting.

We need our system to handle the raycasts that we must perform as efficiently as possible. This means that we should leave raycast-based conditions until late in the position selection process, so that other conditions will screen out as many candidates as possible. We should also limit the number of raycasts that we initiate per frame, so as to avoid spikes, and allow the raycasts to run asynchronously. In many systems, raycast tests are treated specially for this reason—and this may be sufficient for your needs. In the Crytek system and in this discussion, we treat them as one example of a range of expensive and/or asynchronous operations we would like to support in our criteria.

1.7.3 Evaluation Order

The simplest thing we can do that will make a big difference to performance in general is to pay attention to the order we evaluate our criteria. The rule of thumb for evaluation order is:

- *Cheap filters first,* to discard points early
- *Weights,* to allow us to sort into order
- *Expensive filters,* evaluating from highest scoring down, until a point passes

It is reasonable to class many criteria as simply "cheap," because a great many criteria consist of simple Boolean or floating-point operations, with cache misses on data likely the dominant cost. These filters should be run first, as they can be used to quickly eliminate candidates, thus avoiding more expensive criteria. A few criteria, on the other hand, may be many orders of magnitude more costly (such as raycasts). We should defer these tests as long as possible, so as to minimize the number of candidates we have to run them for. By discarding points quickly with cheap filters, then evaluating weights, then performing expensive filters on the remainder in order from the highest-scoring to the lowest, as soon as a point passes we can stop evaluation, returning the correct result but often at much reduced cost.

We note that there is little we can do about expensive weights in this approach (such as a relative exposure calculation or an accurate pathfinding distance); also, that in the worst case we will fully evaluate all of our points before a valid one, or none, is found.

1.7.4 A Dynamic Evaluation Strategy

If we had the ability to skip expensive weights, as well as conditions, this would allow us a greater freedom in the development and use of such criteria. We might measure relative exposure to multiple targets, for example, or make use of accurate path lengths rather than straight-line distance. Of course, we would want to ensure that we return the same results as if full evaluation had been employed. Here, we present an approach that allows this.

We first note that in general we do not need to have the final score of a point to establish that it is better than any other may be. To illustrate this, consider two criteria that return floating-point values, normalized to the 0–1 range: A, assigned a weight of 2/3 in this query and B, assigned a weight of 1/3. If one point gains the full score on weight A, while the second scores less than half of that, then there is no reason to evaluate weight B on these two points; the highest score that B could provide would still not cause the second point to score more highly than the first.

Based on this observation, we should focus our evaluations on the point which currently has the potential to score highest out of all those considered. In order to do this, we need to know how many criteria have been evaluated so far on each point, and the maximum score that each point might achieve. We can use a struct to hold this metadata and the point itself:

```
struct PointMetadata
{
    TPSPoint point;
    int evalStep;
    float minScore, maxScore;
}
```

We employ a binary heap [Cormen et al. 01] to maintain a partial sort of these structures as we proceed, based on the maxScore value. Often used for priority queues, heaps ensure that the maximal element is kept at the top of the heap with a minimum of overhead. In a binary heap, removing the top element (pop_heap) is an O(log *n*) operation and, usually implemented in a single block of memory such as an STL vector, they are also relatively cache friendly.

Nonetheless, we noted earlier that many criteria are inexpensive to evaluate, and in these cases the overhead of heap maintenance would be comparable to the evaluations themselves. Hence, we deal with these "cheap" criteria before forming the heap in a straightforward manner similar to that discussed in the previous section: we evaluate all of the cheap conditions and discard any points that fail, then we score the remaining points based on the cheap weights—that is, summing the products of their normalized return values and the multipliers (weights) specified by the user.

This leaves us with a reduced set of points upon which to evaluate the more expensive conditions and weights. The next step is to establish the minimum and maximum possible score that each remaining point might achieve when all of the weights have been evaluated. Since all weights will be normalized to return values in the [0–1] range, we can do this just by reference to the user-defined multipliers. We sum the values of the negative user-defined multipliers (weights) in the query to find the greatest amount they could subtract from the overall score. We do the same for the positive user-defined multipliers to find the greatest amount they could add to the overall score. We then go through each point and add these amounts to the actual score that was computed when we evaluated the cheap weights, finding the lowest and highest potential scores for that point—the minScore and maxScore metadata described above.

Having dealt efficiently with the cheap criteria and established potential scores, we create the heap from these structs, populated as described above, and all further evaluation is based on that data structure. We now look at the core evaluation loop in detail. The blocks of code in this section can be combined to describe the whole loop, but we have split it into parts so that we can explain each step in the process.

Each iteration begins by checking if we have exhausted all candidates, in which case this query option has failed. Otherwise, we take the top point from the heap and check to see if it has been completely evaluated. If it has, we have a final result and either return immediately (as below) or remove that point from the heap and continue evaluation to find multiple results.

```
while (!empty_heap(pointHeap))
{
    PointMetadata& best = pointHeap[0];
    if (best.evalStep > finalEvaluationStep)
        break;
```

We then check what the next evaluation step is for this point. There is a single defined evaluation order, further discussed in the coming text, which may alternate between conditions and weights. If the next criterion is a condition, we perform that evaluation and then either remove the point from the heap (should the condition fail) or advance to the next evaluation step (should it pass).

```
if (isCondition(best.evalStep))
{
    bool result = evaluateCondition(best);
    if (!result)
        pop_heap(pointHeap);
    else
        best.evalStep++;
    continue;
}
```

When the criterion is instead a weight, we make use of the "heap property." In a binary heap this dictates that the second and third elements, which are the two child nodes of the first element, will each be maximal elements of their subtrees within the heap. Hence, by comparing with these two elements, we can check if the *minimum* potential score of the top element, best, is greater than the *maximum* potential score of any other point. If this is the case, we can skip this and any other weight evaluations on this point—based on our observation at the start of this section—but we must still check any remaining conditions.

```
if (isWeight(best.evalStep))
{
    if (best.minScore > pointHeap[1].maxScore
        && best.minScore > pointHeap[2].maxScore)
    {
        best.evalStep++;
        continue;
    }
}
```

If that is not yet the case, we must evaluate the weight criterion for the point, lookup and apply the defined range to normalize it to the [0, 1] range, and then fetch the user multiplier that will determine its final contribution to the score.

```
float value = evaluateWeight(best.point);
float normalized = normalizeToRange(value, best.evalStep);
float multiplier = getUserMultiplier(best.evalStep);
```

We then need to adjust the minimum and maximum scores for this point. Performing a weight evaluation has narrowed the range of potential scores, in effect resolving some of the uncertainty about the score of this point. Where the user-defined multiplier for this criterion is positive, a weight that returns a high normalized value will raise the minimum score by a lot and lower the maximum score just a little; conversely, a weight returning a low normalized value will raise the minimum score by a little and lower the maximum score by a lot. Note that in both cases, minScore goes up and maxScore goes down.

```
if (multiplier > 0)
{
    //A positive contribution to final score
    best.minScore += normalized * multiplier;
    best.maxScore -= (1 - normalized) * multiplier;
}
```

```
        else
        {
            //A negative contribution to final score
            best.minScore -= (1 - normalized) * multiplier;
            best.maxScore += normalized * multiplier;
        }
```

With the effect of that weight evaluation applied, we now reposition this point in the heap since it may no longer have the maximum potential score. This operation is equivalent to a pop_heap operation immediately followed by a push_heap operation, removing and then replacing the top element. We advance to the next evaluation step and begin the next iteration:

```
        best.evalStep++;
        update_heap(pointVector);
    }//Matches if (isWeight(best.evalStep))
}//Matches while (!empty_heap(pointHeap))
```

In deciding the evaluation order of criteria we are free to interleave weights and conditions. Ordering them by increasing expense is a reasonable strategy, but we might instead evaluate the largest weights earlier and likewise conditions that in practice usually fail. There is scope for considerable gains in performance based on profiling and feedback.

This approach improves over the simpler approach in cases where we have expensive weights that we hope to avoid evaluating. Where we have no such weights, the evaluations it performs will be the same as the approach described in the previous section. In the worst case, when none of the points are valid, it may be able to perform better since the evaluation order can be more freely adjusted, as above. However, if we are to be sure of returning any valid point that exists, this worst case will of course require us to check at least enough conditions to discard every point regardless of the approach we take to do so.

When a query takes significant time to evaluate, due to expensive criteria or a worst-case evaluation on a large number of points, we must be able to spread evaluation over a number of frames. It may also be useful to share evaluation time between multiple agents, to avoid all active agents waiting upon a single slow query. The heap structure described is suitable to pause evaluation at any stage to continue later—as we will exploit in the next section.

1.7.5 Asynchronous Evaluation and Timeslicing

A synchronous approach, returning results in a single function call, is the simplest execution model and the most convenient for the developer, but as we place greater load on our system and provide more powerful criteria, synchronous queries can easily lead to unacceptable spikes in processing time. Further, certain criteria may depend on asynchronous operations—for instance, efficient raycasts, as discussed. As a result, we will almost certainly need to support the ability for queries to be handled asynchronously.

In order to better handle asynchronous queries, we employ a scheduler, which will keep track of which requests are pending and which are currently being processed. *Crysis 2* employed a simple first-come-first-served scheduler working on a single query at any time—however, a scheduler that shared time between agents would be a useful improvement. With a scheduler in place, we can timeslice our evaluation, checking evaluation time periodically during execution and relinquishing control when our allocated budget for the frame has expired.

The Crytek system performs the entire generation phase and evaluates all of the cheap weights and conditions in one pass, before checking evaluation time. Since, by design, these stages are low cost, we do not expect to greatly overrun the budget by this point, and only synchronous operations are supported so we will not need to wait for any operations to complete. Once this is complete, the system forms the heap, which is compatible with timeslicing.

When we continue evaluation of the heap, we evaluate a single criterion—either a weight or a condition—on the point with the highest potential score, and then check the elapsed time before continuing with the next or putting aside the heap until next frame. Since by definition all of the criteria evaluated in this heap stage are of significant expense, the overheads of checking the CPU clock and heap manipulation are acceptable.

The same infrastructure provides the basis to handle criteria that use asynchronous operations such as raycasts. Whenever we reach one of these we start that deferred operation in motion before putting the heap aside much as if we had used up our timeslice. On the next frame we reevaluate the heap in much the same state as before—except this time we find our deferred operation is waiting for a result, which should now be available. We can then complete the results of that criterion on that point just the same as if it has been synchronous—and proceed to the next.

The latencies resulting from criteria that employ asynchronous operations are significant and could limit their use in our queries. There are a number of ways we can address this. First, we should evaluate asynchronous criteria last for each candidate point, so that we will avoid them if we can. Second, if we have remaining time available we could continue evaluation on another query, increasing our throughput. Finally, we could speculatively start deferred criteria on a number of other points near the top of the heap at the same time as the first.

1.8 Tools

As with all such systems, our TPS system is only as effective as the tools we build for it and the workflow we develop around it. The query language is one such tool, but we also need to be able to visualize the query results if we are to effectively develop and tune queries and track down problems.

The Crytek system allows us to render query results for a specific agent in the world in real time. A sphere is drawn for every candidate point, with color indicating their status: white for the highest-scoring point, green for a point that passed all conditions, red for a point that failed a condition, and blue for a point that would have been only partially evaluated. The final score is displayed above each sphere. At the same time, a representation of the parsed query is output to the log, to confirm which query was used and also to allow us to double-check what criteria were used in the evaluation.

While we did experiment with grading the colors by their relative score, we found that the differences in score were often small—though significant—and so very hard to judge visually.

Some criteria have custom debug rendering. For instance, criteria that include raycasts draw the corresponding line in the game world, and more complex dynamic generation criteria could draw indications of where and how they considered generating points.

BulletStorm used a similar visual debugging approach, but also annotated every invalid point with a short text string indicating the specific condition that failed [Zielinksi 13].

1.9 Future Work

There are some avenues for future work that are particularly promising.

As the industry standardizes on efficient navmesh solutions, a family of powerful new criteria become affordable in a TPS system. *Accurate path distances* for individual agents between locations would provide subtly improved movement choices across the board and a greater robustness to dividing obstacles such as walls and fences, compared to the Euclidean distances we take for granted. *Generation of points* could be done only in nav polys connected to our agent, ensuring that points generated in the open, such as the grid method described, are always reachable. *Navigational raycasts* could be very useful for maintaining line-of-sight within a group and might in some cases make a cheap approximation for full physics raycasts.

Game environments continue to become richer, more dynamic, and increasingly they make use of procedural content generation. All these trends represent a scalability challenge to conventional search methods. There is increasing interest in the use of *stochastic sampling*, seen in games such as *Love* [Steenberg 11], which could scale better. This comes at a risk of missing obvious locations, with a cost in believability and immersion that is often unacceptable in current AAA titles, but such games might be tuned to make this very rare, or such points might be used to supplement a conventional database of points.

Finally, when working on a squad-based game, there is currently a stark choice between individual position selection, offering decoupled interaction between members of a group in different roles; and centralized position selection that can coordinate the allocation of points to the advantage of the whole group, but at the cost of tightly coupled behavior code. Work towards *coordination between decentralized queries* would be an area of special interest to the author.

1.10 Conclusion

Tactical Position Selection is a keystone of shooter AI and a potential Swiss army knife of AI and gameplay programming. When we break out of rigid evaluation methods and provide an expressive query language, we can drive a wide variety of behavior with only small data changes. By creating a library of queries specific to the environment and desired behavior, and by considering best practices and making use of specific building blocks, we can keep queries simple and create them quickly. Feedback from our query results to our behavior and query selection allows our AI to adapt when circumstances change.

We have discussed how we can architect such a system, from query specification to final result and how we can integrate it with our behaviors. We have considered performance and tools for debugging that help ensure we make the best use of the system in the final shipped product. In particular, we have referred to details of the system used in *Crysis 2*.

Acknowledgments

The author would like to thank Crytek for their assistance with this article and AiGameDev.com for the valuable resources that they provide. Thanks also to the other developers involved, in particular, Kevin Kirst, Márcio Martins, Mario Silva, Jonas Johansson, Benito Rodriguez, and Francesco Roccucci.

References

[Champandard et al. 11] A. Champandard, M. Jack, and P. Dunstan. "Believable Tactics for Squad AI." GDC, 2011. Available online (http://www.gdconf.com/).

[Cormen et al. 01] T. H. Cormen, C. E. Leiserson, R. L. Rivest, and C. Stein. *Introduction to Algorithms*. MIT Press, 2001, pp. 127–144.

[Crytek 11] Crytek. "The Tactical Point System." http://freesdk.crydev.net/display/SDKDOC4/Tactical+Point+System, Crytek, 2011.

[Crytek 12] Crytek. "Crydev.net." http://www.crydev.net. 2012.

[Evans 11] R. Evans et al. "Turing Tantrums: AI Developers Rant." GDC 2011. Available online (http://www.gdcvault.com/play/1014586/Turing-Tantrums-AI-Developers-Rant).

[Graham 13] David "Rez" Graham. "An introduction to utility theory." In *Game AI Pro*, edited by Steve Rabin. Boca Raton, FL: CRC Press, 2013.

[Mark 09] D. Mark. *Behavioral Mathematics for Game AI*. Boston, MA: Course Technology PTR, 2009.

[Martins 11] M. Martins. Paris Shooter Symposium 2011. Available online (https://aigamedev.com/store/recordings/paris-shooter-symposium-2011-content-access.html).

[Mononen 11] M. Mononen. "Automatic Annotations in Killzone 3 and Beyond." Paris Game/AI Conference. 2011. Available online (http://aigamedev.com). Slides available online (http://www.guerrilla-games.com/publications).

[Nelson 11] J. Nelson. Paris Shooter Symposium 2011. Available online (https://aigamedev.com/store/recordings/paris-shooter-symposium-2011-content-access.html).

[Steenberg 11] E. Steenberg. "Stochastic Sampling and the AI in LOVE." Paris Game/AI Conference. 2011. Available online (http://aigamedev.com).

[Sterren 01] W. van der Sterren. "Terrain reasoning for 3D action games." In *Game Programming Gems 2*, edited by Steven Rabin. Boston, MA: Charles River Media, 2002.

[Straatman et al. 06] R. Straatman, A. Beij, and William van der Sterren. "Dynamic tactical position evaluation." In *AI Game Programming Wisdom 3*, edited by Steve Rabin. Boston, MA: Charles River Media, 2006.

[Zielinski 13] M. Zielinski. "Asking the environment smart questions." In *Game AI Pro*, edited by Steve Rabin. Boca Raton, FL: CRC Press, 2013.

Tactical Pathfinding on a NavMesh

Daniel Brewer

2.1 Introduction

Traditional pathfinding has been focused on finding the *shortest* route from A to B. However, as gamers demand more realism, this is no longer sufficient. Agents should instead find the most *appropriate* route from A to B. In action-shooter or strategy games, this usually means the most tactically sound route—the route that provides the most concealment from the enemy and avoids friendly lines of fire, rather than the shortest, most direct path.

Many tactical pathfinding solutions require a regular waypoint grid and numerous line-of-sight raycast checks to determine the safer, more concealed route between two points. However, regular waypoint grids are known for poor memory efficiency and the large number of waypoints to check increases the run-time pathfinding load, especially with the numerous visibility checks required for tactical pathfinding.

Navigation meshes (NavMeshes) are an alternative approach to grids and have become a widely used, efficient representation of navigable space. This article will present a method of cover representation and modification to the A* algorithm to perform tactical pathfinding directly on a NavMesh.

2.2 Other Methods

At its core, tactical A* pathfinding can be achieved by modifying the cost of nodes in your navigation graph [van der Sterren 02]. A node that is visible or exposed to the enemy should have a higher cost, while a node that is concealed from the enemy should have a lower cost. This way, the A* algorithm will favor the lower cost, more concealed nodes over the high cost, exposed nodes. An agent following such a path will seem more cautious, preferring to keep out of line-of-sight of his enemy as much as possible.

The common practice in tactical pathfinding is to use a grid or a regular waypoint graph. The high resolution and regular spacing of nodes allows the A* algorithm to better take into account the differing costs for exposed versus concealed nodes over the distance traveled. The accuracy of these techniques depends on the density of the grid; the tighter the grid spacing, the greater the number of nodes and the better the accuracy of the paths generated. A high grid density has significant costs, not only in memory for storing all the nodes, but also in processing at run-time when the A* algorithm has many more nodes to compute.

There are a number of possible methods to determine how exposed a particular node is to an enemy threat. The crucial question is "Can an enemy standing at position A see me at position B?" Performing visibility raycast checks at run-time during pathfinding can drastically hamper performance. Exhaustive visibility calculations can be performed offline and stored for use in game via look-up tables [Lidén 02]. As the environment increases in size and the number of nodes grows, this $O(n^2)$ approach requires exponentially larger amounts of memory.

An alternative to relying on exact line-of-sight raycast checks is to use approximations. A possible approximation is to store a radial distance field for each node [Straatman 05]. This approach can be extended to 3D with depth-buffer cube-maps [van der Leeuw 09]. This allows a quick look-up to approximate how far an agent can see in a particular direction from a specified point in the world. By comparing the distances in each direction between two points, it is possible to determine if these points are visible to each other. Another form of approximation is to rasterize cover objects into a grid [Jurney 07]. The enemy's view cone can then be rasterized into the grid to add a weighting factor against waypoints that are exposed to his line-of-sight. This rasterizing approach can be used to deal with dynamic, destructible cover, too. After an object is destroyed, simply perform the rasterization again with the remaining objects, and the navigation grid will reflect the current run-time changes.

These approximations actually enhance the robustness of the solution against small movements of the enemy threat. In an environment filled with complex geometry it is possible for a raycast to pass through a tiny gap in an object and so report a clear line-of-sight, when in fact the location would be concealed. The opposite can also occur, reporting an obscured line-of-sight when the location would in fact be visible. Even with simple geometry, a small adjustment of the raycast origin could return different results. The low resolution of the distance fields, or rasterized cover grids, makes these approximations much less susceptible to these slight variations in position.

Navigation meshes are a popular, efficient method of representing navigable regions of a virtual environment [Tozour 04]; however, it is not as straightforward to perform tactical pathfinding on these navigation representations. The irregular spacing and large area covered by the navigation polygons results in poor overall visibility accuracy from raycast tests. To overcome this drawback, it is possible to dynamically calculate a regular waypoint graph at run-time by sampling positions from a static NavMesh [Bamford 12]. This tactical graph need only be generated locally for the areas of the world where combat encounters take place. However, this does lead to a duplication of navigation information and at worst case may even require a separate, independent pathfinding code for the two different representations.

The following section presents an approach to tactical pathfinding that can work directly on a NavMesh without requiring the duplication of navigation information.

2.3 Tactical Pathfinding Method

The technique is split up into three parts. The first part will deal with ways to partition and annotate the NavMesh. The second part will deal with cover representation, and the final part will deal with calculating the cost of navigation polygon traversal in A* in order to calculate a more appropriate route.

2.3.1 Tessellating and Annotating the NavMesh

There has been a lot of work on creating an optimal NavMesh representation of a virtual environment [Tozour 02, Farnstrom 06], though this is not necessarily required for the purposes of tactical pathfinding. The NavMesh can be more finely tessellated to provide increased detail in areas of different movement properties or tactical significance.

Polygons in which it is more difficult, or more tactically unsafe, to move can be flagged with additional costs, just as in a regular grid representation. Areas of water could be flagged as "slow movement" or "only passable by amphibious units." Regions of high grass could be flagged with "provides concealment." Dense undergrowth could be flagged as "slow movement" and "provides concealment." The center of a courtyard with overlooking balconies can be flagged as "vulnerable" or "unsafe" so that agents will move through the area while staying near the edges. These flags and costs modify the traversal costs for the pathfinding algorithm to get agents to follow more appropriate paths rather than simply the shortest route.

An optimal NavMesh will be made up of large, convex polygons in order to provide the most coverage of the navigable space with the least number of polygons. The aforementioned courtyard could be represented by a single polygon as shown in Figure 2.1. This would prevent the differentiation between the exposed center and the covered edges under the balconies. Additional polygons are required in order to represent the tactical difference between these areas.

A quick and easy way to achieve these benefits is to provide tools allowing level designers to mark-up areas of the NavMesh with this extra detail. The designers need to be able to specify the contour boundaries of the marked up areas, and then these boundaries need to be kept fixed in the polygonal tessellation of the map. It is possible to use terrain analysis algorithms during NavMesh generation to automate some of the tedium of manual mark-ups, but this is beyond the scope of this article. In most cases, this manual mark-up may only be necessary in very specific game-play instances and the general cover approach below will suffice for most tactical pathing needs during combat.

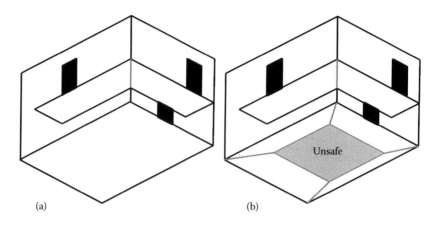

Figure 2.1

Optimal NavMesh for a courtyard with an overhanging balcony (a). The same courtyard is shown with an exposed designer region flagged as "unsafe" (b).

2.3.2 Cover Representation

Cover spots in game levels can be represented as discrete points. This is often the case with waypoint graph navigation representations. Connected areas of cover are represented by links between these cover waypoints. It can be beneficial to instead consider cover as connected, linear segments rather than discrete points. These line segments follow the contour of the cover-providing obstacle and a height property can differentiate between tall, standing cover and waist-high, crouching cover. This annotated line segment is called a "cover segment" and provides a simple polygon approximation of the line-of-sight blocking obstacle.

It is important to quickly be able to look up which pieces of cover can provide concealment to an avatar at a given location in the world. Each polygon in the NavMesh can store a small table with the indices to the most significant cover segments affecting that polygon. This table of cover segments per polygon is called the Cover Map (CoverMap). This allows a quick look-up of the objects that could provide cover or block line-of-sight to a character on a particular polygon in the NavMesh (Figure 2.2).

This data is only an approximation of the line-of-sight blockers, since only the most relevant cover for each NavMesh polygon is stored. A heuristic for selecting cover segments for a navigation polygon should take into account the direction of cover provided, the distance of the cover segment from the polygon, and whether that cover is already occluded by other cover segments. For the purposes of allowing agents to make better tactical choices during combat, this approximation is sufficient. It is possible to improve the accuracy by increasing the number of cover segments stored per polygon and by tweaking the selection criteria.

2.3.3 Pathfinding

When searching for the shortest path, the primary concern is distance or movement time. Tactical pathfinding, on the other hand, is concerned more with finding a safe path. This can be accomplished by taking a standard pathfinding algorithm and biasing the node

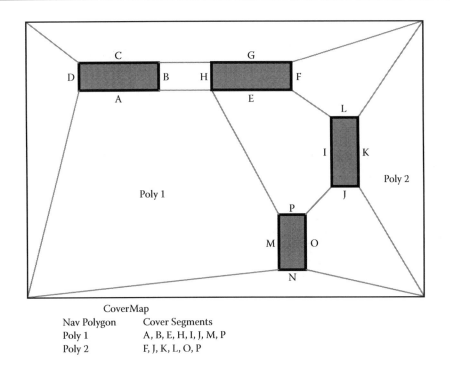

CoverMap

Nav Polygon	Cover Segments
Poly 1	A, B, E, H, I, J, M, P
Poly 2	F, J, K, L, O, P

Figure 2.2

Example NavMesh showing some cover segments and how they are stored in the CoverMap.

traversal cost by how exposed or concealed that node is to the enemy. By increasing the cost of exposed nodes, the pathfinding algorithm will return a route that avoids more of these exposed nodes and thus one that is more concealed. The method below will not cover how to perform A* on a NavMesh, which can be found elsewhere [Snook 00], but will focus on how to modify the A* costs to take cover into account in order to find a safer path. The core of the algorithm is first presented in a simpler, 2D form in order to clearly illustrate the concept. The next section will explain some extensions to the algorithm to operate in more complex environments.

To start finding a safe path from an enemy, the algorithm requires a list of cover segments that can potentially shield the agent from his enemy. The navigation polygon containing the enemy's position can be used to index into the CoverMap and obtain the list of cover segments. When considering a potential path segment, it is now possible to calculate how much of that path segment is concealed from the enemy.

The next step is to construct a 2D frustum from the cover segment (A–B in Figure 2.3) and the lines joining the enemy's position to each end of the cover segment (C–A and C–B). The normals of all these planes should point inwards to the leeward area behind the cover. The path segment is then clipped by this frustum. The portion of the segment left in front of all three planes is the concealed portion of the path segment.

These steps are repeated for each cover segment in the enemy's CoverMap. By comparing the total clipped length to the original segment length, the proportion of exposed to

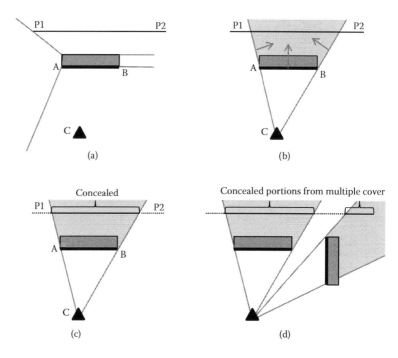

Figure 2.3

Calculating the proportion of the path segment that is concealed from an enemy (a) by first constructing a frustum from the cover segment (b) and then clipping the path segment by this frustum (c) and repeating for each cover segment in the CoverMap (d).

concealed is calculated. This is then multiplied by the cover-bias factor and added to the base cost of the segment, as shown in Listing 2.1. The A* search will thus be biased away from exposed segments. The greater the cover-bias factor, the more it will cost the agent to move along exposed segments and this will result in him going further out of his way to find a safer, more obscured path.

Listing 2.1 also shows how designer mark-ups and agent biases can affect the pathing costs. When dealing with these, it is important to remember that biases above 1.0 will increase the cost of traversing the polygon, while biases below 1.0 decrease it and may cause the cost of traversing the node to drop below the actual straight-line distance. In general, this should be avoided as it is preferable to keep the heuristic admissible and always modify the costs to make nodes more expensive. Care should also be taken not to increase the costs too much, as if the heuristic is drastically different to the cost, the A* algorithm will explore many more nodes than necessary.

2.4 Extending the Technique to 3D

The previously presented algorithm is good for 2D or slightly undulating terrain. This is to present the core algorithm in a simple, digestible manner. However, not all environments are this simple. A character on a tall hill will be able to draw a line-of-sight over some intervening cover. Vertical structures can prove problematic as a character may not be able

```
Line ClipLineByPlane(Line, Plane)
    returns the segment of the input Line in front of the Plane

float GetSegmentExposedLength(Line pathSegmentP1P2, Point C)
    float ConcealedLength = 0
    For each Line coverSegmentAB do
        Plane planeAB = CalcPlaneFrom3Points(A, B, A + up_axis)
        Plane planeAC = CalcPlaneFrom3Points(A, C, A + up_axis)
        Plane planeCB = CalcPlaneFrom3Points(C, B, C + up_axis)
        Line clippedLine = ClipLineByPlane(pathSegmentP1P2, planeAB)
        clippedLine = ClipLineByPlane(clippedLine, planeAC)
        clippedLine = ClipLineByPlane(clippedLine, planeCB)
        ConcealedLength += Length(clippedLine)
        ExposedLength = Length(pathSegmentP1P2) - ConcealedLength
        return ExposedLength

float CostForSegment(Line pathSegmentP1P2, polyFlags)
    float segmentLength = Length(pathSegmentP1P2)
    float exposedLength =
        GetSegmentExposedLength(pathSegmentP1P2, enemyPosition)
    float cost = exposedLength * agentCoverBias +
        (segmentLength - exposedLength)
    cost += segmentLength * polyFlags.isUnsafe * agentSafetyBias
    return cost
```

to draw a clear line-of-sight through the floor or ceiling, but if the visibility approximation only considers cover segments, it will not take the floor or ceiling into account. Fortunately, the technique can be extended to work with these more complex environments.

If the terrain has large height variance, a more accurate result can be obtained by treating the cover segment as a rectangular polygon representing the length and height of the cover. A frustum can be constructed from the enemy's position and the edges of the cover polygon, as shown in Figure 2.4. This frustum can be used to clip the path segments to determine how much of the segment is obscured, just as in the planar example presented above. If the environment includes more vertical structures, it may be necessary to add extra cover planes for floors and ceilings into the CoverMap.

2.5 Conclusion

Agents that can navigate an environment in a tactically sound manner can greatly enhance a video game experience. A good approximation of cover is crucial for run-time tactical pathfinding. Using linear cover segments is an effective way of reasoning about cover and line-of-sight blocking obstacles. This representation makes it simple to calculate how much of a path segment is obscured by each cover segment. By combining this cover representation with a NavMesh, it is possible to perform fast tactical pathfinding without having to resort to high memory usage grids, regular waypoint graphs, or comprehensive visibility look-up tables.

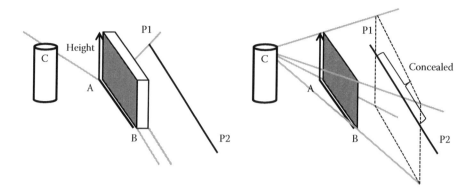

Figure 2.4

To extend the algorithm into 3D, a full frustum needs to be created from the edges of the cover segment polygon to clip the path segment.

References

[Bamford 12] N. Bamford. "Situational Awareness: Terrain Reasoning for Tactical Shooter A.I." AI Summit, GDC 2012. Available online (http://www.gdcvault.com/play/1015443/Situational-Awareness-Terrain-Reasoning-for).

[Farnstrom 06] F. Farnstrom, "Improving on near-optimality: More techniques for building navigation meshes." In *AI Game Programming Wisdom 3*, edited by Steve Rabin. Charles River Media, 2006, pp. 113–128.

[Jurney 07] C. Jurney and S. Hubrick. "Dealing with Destruction: AI From the Trenches of Company of Heroes." GDC 2007. Available online (http://www.chrisjurney.com/).

[Lidén 02] L. Lidén. "Strategic and tactical reasoning with waypoints." In *AI Game Programming Wisdom*, edited by Steve Rabin. Hingham, MA: Charles River Media, 2002, pp. 211–220.

[Snook 00] G. Snook. "Simplified 3D movement and pathfinding using navigation meshes." In *Game Programming Gems*, edited by Mark DeLoura. Charles River Media, 2000, pp. 288–304.

[Straatman 05] R. Straatman, W. van der Sterren, and A. Beij. "Killzone's AI: Dynamic Procedural Combat Tactics." GDC 2005. Available online (http://www.cgf-ai.com/docs/straatman_remco_killzone_ai.pdf).

[Tozour 02] P. Tozour, "Building a near-optimal navigation mesh." In *AI Game Programming Wisdom*, edited by Steve Rabin. Hingham, MA: Charles River Media, 2002, pp. 171–185.

[Tozour 04] P. Tozour, "Search space representations." In *AI Game Programming Wisdom 2*, edited by Steve Rabin. Charles River Media, 2004, pp. 85–102.

[van der Leeuw 09] M. van der Leeuw. "The PlayStation 3's SPU's in the Real World—A KILLZONE 2 Case Study." GDC 2009. Available online (http://www.gdcvault.com/play/963/The-PlayStation-3-s-SPU).

[van der Sterren 02] W. van der Sterren. "Tactical path-finding with A*." In *Game Programming Gems 3*, edited by Dante Treglia. Hingham, MA: Charles River Media, 2002, pp. 294–306.

3

Beyond the Kung-Fu Circle
A Flexible System for Managing NPC Attacks

Michael Dawe

3.1 Introduction

Action games featuring real-time combat have an interesting balance to strike when approaching difficulty and player challenge. Frequently, such games may have encounters featuring several adversaries in a group attacking the player, often with differing types of attacks. This can be desirable from a game design standpoint, for reasons ranging from total combat duration to narrative requests. However, inexperienced players may become overwhelmed by the sheer number of enemies attacking simultaneously, and so these games typically restrict opponents to attacking one at a time.

For *Kingdoms of Amalur: Reckoning*, the game design called for an authentic action game inside a traditional RPG setting, complete with a large number of enemies taking on the player at once. After evaluating several approaches of restricting attackers within a combat encounter, we used a technique capable of changing the number of attackers and even the types of attacks allowed against the player dynamically based on the attackers themselves and the player's chosen difficulty level.

3.2 The Kung-Fu Circle

Requiring that opponents attack the player one at a time is a technique known as the Kung-Fu Circle, named after classic scenes from martial arts movies in which the protagonist faces off against dozens of foes who launch their attacks one at a time. This is a simple algorithm to write and employ, and can make sense in games where focusing on a single opponent is desirable. However, this restriction may be too strict for a game with quick-flowing combat. To allow for a faster pace of combat and to give the player opportunities to use wider-affecting area attacks, it is advantageous to ease these restrictions and allow more than one enemy to attack at a time. A naïve approach might be to simply allow two or three enemies to attack simultaneously, but this will not account for different enemy types or the relative strength of their attacks. For *Reckoning*, we employed an approach known internally as the "Belgian AI" system (so-called for the iconic sketches of waffles used to describe the algorithm) to allow the combat team to design encounters utilizing a variety of creatures while always employing the same underlying rules to determine the number and types of creatures allowed to attack at the same time.

3.3 Belgian AI

At a high level, the Belgian AI algorithm is built around the idea of a grid carried around with every creature in the game. While every NPC had a grid for itself, in practice the player is the game entity we are most concerned about, so we will use the player as our example throughout this article. The grid is world-space aligned and centered on the player with eight empty slots for attacking creatures, much like a tic-tac-toe board with the player at the center. In addition to the physical location of those slots, the grid stores two variables: *grid capacity* and *attack capacity*. Grid capacity will work to place a limit on the number of creatures that can attack the player at once, while attack capacity will limit the number and types of attacks that they can use.

Every creature in the game is assigned a *grid weight*, which is the cost for that creature to be assigned a spot on someone's grid. The total grid weight of the creatures attacking a character must be less than that character's grid capacity. Similarly, every attack has an *attack weight*, and the total weight of all attacks being used against a character at any point in time must be less than that character's attack capacity.

The easiest way to show the impact of these variables is to describe an example of them in action. Let's look at a situation where an enemy soldier has become aware of the player and decides to launch an attack. Before doing so, the soldier needs to request a spot from which he can attack the player. For *Reckoning*, we kept all spatial reasoning out of the individual creatures and had a centralized AI responsible for handling the positioning of creatures in battle called the *stage manager*. Our soldier will therefore register a request to attack the player with the stage manager and wait to be assigned a spot. On its next update, the stage manager will process the request and compare the soldier's grid weight against the player's current grid capacity. For our example, we'll say that the soldier's grid weight is 4 and the player's grid capacity is 12. Since the grid weight of the soldier is less than the available grid capacity, the stage manager will assign the soldier the closest available grid position and reduce the player's available grid capacity to 8. The soldier now has

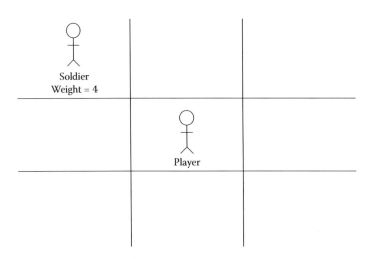

Available Grid Capacity = 12 − 4 = 8

Figure 3.1

A soldier is granted permission to attack the player and takes up position on the grid, reducing the player's available grid capacity.

permission to approach the player and launch an attack. Figure 3.1 shows an example of what the grid might look like at this point.

Next, suppose a troll notices the player. Similarly to the soldier, the troll must request of the stage manager a position on the grid, but since trolls are larger and more powerful than mere humans a troll's grid weight is 8, double that of our ordinary soldier. Since that's still within the player's available grid capacity, the stage manager can assign a slot to the troll and reduce the player's available grid capacity to 0. Now when another soldier comes along (Figure 3.2), he can request a spot to attack the player, but the stage manager will not assign him a slot, since his grid weight is larger than the player's available grid capacity. This second soldier cannot approach the player and must wait outside the grid area.

Attack capacity and weight work similarly, but for individual attacks. So far in our example, both a troll and a soldier have been granted permission to attack the player, but they haven't picked out an attack to use yet. Suppose the player's attack capacity is 10. The troll may have two attacks to pick from: a strong charge attack with an attack weight of 6, and a weaker club attack with a weight of 4. Since the player's attack capacity is 10, the troll can pick the charge attack and inform the stage manager, which reduces the player's attack capacity to 4. Now the soldier picks from his attacks: a lunge with cost 5 or a sword swing with cost 3. Since the player's current attack capacity is 4, he's unable to use the lunge attack, so he'll have to settle for the sword swing this time.

3.3.1 Grid Sectors, Inner Circles, and Outer Circles

Though the algorithm often refers to grid positions, it is more natural to think of the grid slots as defining positions equidistant from the player, forming a circle some arbitrary distance away. For Reckoning, we further subdivided the grid into inner and outer circles, which we called the "attack" and "approach" circles. The radius of the attack circle

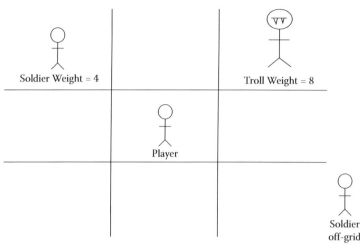

Available Grid Capacity = 12 − 4 − 8 = 0

Figure 3.2

A troll is also granted permission to attack, bringing the grid capacity down to 0. The second soldier is not allowed to approach the player to attack.

is defined by the minimum and maximum distances for melee attacks. When a creature first passes the grid capacity check and is granted permission to approach the player, it will move to stand inside the approach circle. When it is granted permission to perform a particular attack (such as the troll's charge or the soldier's sword swing), it will move into the attack circle to do so. Meanwhile, characters that have not yet passed the grid capacity check (such as the second soldier in our previous example) will stand outside the approach circle, awaiting their chance to step in. This helps the player to determine which creatures are immediate melee threats. Figure 3.3 shows what it might look like.

3.4 Behavior Integration

To fully take advantage of the grid system, creatures in *Reckoning* had a series of specific common behaviors to enforce positioning and attack rules. This also increased behavior reuse, as any creature that could use melee attacks would share these common behavior sets.

First, any creature that was within the distance defined by the outer circle but without permission to attack had to leave the circle as quickly as possible. This helped make it clear to the player which creatures were attacking. Additionally, it prevented monsters from getting in the way of each other when making their actual attacks.

Creatures waiting on the outside of the grid but not assigned grid slots were not given permission to approach, but would instead be given the location of a slot on the grid that was not currently occupied. The creatures would attempt to stand in front of their given slots, even if they did not have permission to attack, which made for natural flanking behavior without any creature explicitly needing to know about any other creature in combat.

Finally, creatures would relinquish control of their grid slot back to the stage manager immediately after launching an attack. Thus, the stage manager could queue requests for

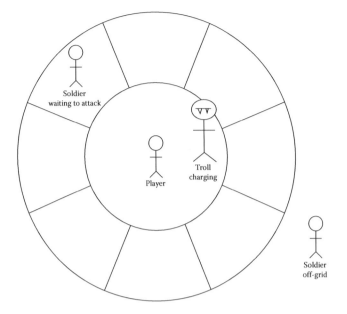

Figure 3.3

The inner- and outer-circle approach. Creatures assigned a grid slot move to their assigned section on the outer circle, but only creatures launching attacks are allowed inside the innermost circle. Any creature not assigned a slot must wait outside the outer circle.

attack slots and rotate the creatures allowed to attack throughout a combat encounter. This kept creatures moving into and out of immediate melee range of the player and ensured no single creature could monopolize attack opportunities. In the case of encounters with a small number of creatures, any creature that gave up its position after making an attack could immediately be assigned a slot again.

3.5 Scaling Difficulty

Grid capacity and attack capacity work together to limit both the number and types of creatures and attacks that can be thrown at the player at any given time. One advantage of this system is the immediate difficulty scaling that can come out of changing the player's grid capacity and attack capacity, all without changing the carefully balanced individual grid and attack weight set for each creature. As the player increased the difficulty in *Reckoning*, we scaled up the grid and attack capacities accordingly. The change to grid capacity allowed more creatures to surround the player during combat, while the change to attack capacity allowed more of those creatures to attack simultaneously and to use more powerful attacks as well.

3.6 Additional Concerns

While the Belgian AI is straightforward enough, care needs to be taken to ensure that it works well with a fast-paced action combat game. Additionally, there may be other design goals concerning creatures and their attacks that the system can be adapted to.

3.6.1 Maintaining Grid Assignments in the World

As mentioned previously the grid is world-oriented, so slots on the grid move around with the player. Sometimes, this would lend itself to situations where the slot that creatures had been assigned would no longer be the closest slot to them. This would frequently occur when the player rolled out of the way of an attack towards other creatures.

To solve this, we gave the stage manager full control over the assignment of the slots on the grid. On any given frame, it could decide which creatures to assign to slots in order to make the best use of the player's grid capacity. In the case of an empty grid, creatures could be assigned the slot closest to their current position. If creatures were already on the grid, the stage manager could assign a slot that was not the closest, or perhaps shift assignments of creatures already granted slots to make room for the newcomers. Creatures would never remember their grid slot assignments and were responsible for checking with the stage manager to get their current slot assignments every frame.

Creatures that had previously been determined to be in the best position to attack could also suddenly not be the best choice to attack the player. For a concrete example, suppose the player had encountered the troll and soldier as before, with a second soldier waiting to attack on the outside of the grid. If the player suddenly moves towards the second soldier who is currently without permission to attack, it would be best if the stage manager could move permission from the first soldier to the second to take advantage of the second soldier's new position.

To solve this, the stage manager could "steal" slot assignments from one creature to give to another or otherwise reassign creatures as it saw fit. In practice, this was tweaked such that it tended to leave creatures with permission to attack alone, unless the assigned creature was outside of the attack grid while some other creature was within the space of the grid, in which case the creature assignment would shift. Shifting could also occur in order to move attacking creatures to different positions on the grid. This shifting would attempt to reduce the total travel time for all creatures to their assigned places in combat. Further, creatures that were actively launching an attack would "lock" their assignment with the stage manager, so they wouldn't lose their slot during an attack and accidentally overload the player's attack capacity. Such an algorithm might look like the following:

```
Attacking list = all attacking creatures
For each creature in Attacking list
    Find closest slot for creature
    If closest slot is locked, continue
    Assign closest slot to creature
    Remove creature from Attacking list
    If closest slot was already assigned,
    Remove assignment from that creature
```

3.6.2 Further Restrictions on Enemy Attacks

While the attack capacity restricts the total number of attacks that can be launched at the same time, it doesn't prevent many creatures from launching the same type of attack simultaneously, especially at higher difficulty levels where the attack capacity is increased, and especially in encounters with many of the same type of creature. In order to help ensure that a variety of attacks occur in a given combat encounter, *Reckoning* also imposed cooldowns on individual, creature-wide, and global bases to prevent creatures from launching too many of the same attacks within a certain window of each other. This helped tremendously in preserving game balance at the most difficult setting, as even with an increased attack capacity, particular enemies could be prevented from using too many area-of-effect type attacks at once.

3.7 Conclusion

Managing game difficulty is an area worthy of serious consideration and research. While it's important to not overwhelm a player learning the game, flexible systems are imperative in order to provide challenging gameplay for more experienced players. Simple approaches, like the grid-based one presented here, can help empower game designers to create different and interesting encounters that can scale for a multitude of difficulty levels simply by adjusting a small set of initial values.

While the implementation of this algorithm is simple enough, its real strength lies in how the positioning logic is centralized to the stage manager. Simply having behaviors to move characters out from slots they aren't assigned to can work to get characters to flank and avoid each other, but it's easy to see how this algorithm could easily be paired with an influence map technique to help characters avoid each other and move around the battlefield more naturally. Other techniques could similarly be combined with the idea of a battle grid to tailor the technique to the needs of an individual game while maintaining the flexibility of adaptive difficulty levels.

4

Hierarchical AI for Multiplayer Bots in Killzone 3

Remco Straatman, Tim Verweij, Alex Champandard,
Robert Morcus, and Hylke Kleve

4.1 Introduction

First-person shooter (FPS) games often consist of a single-player campaign and a large competitive multiplayer component. In multiplayer games, some players' slots can be taken by *bots*, AI controlled players that mimic human players for training purposes. This section describes the AI techniques used to create the bots for Killzone®3, a tactical FPS released on the Playstation®3.

Killzone bots have been used both in an offline training mode with only one or two human players in the game and in multiplayer games with any number of human and bot players. Killzone's main multiplayer mode, *Warzone*, has a number of features, such as multiple team-based game modes being played on the same map in succession and class-based player abilities, which lead to specific requirements for the AI. The chosen approach is inspired by AI techniques from strategy games (hierarchical chain-of-command AI, use of influence maps) and leans heavily on planning and position picking techniques developed for our single-player campaigns.

In this article we describe the scope of the system, the chosen architecture, and the three layers of the architecture. We provide details on the techniques that make up the various layers and describe how we model behaviors. We conclude by describing our experiences, experiments, and future directions.

4.2 Scope

Warzone pits two teams (called *ISA* and *Helghast*) of up to 12 players against each other. During one round on a single map, seven different game modes play out in random order and the team that wins the most game modes wins the round. The game modes are:

- *Capture and hold* (teams gain points by controlling objects on the map)
- *Body count* (teams compete for the most kills)
- *Search and retrieve* (both teams try to return an object to their respective return point)
- *Assassination* (attacking team tries to eliminate one specific player on the other team)
- *Search and destroy* (attacking team tries to destroy an object of the defending team)

The last two game modes are played twice, with each team playing the defending role once.

Players and bots can pick one of five classes which give them access to specific weapons and abilities. For example, the engineer class can place automated turrets, while the medic class can heal teammates. Other abilities include calling in flying drones, disguising as an enemy, cloaking, placing mines, etc.

Each map contains a number of tactical spawn points (TSPs) that can be captured by the tactician class. Team members can spawn at captured TSPs. Mounted guns, ammo boxes, and vehicles (exoskeletons called Exos) are placed at fixed spots on the maps; these can be destroyed or repaired by engineers so that they are usable by the team. For a new player joining *Warzone*, there are many things to learn. To assist in the players' learning process, the bots should mimic experienced human players, master the maps, use the abilities, and work together to win each specific game mode. They should show high level strategies, tactics, and appropriate use of abilities.

4.3 Architecture

The multiplayer AI system is set up as a three-layered hierarchy, where each layer controls the layer below it and information flows back from the lower layers to the higher one. Figure 4.1 illustrates the architecture. Each team has a hierarchy responsible for its bot players. The *strategy layer* is responsible for playing the current game mode, and contains the *commander* AI. The commander monitors the state of the game mode, assigns bots to squads, and issues objectives. The *squad layer* contains the AI for each of the squads. The *Squad AI* is responsible for translating objectives into orders for its members, group movement, and monitoring objective progress. At the lowest level, the *individual layer* consists of the individual AI of the bots. The *bot AI* follows squad orders, but has freedom in how to execute those orders. Bot AI mainly deals with combat and using its class abilities.

The communication between the layers consists of orders moving downward and information moving up. The commander can order squads to *Attack area*, *Defend area*, *Escort player*, or *Advance to regroup point*. Squads will report to the commander on successful completion of orders or imminent failure—for instance, when the squad has been decimated during an attack. Squads will order their members to move to an area, attack a target, use a specific object, or restrict bots to specific areas. Bots will report back completion of orders and send information on observed threats.

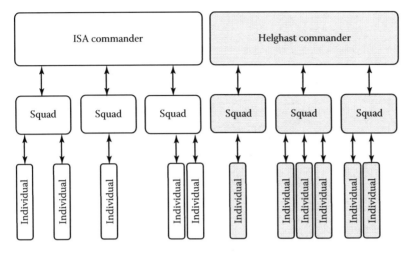

Figure 4.1

Hierarchical layered AI for both teams.

The previous sections have shown the scope and overall architecture. The following sections describe the individual, squad, and commander AI layers in more detail.

4.4 Individual Bot AI

At the lowest level in the hierarchy we find the individual AI for each bot. Even though the bots get orders from their squad, they are still highly autonomous agents. The squad does not micromanage each bot; bots gather information and decide how to fulfill their role. For example, bots can select their own attack target, the position to attack from, the weapon to use, and so forth. They can also decide to temporarily ignore orders in order to survive. Bots have the same weapons and abilities as human players.

4.4.1 Individual Update Loop

The bot AI takes a typical agent-based approach, as shown in Figure 4.2. First, the NPC gathers information about the current world state, either through *perception* or by messages from other team members. Agents perceive *stimuli* in the game world through various *sensors*. There are different sensors for seeing, hearing, and feeling, and different types of stimuli (visual, sounds, and contact). The sensors have limitations such as view cones and maximum distance. See [Puig08] for general information on perception systems. Abilities such as cloaking and disguise further influence perception and make the AI react believably. The information on threats derived from perception is placed in each individual's *world database*. Because of the limitations in perception, the bot's idea of the world may be believably wrong. Besides perception and messages from other agents, a number of *daemons* fill the agent's database with other data. A daemon is a component that adds facts about a specific type of information such as the state of the bot's weapons and health.

In the next step, the *planner* either generates a *plan* or continues execution of the current plan. A plan consists of a sequence of *tasks*. The set of tasks available to the bots is typical for a shooter (such as move to destination, select weapon, reload weapon, etc.).

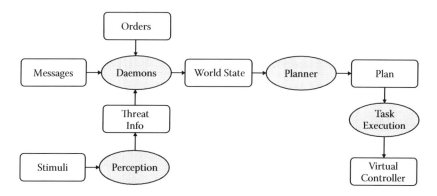

Figure 4.2

Individual update loop.

Each update, the current task of the plan gets executed. Completion of the task advances the plan to the next task, while failure will invalidate the whole plan. Executing a task updates the lower level *skill planner* that takes care of coordinating lower granularity actions such as looking, aiming, walking, crouching, etc. The skills finally update the bots' *virtual controller*, the interface both bots and players share to control their humanoid game avatar. The virtual controller enforces a strict separation between AI and the game engine, so that AI code does not directly control animations or guns, and thus ensures that the bots' capabilities are identical to those of the player.

4.4.2 Individual Planner

We use a custom planner that is based on the Hierarchical Task Network (HTN) planner architecture [Nau 00]. This planner was chosen because it provides good control over what plans can be generated and a clear definition of priorities between plans.

The individuals' behavior is defined in HTN by a *domain*, which consists of *constants* and *methods*. A method defines one or more ways to achieve a *task* by defining a list of *branches*. Each branch has a *precondition* and a *decomposition* consisting of a list of tasks. A task can be *primitive*, meaning it can be executed by the agent, or *compound*, meaning it needs to be further decomposed using a method.

Planning begins by instantiating a plan for a top-level task. The branches of the method for this task are attempted in listed order. When a branch's precondition matches, the planner recursively tries to create plans for all compound tasks in the branch's plan. The planner will backtrack over branches, variable bindings of preconditions, and plan instantiations for compound tasks. The resulting plan is the first one fully consisting of primitive tasks.

The primitive tasks modify their agent's memory, make the bot do things in the world, and add information for debugging. Table 4.1 shows some of the primitive tasks.

Listing 4.1 shows the method that turrets (which use the same planner as the bots) use for selecting a weapon to fire at some threat (represented by the variable ?threat). Variables are prefixed by a question mark, constants by an @ sign, and the keyword call precedes C++ function calls. Each of the weapons of the turret has its own branch, with preconditions matching against facts in the agent's world database (e.g., distance_to_threat), resulting in the instantiation of local variables (e.g., ?dist). The plan of both branches

Table 4.1 Example of primitive tasks (prefixed with!) for individual bots

Primitive task	Description
!remember	Add a (temporary) fact to agent database.
!forget	Remove fact(s) from agent database.
!fire_weapon_at_entity	Fire current weapon at specified entity.
!reload_weapon	Reload current weapon.
!use_item_on_entity	Use current inventory item on other entity.
!broadcast	Send a message to nearby bots.
!log_color	Add text to the debug log of an agent.

Listing 4.1. Example methods for selecting a weapon to fire. The syntax is based on the SHOP HTN planner, which was written in Lisp. Our HTN compiler converts this domain description into C++ code.

```
(:method (attack ?threat)
    (:branch "use bullets"
        (and (distance_to_threat ?threat ?dist)
            (call le ?dist @bullet_rng)
            (call request_line_of_attack ?threat bullets)
            (line_of_attack ?threat bullets) )
        (   (!begin_plan attack_using_bullets)
            (select_weapon bullets)
            (!fire_weapon ?threat)
            (!end_plan) )
    )
    (:branch "use missiles"
        (and (distance_to_threat ?threat ?dist)
            (call ge ?dist @bullet_rng)
            (call le ?dist @missile_rng)
            (call request_line_of_attack ?threat missiles)
            (line_of_attack ?threat missiles) )
        (   (!begin_plan attack_using_missiles)
            (select_weapon missiles)
            (!fire_weapon ?threat)
            (!end_plan) )
    )
)
```

contains a number of primitive tasks and one compound task (select_weapon). To form an instantiated plan that compound method needs to be decomposed further by another method.

The example in Listing 4.1 also shows how a request for information (request_line_of_attack) can be part of the precondition; the result will be placed in the database and is tested in the next condition (line_of_attack).

For bots, plan generation always starts with a root task (called behave). The methods in the domain determine the plans that can be generated and in which order they are tried. Listing 4.2 shows the final decomposition that led to a medic bot's plan to use the revive

```
behave
+ branch_mp_behave
    - (do_behave_in_vehicle_mp)
    + (do_behave_on_foot_mp)
        - branch_self_preservation
      + branch_medic_revive
          + (do_medic_revive)
              - branch_medic_revive_abort
              - branch_medic_revive_continue
              + branch_medic_revive
                  (!begin_plan medic_revive [Soldier:TimV])
                  (!log_color magenta "Medic reviving nearby entity.")
                  (!broadcast 30 10 medic_revives [Soldier:TimV])
                  (!select_target [Soldier:TimV])
                + (walk_to_attack 5416 crouching auto)
                + (wield_weapon wp_online_mp_bot_revive_gun)
                    - branch_dont_switch_weapon
                    + branch_switch_weapon
                        (?wp = wp_online_mp_bot_revive_gun)
                        + (wield_weapon_internal wp_mp_bot_revive_gun)
                  (!use_item_on_entity [Soldier:TimV] crouching)
                  (!end_plan)
```

tool on a teammate. The decomposition illustrates the way the HTN planner solves a plan, but also illustrates the way the domain is structured.

The final plan consists of all the primitive tasks in the decomposition. Starting at behave, the first branches decide between behavior in a vehicle or on foot, followed by a choice between self-preservation behavior (such as fleeing a grenade) and doing one of its class abilities, revive.

As described above, planning starts at the root node, generating a plan for behave. It does this by going through behave's branches in the order specified, so that branches pertaining to self-preservation are considered before those for healing friendlies for instance. If it selects a branch that contains composite tasks, the planner recursively generates a plan for that branch.

Once the planner has finished, the agent can execute the plan. Each update the current task in the plan is executed. The current task can continue running for multiple updates before succeeding and moving to the next task in the plan, or fail. If the plan has reached the end or a task has failed the agent needs to generate a new plan.

In practice, making sure the agents' plan is still the best one given the ever-changing situation is more complicated. Because of this, the agent reruns the planner at a fixed rate and replaces the current plan if it finds one which is better (that is, one that traverses branches that are farther up the list than those in the current plan). For example, if the AI is in the process of healing a buddy when it replans, and it discovers that there is a grenade nearby, it will abort the heal in favor of a self-preservation branch (such as fleeing from the grenade).

Plans will also be interrupted if they are no longer relevant. For example, if the AI is running toward a buddy that it wants to heal, but that buddy has since died, then it is time to select a different plan. This is implemented by adding extra branches to the domain that contains the "continuation conditions." These branches are selected when a plan is active and the plan's continuation conditions are met. They contain a single `continue` task, which lets the planner know that further planning is unnecessary, and the current plan is still the best.

Within this general planning and reasoning framework the domains need specific information to make good tactical decisions. The next section briefly describes the types of information that are available, and how they are used.

4.4.2 Individual Tactical Reasoning—Waypoint Graph and Cover Data

The basis for the combat reasoning of our single and multiplayer bots is a combination of *waypoints* and *cover data*. The *waypoint graph* defines waypoints, positions for which tactical data is available, and links between them that allow the AI to plan paths and navigate. This waypoint graph is generated by our automated tools (described in [Mononen 11]). For each waypoint, cover data is stored that describes the cover available in each direction. The cover data is automatically created in an offline process.

This data, in combination with dynamic information on threats, is used for various tactical decisions. For instance, selecting a suitable position to attack a threat is done by *position picking*, where the waypoint graph is used to generate nearby potential waypoints and score these candidates based on a number of properties. Properties can include cover from known threats, distance from threats or friendlies, line of fire to threats, travel distance to reach the position, etc. The properties that are used and how they influence the score can be specified differently for different behaviors. Another use of this data is *threat prediction*, where the most likely hiding waypoints for a hidden threat are calculated. Our agents' tactical reasoning has been discussed in more details in our previous work [Straatman 06, Van der Leeuw 09].

These tactical services are available to the domains in a number of ways. Position picking or path planning queries can be used in preconditions of branches and will instantiate variables with the best position or path (if any). Predicted positions of threats can be queried in preconditions of branches and plans can use the resulting lists of hiding waypoints in a variety of ways—for example, to search or scan for the threat. In this way we combine a more specific, optimized tactical problem solver with the general HTN planner to generate tactical behavior.

4.5 Squad AI

The previous section described how our autonomous bots make decisions on combat and ability use. We now turn to squads, which will make these bots work together as a group to achieve a goal. A *squad* is an agent that controls a collection of bots. The squad AI structure is similar to an individual's: it collects information into a world state, generates and monitors a plan using the HTN planner, and executes the tasks in that plan. The difference lies in the data collected, domains, and primitive actions.

4.5.1 The Squad Update Loop and Planning Domain

During data collection, the squad AI gathers information on the state of its members. Instead of using perception to collect this information, however the squad bases its world

Table 4.2 Primitive tasks (prefixed with !) for squads

Primitive task	Description
!start_command_sequence	Start a sequence of commands to send to an agent
!order	Send command to agent's queue
!end_command_sequence	End a command sequence
!clear_order	Pop current command from own command queue

state on messages received from its members. Based on this state and the orders given to it by the commander AI, the squad planner generates a plan. The squad does not act directly, but through its members. As a result, most of its primitive tasks simply send an order to a member's *command queue*. Table 4.2 shows some of these primitive tasks.

Each squad and individual has a command queue (similar to RTS units). Newly arriving orders overwrite existing orders, unless they are part of a sequence, in which case they are queued. The individual's domain will try to handle the current command and removes it from the queue when the order is completed.

Listing 4.3 shows a part of the squad method for making one member defend an area. The branch advance takes care of the case where the squad needs to move to the area that must be defended. The plan starts by resetting the squad's bookkeeping on what the member is doing, and then commands the member to stay within the areas the squad pathfinder defines (discussed below), orders the member to move to defend, orders the member to send a message to the squad (so the squad knows it arrived), and on arrival orders the member to stay within the defending area.

Listing 4.3. Part of a squad method showing one branch for defending an area.

```
(:method (order_member_defend ?inp_mbr ?inp_id ?inp_level ?inp_marker
?inp_context_hint)
    ...
    (:branch "advance"
        ()//no preconditions
        (   (!forget member_status ?mbr **)
            (!remember - member_status ?inp_mbr go_defend ?inp_id)
            (!start_command_sequence ?inp_mbr ?inp_level 1)
            (do_announce_destination_waypoint_to_member ?inp_mbr)
            (!order ?inp_mbr clear_area_filter)
            (!order ?inp_mbr set_area_restrictions
                (call find_areas_to_wp ?inp_mbr
                (call get_entity_wp ?inp_marker)))
            (!order ?inp_mbr move_to_defend ?inp_marker)
            (!order ?inp_mbr send_message completed_advance ?inp_id)
            (set_defend_area_restriction ?inp_mbr
                (call get_entity_area ?inp_marker))
            (!order ?inp_mbr defend_marker ?inp_marker)
            (!end_command_sequence ?inp_mbr)
        )
    )
)
```

As stated before, when the individual bot AI has `DefendMarker` as its current order its planner can make different plans to achieve this. The branches of the method that deals with this order specify both character class specific plans and generally applicable plans. The engineer specific branch specifies: "move there, place a turret nearby," the tactician specific branch specifies "move there, call in a sentry drone," and the generic branch just specifies "move there, scan around." The generic branch is always available, so after an engineer placed his turret he can generate a plan to scan around.

Similar to the individual bots, the squad planner needs information about static and dynamic aspects of the world to make tactical plans. The next section will describe the tactical reasoning available to squads.

4.5.2 Squad Tactical Reasoning—Strategic Graph and Influence Map

The squad AI reasons about the terrain using the *strategic graph*. This is a hierarchical summary of the waypoint graph and consists of *areas* (groups of waypoints) and connections between areas. A connection between two areas exists when there is a link between the waypoints of the two areas in the waypoint graph. This ensures that when a path exists between areas in the strategic graph, it also exists in the waypoint graph, and vice versa. The abstraction of detail the strategic graph provides makes squad reasoning more efficient. This is necessary because the squad's plans typically cover larger areas, and sometimes even the entire map, which would be prohibitively expensive if done on the waypoint graph. Since we do not want to micromanage the individual bots, reasoning at the area level also leaves choices for individual bots, when doing their tactical reasoning at the waypoint level.

The strategic graph is automatically generated from the waypoint graph at export time. The clustering algorithm incrementally groups areas together, starting at one area per waypoint. Clustering is done based on connection properties, number of waypoints in an area, and area surface. This process leads to logical areas that have good pathfinding properties. Similar clustering algorithms have been described elsewhere [van der Sterren 08].

An *influence map* provides dynamic information to complement the strategic graph. Each of the factions updates its own influence map. The map assigns an influence float value to each area expressing whether the area is under enemy or friendly control. Influence maps are a standard technique in strategy games and have been documented in detail [Tozour 01]. The influence map is calculated by counting the number of friendly and enemy bots and players in an area as well as automated turrets and drones. Recent enemy and friendly deaths also change the influence values. Next the values are smoothed based on distance and combined with the previous values in the influence map for temporal smoothing.

Each squad has a strategic pathfinder. Using the influence values in strategic pathfinding allows the squads to avoid enemy controlled areas. Another use is the selection of *regroup markers*, which are safe locations near the objective where squads will gather an attack. Choosing between regroup markers is done by taking the influence map values of the area containing each marker into account. Additionally a penalty is given to areas chosen by any friendly squad as part of their paths, which provides variation for repeated attacks and spreads out simultaneous attacks.

The pathfinder is implemented as a single source pathfinder which calculates the cost towards all areas in the level using the position of the squad as source. Figure 4.3 illustrates the results of this pathfinder.

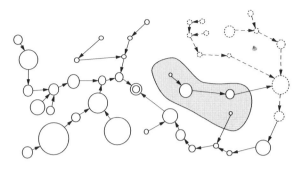

Figure 4.3

The spanning tree of the squad pathfinder in a section of the Salamun Market map. The ultimate destination of the squad is the double circle. The left section of the figure shows a spanning tree that follows the shortest Euclidean path. The shaded dotted zone in the middle right is marked as high cost for the squad, so the dotted nodes on the right avoid that area due to the pathfinder taking into account the costs from the influence map.

The approach allows the squad HTN planner to do many position and path queries as it plans. The squad pathfinder returns a *strategic path* (a sequence of areas) which is then used as a corridor for the squad members by restricting them to these areas. These restrictions constrain the portion of the waypoint graph available for individual path planning and position picking, which allows the individual bots to make their own decisions while still taking the more global tactical decisions of the squad into account. Furthermore the corridor restricts the search space of individual path planning, thus improving performance.

The strategic path planners are updated incrementally using an anytime algorithm to minimize performance impact [Champandard 02]. The incremental nature is less of an issue at the squad level as updates are less frequently needed.

4.6 Commander AI

The highest layer in our AI system is the commander AI for each of the two factions (Helghast and ISA). The commander understands how to play the game modes, and will assign objectives and bots to squads as appropriate for the particular mode being played. Because of the varying number of bots in a faction, the multiple objectives in the game modes, and aspects such as tactical spawn points (TSPs) and vehicles, the commander must be able to create new variants of strategies; a fixed policy for a game mode will not do.

4.6.1 Commander Objectives and Assignment

The commander consists of three parts:

1. A game mode specific part that generates objectives
2. A system for assigning objectives and bots to squads
3. A system for monitoring the objectives assigned to squads

The commander can create squads, delete squads, reuse previous squads, assign a bot to a squad, reassign a bot, and assign objectives to squads and to individual bots. There are four types of objectives: `AdvanceToWaypoint`, `DefendMarker`, `AttackEntity`, and `EscortEntity`. Each objective has a weight, which expresses its importance relative to the other objectives, and an optimal number of bots.

The mission specific AI consists of C++ classes, one for each mission type. These classes use the current information from the game state to add and remove objectives. For example, the class for the Capture and Hold mode needs objectives for attacking or defending the three conquerable areas. Initial objectives will be created to capture all three areas, but if a faction is ahead in score and owns two of the three areas, it can decide to only generate defend objectives for the areas it has already captured.

For Search and Destroy, objectives are added for each of the two destructible targets. The type of objective depends on whether the commander's faction is the defending or attacking side.

In Search and Retrieve there is one object that both factions want to return to their base. When the object has not been claimed, an objective will be generated to advance on the location of the object. If it is claimed, the holding faction will create an escort objective for the carrier, and the other faction will create an objective to attack the carrier to reclaim the object. Both factions may decide to add objectives to defend the enemy's base to prevent returning the object, or to attack their own base to make it easier for the (future) carrier to return.

Some objectives are relevant for all game modes. The tactical spawn points are important because of the shorter travel distances to objectives for re-spawning team members, so capturing or defending them is also a lower priority objective. Furthermore, one level contains vehicles (called Exo's), so there is a *Harass with vehicle* objective that will make a bot in a vehicle attack enemies near the most important objective.

The commanders are custom coded based on input from the multiplayer designers and QA testers. By specifying a list of current objectives, one can make the commanders for a game mode as simple or subtle as needed while the code for the commander stays small.

The algorithm for assigning bots and squads to objectives is as follows:

1. Calculate the ideal distribution of bots, then squads.
2. Create new squads if necessary.
3. If the previous assignments had too many squads assigned to any one objective then remove the excess squads.
4. Assign the best objective to each squad.
5. If too many bots are assigned to a particular squad or objective then unassign them.
6. Assign each free bot to the best squad.

In step 1, all active objectives' weights and desired number of bots are used to calculate the desired number of squads and their sizes. Step 2 and 3 ensure that the actual number of squads matches the desired number as closely as possible. Step 4 prefers to keep squads assigned to previously assigned objectives and otherwise assigns them based on the distance between the squad and the objective. Squads reassigned to new objectives may have too many bots, so step 5 makes these extra bots leave their squad. Step 6 takes care of assigning all bots without a squad to the closest squad in need of more bots. Bots can be assigned to a squad when they are about to re-spawn and then will select the spawn point with the best travel cost (including influence map cost) to their squad. Class selection on spawning by bots is done by a fixed heuristic. This ensures that there are some tacticians and engineers because of their importance for achieving objectives, and randomly assigns a class to the rest of the bots.

4.6.2 Commander Strategic Data

The Commander AI uses a number of *level annotations* to make better map-specific strategic decisions. We chose to manually place these, because they would require complex terrain reasoning to generate automatically but can be identified easily for each map by observing play tests. Some of the annotations are also used by the squad and individual AI at the lower layers when formulating their plans.

Generic level annotations include:

- *Regroup locations*, which are strategic locations that are good to control. Squads are sent here to form up before attacks.
- *Sniping locations*, which specify areas that have good visibility over key locations. Squads are sent here to help defend or attack objectives.

Mission specific annotations include:

- *Assassination hiding locations*. These are markers that specify good locations for the target bot to hide during Assassination missions. Good locations are typically inside defensible buildings. The commander for the defending team initially picks one of these locations, and may decide to move the target to another one based on distance and the influence map later.
- *Defend locations*. Missions with static objectives, such as Capture and Hold, use these locations to define where the defenders should stand or patrol.

Our previous work includes more details on the use of annotations [Straatman 09], as well as on the architecture itself [Verweij 06].

4.7 The AI in Action

As an example, in a Capture and Hold mission the ISA commander might send a squad to defend a capture point, another squad to take the nearby Tactical Spawn point (TSP), and a third squad (which consists of a bot manning an Exo vehicle) to harass any enemies in the areas near the capture point. The squad attacking the TSP plans a path from the base, avoiding another capture point that is owned by the Helghast. Once it has arrived, the tactician captures the TSP and the engineer places a turret on a defend marker near the TSP. After capturing the TSP, the tactician and engineer will patrol and scan the area to defend it. Meanwhile, the squad defending the capture location has come under attack. In response, the tactician calls in drones to help with the defense. Individual bots use the cover data to find cover and attack locations. ISA medics use their revive tool to revive wounded comrades. Engineers repair the supporting Exo when needed. ISA defenders that did not survive will spawn at the nearby TSP to get back to defending the capture point. The overall result is that, by using the architecture described in the sections above, the bots master all gameplay aspects of the *Warzone* mode.

4.8 Future Work

The process of shipping a title always brings new lessons and ideas. Based on what we learned creating *Killzone 3* we are considering the following improvements:

- The squad assignment component of the Commander AI was much harder to get working than it was for *Killzone 2*. This was probably because in *Killzone 3* there are more objectives to consider, but fewer bots to accomplish them with. Therefore we created an agent-based Commander AI that uses the same HTN planner. We expressed our current capture and hold commander and squad assignment in an HTN-based commander and would consider using this approach in future titles.
- It is relatively easy to express different strategies for a game mode using either the objective system or the HTN commander described above. Interviews with our internal testers, game designers, and watching games in public beta will lead to many possible strategies. However, deciding between strategies is harder. We have used reinforcement learning to adapt branch ordering and preconditions in the commanders' HTN domain based on the outcomes of bot versus bot games.

Both these changes are described in more detail in a paper by Folkert Huizinga [Huizinga 11].

4.9 Conclusion

This article described the AI systems we use for our multiplayer bots. We have shown the architecture, algorithms, the way we structure the planning domains, and the extra data (both static and dynamic) involved in making decisions. This approach divides the responsibility for decisions in a hierarchical manner that reduces complexity and maximizes opportunities for adding interesting dynamic behavior.

The use of hierarchical layers is one way we reduce complexity and maximize reuse. Within one agent we often combine static terrain data, a generic problem solver, and dynamic game state data to achieve a nice combination of predictability and reactiveness. Between hierarchical layers the translation from commands to behavior introduces choice and character-specific ways of achieving a goal.

We use various existing techniques in a complementary way. In some places we automatically generate tactical data whereas in others we rely on designer-provided input. We use a generic domain-independent HTN planner to define most of our behavior, but use specific problem solvers for position picking, squad path planning, and lower level humanoid skill planning.

We believe this section shows a way in which various established techniques can be used for combined effect, and that the architecture described here can be applied to many AI engines.

Acknowledgments

The work described here is the result of development over a number of projects and collaboration with numerous other developers. We want to thank the developers at Guerrilla, especially Arjen Beij and the multiplayer design team, for their contributions, feedback, and support. Furthermore, we thank Guerrilla and Sony Computer Entertainment for providing us with the environment that led to the development of the techniques described above.

References

[Champandard 02] A. J. Champandard. "Realistic Autonomous Navigation in Dynamic Environments." Masters Research Thesis, University of Edinburgh, 2002.

[Huizinga 11] F. Huizinga. "Machine Learning Strategic Game Play for a First-Person Shooter Video Game." Masters Research Thesis, Universiteit van Amsterdam, 2011. Available online: (http://www.guerrilla-games.com/publications/index.html#huizinga1106).

[Mononen 11] M. Mononen. "Automatic Annotations in Killzone 3 and Beyond." Paris Game/AI Conference 2011, Paris, June 2011. Available online: (http://www.guerrilla-games.com/publications/index.html#mononen1106).

[Nau 00] D. S. Nau, Y. Cao, A. Lotem, and H. Muñoz-Avila. "SHOP and M-SHOP: Planning with Ordered Task Decomposition." Tech. Report CS TR 4157, University of Maryland, College Park, MD, June, 2000.

[Puig 08] F. Puig Placeres. "Generic perception system." In *AI Game Programming Wisdom 4*, edited by Steve Rabin. Hingham, MA: Charles River Media, 2008, pp. 285–294.

[Straatman 06] R. Straatman, A. Beij, and W. van der Sterren. "Dynamic tactical position evaluation." In *AI Game Programming Wisdom 3*, edited by Steve Rabin. Hingham, MA: Charles River Media, 2006, pp. 389–403.

[Straatman 09] R. Straatman, T. J. Verweij, and A. Champandard. "Killzone 2 multiplayer bots." *Paris Game/AI Conference 2011*, Paris, June 2011. Available online (http://www.guerrilla-games.com/publications/index.html#straatman0906).

[Tozour 01] P. Tozour. "Influence mapping." In *Game Programming Gems 2*, edited by Mark Deloura. Hingham, MA: Charles River Media, 2001, pp. 287–297.

[Van der Leeuw 09] M. van der Leeuw. "The PlayStation®3's SPUs in the Real World: A KILLZONE 2 Case Study" Presentation GDC 2009, San Francisco, March 2009. Available online (http://www.guerrilla-games.com/publications/index.html#vanderleeuw0903).

[van der Sterren 08] W. van der Sterren. "Automated Terrain Analysis and Area Generation Algorithms." http://aigamedev.com/premium/masterclass/automated-terrain-analysis/

[Verweij 06] T. J. Verweij. "A Hierarchically-Layered Multiplayer Bot System for a First-Person Shooter." Masters Research Thesis, Vrije Universiteit Amsterdam, 2006. Available online: (http://www.guerrilla-games.com/publications/index.html#verweij0708).

5

Using Neural Networks to Control Agent Threat Response

Michael Robbins

5.1 Introduction

Neural networks are one of the oldest and most widely used machine learning techniques, with a lineage dating back to at least the 1950s. Although there has been some concern within the game AI community that they might not be the right fit for games, our experience with using them in *Supreme Commander 2* has been tremendously positive. Used properly, they can deliver compelling behaviors with significantly less effort than it would take to hand-code them. In *Supreme Commander 2*, neural networks were used to control the fight or flight response of AI controlled platoons to great effect. Far from being useless, neural networks added a lot of value to the AI without an exorbitant amount of effort.

There are numerous resources both in print and on the web that describe the basics of neural networks, and even provide sample code. The books *Artificial Intelligence for Games* [Millington 09] and *AI Techniques for Game Programing* [Buckland 02] are great resources for getting started, while *Game Programming Gems 2* [Manslow 01] provides sample code and a wide range of practical hints and tips. This article will focus on the specifics of how neural networks were used in *Supreme Commander 2*.

5.2 What Is a Neural Network

There are many different types of neural networks but this article will focus on multilayer perceptrons (MLPs), which were chosen for *Supreme Commander 2* because they're relatively easy to implement and simple to use.

MLPs typically consist of three layers of neurons or "nodes," as they are often called in the neural network literature. These layers are the input layer, the hidden layer, and the output layer. Each node has a value associated with it that lies in the range zero to one and indicates its level of excitation. Nodes are connected to other nodes by unidirectional "weights," which are the analog of biological synapses and allow the level of excitation of one node to affect the excitation of another. In an MLP, each node receives stimulation only from nodes in the preceding layer and provides stimulation only to nodes in the next layer.

Data is fed into an MLP by setting the levels of excitation of the nodes in the input layer. Each node in the hidden layer then receives an amount of stimulation that is equal to an internal bias plus the sum of the products of the levels of excitation of each node in the input layer and the weight by which it is connected to it. The excitation of each node in the hidden layer is then calculated by applying a nonlinear activation function to the value that represents its level of stimulation. The logistic function is the standard choice of activation function for MLPs and produces a level of excitation in the range zero to one.

This process is repeated with each layer in the network receiving stimulation from the preceding layer until the levels of excitation of the network's output nodes have been updated; these levels constitute the network's output and hence its response to the earlier input. The behavior of an MLP is determined entirely by the values of its weights and biases, and the process of training it consists of finding the values of the weights and biases that minimizes some measure of the difference between the network's outputs and some ideal target values.

5.3 Setting Up a Neural Network

For *Supreme Commander 2*, it was decided to use an MLP to control a platoon's reaction to encountering enemy units. We decided to use a total of four MLPs, one for each platoon type: land, naval, bomber, and fighter. We split the MLPs this way so that each platoon type could learn what it needed to without interfering with the other platoon types.

The bulk of the AI's platoon logic would exist inside of a finite-state machine that would use the MLP to decide what to do when the platoon encountered enemy resistance and would continue to use the MLP to reevaluate the constantly changing situation. MLPs provide a great way to accomplish this because they can quickly size up a situation based on their training. In any situation, an MLP can give an AI the ability to determine which enemy targets it should attack first or to retreat if it found itself outmatched. To accomplish this, the first thing that needs to be done is to decide what information the MLP needs to make these decisions and how it should be represented.

5.3.1 Choosing Inputs

Inputs are supplied to an MLP by setting the values that represent the levels of excitation of its input nodes. These values are typically bounded to lie in the range zero to one, though the range minus one to plus one also works well with MLPs. For *Supreme Commander 2*, inputs were created by taking the ratio between the friendly and enemy values of certain statistics which included number of units, unit health, overall damage per second (DPS), movement speed, resource value, shield health, short-range DPS, medium-range DPS, long-range DPS, and repair rate. All input values were clamped to lie in the range zero to one, so the reciprocals of the ratios were also included to provide the network with useful information about the relative sizes of the statistics even when the friendly statistic exceeded the enemy statistic. These statistics were gathered from friendly and enemy units in a radius around the AI's platoon. Altogether, 17 ratios were calculated, and hence the network had 34 inputs.

This relatively large number of inputs worked well in *Supreme Commander 2* but could be problematic in other applications, particularly if there were only a few thousand examples that could be used in training. This can lead to what is called "overfitting," which is where a network effectively learns certain specifics of the training data rather than the general patterns that lie within it. Overfitting is apparent when a network performs significantly better during training than it does when tested. Overfitting is most easily prevented by retraining with a simpler network (or by providing a larger set of training data, of course). Thus, in general, it's a good idea when choosing inputs to find as small a set as possible. At the same time, the MLP will only be able to account for information that you provide to it, so the desire to have a small input set needs to be balanced against a desire to include as much of the relevant information as possible. At the end of the day, you'll need to experiment to find what works for your project.

5.3.2 Choosing Outputs

When inputs are applied to an MLP, it computes outputs in the form of values between zero and one that represent the levels of excitation of its output nodes. For *Supreme Commander 2*, it was decided that each output node would represent the expected utility of one of the actions that the platoon could take. These actions included attack the weakest enemy, attack the closest enemy, attack the highest value enemy, attack a resource generator, attack a shield generator, attack a defensive structure, attack a mobile unit, attack an engineering unit, and attack from range. Although the platoon could run away, the act of running away was not associated with any individual output. Instead, it was decided that the platoon would run away if none of the network's outputs were above 0.5, because that indicated that no individual action was expected to have particularly high utility.

5.3.3 Choosing the Number of Hidden Nodes

It is the hidden nodes in an MLP that are responsible for its ability to learn complex nonlinear relationships, and the more hidden nodes a network has, the more complex are the relationships that it can learn. Unfortunately, increasing the number of hidden nodes also comes at the cost of increased training time and, as with increasing numbers of inputs, an increased risk of overfitting. Unfortunately, the optimum number of hidden nodes is problem dependent and must be determined by trial and error. One approach is to initially test your network with only two or three hidden nodes, and then add more until acceptable performance is achieved. For more complex decisions, it's reasonable to start with a larger network, but you will want to ensure that the trained network is thoroughly tested to make sure that its performance under test is consistent with its performance during training.

For *Supreme Commander 2*, we found that a network with 98 hidden nodes achieved good and consistent performance during both training and testing. Such a network would be too large for many other applications, particularly when the amount of training data is limited, but given our ability to generate arbitrarily large amounts of training data and the complexity of the decision being made, this worked well for us.

5.4 Training a Neural Network

Training an MLP usually involves repeatedly iterating through a set of training examples that each consist of a pairing of inputs and target outputs. For each pair, the input is presented to the network, the network computes its output, and then the network's weights and biases are modified to make its output slightly closer to the target output. This process is repeated for each example in the training set, with each example typically being presented hundreds or thousands of times during the course of training.

In *Supreme Commander 2*, we decided not to create a fixed set of training examples but to generate examples dynamically by making the AI play against itself. This was achieved by putting two AI platoons on a map and having them battle against each other as they would in a regular game, except we would run the game as fast as possible to speed up iteration time. During the battle, the AI's platoons would act the same as they would in a regular game. The AI's neural networks would make a decision as to which action should be performed whenever opposing platoons met on the battlefield by gathering data about the friendly and enemy units in a radius around the platoon and feeding that data into the MLP. Instead of actually taking the action suggested by the network, however, each platoon was made to perform a random action and a measure of how good those actions were—a measure of their utility—was derived using a fitness function. The utility measure then formed the target output for the output node corresponding to the random action, and the target outputs for all other output nodes were set to each node's current level of excitation; in this way, the network updated its weights and biases to improve its estimate of the utility of the random action but didn't attempt to change any other outputs. Random actions were used instead of the actions suggested by the networks to ensure that a good mix of actions were tried in a wide range of circumstances. An untrained network will typically repeatedly perform the same action in a wide range of circumstances and hence will learn extremely slowly—if it learns at all.

This training process produced an MLP that responded to an input by estimating the utility of each of the different actions. Choosing the best action was then a simple matter of choosing the action associated with the output that had the highest level of excitation. The key to ensuring that these actions were appropriate was to make sure that the fitness function—which assessed the utility of actions during training—assigned the highest utility to the action that was most appropriate in each situation.

5.4.1 Creating the Fitness Function

The fitness function's job is to evaluate the results of the selected action to determine how much better or worse the situation became as a result of its execution. For *Supreme Commander 2*, this was achieved by gathering the same set of data (number of units, DPS values, health, etc.) that were used to make the initial decision, and then examining how those data values changed when the action was taken.

```
float friendRatio = 0.0f;
int numData = 0;
for (int i = 0; i < mFriendData.size(); ++i)
{
    if (mFriendData[i] > 0.0f)
    {
        ++numData;
        friendRatio += (newFriendData[i]/mFriendData[i]);
    }
}
if (numData > 0)
    friendRatio /= numData;
float enemyRatio = 0.0f;
numData = 0;
for (int i = 0; i < mEnemyData.size(); ++i)
{
    if (mEnemyData[i] > 0.0f)
    {
        ++numData;
        enemyRatio += (newEnemyData[i]/mEnemyData[i]);
    }
}
if (numData > 0)
    enemyRatio /= numData;
DetermineNewOutputs(friendRatio, enemyRatio, mOutputs, mActionIndex);
network->FeedAndBackPropagate(mInputs, mOutputs);
```

Listing 5.1 gives a snippet of the fitness function we used on *Supreme Commander 2*. It first takes the ratio between the new and old values for each type of data. Note that since all of these values are likely to have stayed the same or gone down, all of these ratios should be between 0 and 1, which constrains the magnitude of the later calculations to something reasonable. Next, we take the average of the ratios for the friendly units and for the enemy units. This gives a sense of how much the overall tactical situation has changed for each side not only in terms of damage taken, but also in terms of every significant capability—shields, damage output, number of units remaining, and so forth. The resulting averages are passed into `DetermineNewOutputs` which determines what the correct output—called the *desired output*—value should have been using Equation 5.1.

$$desiredOutput = output \times \left(1 + \left(friendRatio - enemyRatio\right)\right) \tag{5.1}$$

This desired output value is then plugged into the corresponding output node of the MLP, and the MLP goes through a process of adjusting weights and biases, starting at the output layer and working its way back to the input layer in a process called *back propagation*. This is how an MLP learns.

5.4.2 Adjusting Learning Parameters

The training of an MLP is typically controlled by a learning rate parameter that controls the sizes of the changes the network makes when adjusting its weights and biases. A higher learning rate allows for larger changes, which can lead to faster learning but increases the risk of numerical instability and oscillations as the network attempts to zero in on optimum values; a lower rate can make training impractically slow. One common trick is therefore to start training with a higher learning rate and decrease it over time—so you initially get fast learning but, as the weights and biases approach their optimum values, the adjustments become more and more conservative. For *Supreme Commander 2*, we initially started with a learning rate of 0.8 and gradually lowered it down to 0.2.

MLP training algorithms usually also have a parameter called *momentum*, which can be used to accelerate the learning process. Momentum does this by reapplying a proportion of the last change in the value of a weight or bias during a subsequent adjustment, thereby accelerating consistent changes and helping to prevent rapid oscillations. As with the learning rate, a higher value for the momentum parameter is good initially because it accelerates the early stages of learning. For *Supreme Commander 2* we started with a momentum value of 0.9 and eventually turned momentum off entirely by setting it to zero.

5.4.3 Debugging Neural Networks

A neural network is essentially a black box, and that makes debugging them difficult. You can't just go in, set a breakpoint, and figure out why it made the decision it did. You also can't just go in and start adjusting weights. This is a large part of the reason why neural networks are not more popular. In general, if an MLP is not performing as desired, then it's usually a problem with the data its receiving as input, the way its outputs are interpreted, the fitness function that was used during training, or the environment it was exposed to during training.

For example, if an MLP performs well during training but performs less well during testing, it could be because the environment the network was exposed to during training wasn't representative of the environment it experienced during testing. Maybe the mix of units was different, or something changed in the design? It could also be due to overfitting, in which case a network with fewer inputs or fewer hidden nodes might perform better. If an MLP performed well during training but its behavior isn't always sensible, then it might be that the fitness function that was used during training was flawed—perhaps it sometimes assigned high utility to actions that were inappropriate or low utility to actions that were appropriate—more on this point later. If an MLP fails to perform well even during training, then it's usually because either its inputs provide too little relevant information or it has too few hidden nodes to learn the desired relationships.

If you are using neural networks in a game, these points need to be stressed. When debugging neural networks, the solution is usually not to find the point of failure by setting a breakpoint. You have to think about the network's inputs, its outputs, and how your fitness function is training your neural network.

5.4.4 Case Study: Repairing a Bug in the Fitness Function

In *Supreme Commander 2,* each player starts with a unit called an ACU and whichever player destroys their opponent's ACU first wins the game. However, when an ACU is destroyed, it blows up in a large nuclear explosion, taking out most of the smaller units and buildings in a wide area. For the neural network this posed a problem: since the network was trained on tactical engagements, it didn't know about winning or losing. All it saw was that when it sent units up against an ACU, most of them were destroyed.

This introduced a bug that made the AI unwilling to commit troops to attack an ACU. It would overwhelm players with massive groups of units but, as soon as it saw an ACU, it would turn tail and run. The problem wasn't in the behavior code, and it wasn't something that could be tracked down by setting a breakpoint; the problem was in the fitness function.

Once we realized what the problem was, the solution was simple: we needed to modify the fitness function to take into account the destruction of an enemy ACU. Basically, we needed to teach the neural network that it was worth taking out an ACU whatever the cost. This was done by modifying the fitness function to provide a very positive measure of utility whenever an enemy ACU was destroyed. Instead of relying on the results of Equation 5.1, the fitness function would return a desired output of double whatever the original MLP output was, clamped to a maximum of 1.0. After retraining the network with the new fitness function, we saw a huge improvement. The AI would run from the ACU if it only had a small number of units but, if it had a large enough group to take it down, it would engage, winning the game as the enemy's ACU blew up in spectacular fashion.

5.5 Adjusting Behavior

Even though the behavior of an MLP is fixed once it's been trained, it's still possible to use it to generate AI that exhibits a variety of different behaviors. In *Supreme Commander 2*, for example, we added an aggression value to the AI personality. This value was used to modify the ratios that were input to the MLP to mimic the effect of the AI's units being stronger than they actually were. This made the MLP overestimate the utility of more aggressive actions, producing an overall more aggressive AI.

Rather than always having the AI perform the action for which the MLP estimated highest utility, different action selection schemes could be considered. For example, the AI could select one of the N highest utility actions at random or select an action with probability proportional to its utility. Both of these schemes would produce behavior with greater variety though they both involve selecting actions that are probably suboptimal and hence would probably produce AI that is easier to beat.

5.6 Neural Network Performance

The run-time performance of an MLP is determined by how many nodes it has. In *Supreme Commander 2*, each MLP has 34 input nodes, 15 output nodes, and 98 hidden nodes and we never saw a network take longer than 0.03 ms to compute its output (during an eight-player AI match). Since feeding a MLP forward is basically just a bunch of floating-point math, this is not surprising. Performance will, of course, vary depending on hardware and the details of your implementation, but it is unlikely that the time taken to query an MLP will be a problem.

5.7 Benefits of Using a Neural Network

Probably the most notable benefit of using a neural network over something like a utility based approach is that you don't have to come up with the weights yourself. You don't have to figure out whether health is more important than shields in any particular decision or how they compare to speed. This is all worked out for you during training. Each of *Supreme Commander 2*'s neural networks took about an hour of training to reach a shippable level of performance. We did, however, have to complete the training process several times before we ended up with a set of neural networks that worked well, mostly due to snags such as the ACU problem that was mentioned earlier.

A major benefit of the input representation that was used in *Supreme Commander 2* was that it provided an abstract representation of the composition of a platoon that remained valid even when the statistics of individual units changed; the neural network is not looking at specific units, only their statistics. As long as there weren't any radical changes in the game's mechanics, the networks were able to continue to make good decisions as the statistics of individual units were modified to produce a well-balanced game.

5.8 Drawbacks of Using Neural Networks

Like most things in life, using a neural network solution doesn't come free. There are certainly some drawbacks to using them over more traditional methods, the foremost of those being their black box nature. With most solutions you can come up with a tool that designers can use to adjust the behavior of the AI; at the very least you can make small adjustments to alter its behavior to suit their needs. With neural networks this is difficult, if not altogether impossible. On *Supreme Commander 2*, we got lucky because we had a separate AI system for the campaign mode than we did for skirmish mode. The designers could make any changes they wanted for the campaign but they did not want to have control over skirmish mode. Unfortunately, most projects are not that lucky.

The other issue is the training time. Unlike with other techniques, where you can easily make small changes, if you change anything to do with a neural network—its inputs, the interpretation of its outputs, the fitness function, and the number of hidden nodes—you have to start training from scratch. Even though training is hands-off, the time it takes makes it difficult to quickly try things out.

5.9 Conclusion

Whenever the subject of neural networks in *Supreme Commander 2* comes up, two questions are frequently asked: Was it worth using them, and would you use them again? The answer to both is yes. We firmly believe that the AI in *Supreme Commander 2* would not have had the same impact without the use of neural networks. Moreover, if someone proposed doing *Supreme Commander 3*, you can bet neural networks would play a part.

That being said, neural networks are not for every project, and they are certainly not the be-all and end-all of AI. Neural networks are a tool like any other in that they have specific strengths and weaknesses. They are very handy if you have a well-defined set of actions or responses and designers don't require a lot of control. If your designers are going to want to fine-tune things or you have to work with multiple sets of responses to accommodate things like different AI personalities, however, you may want to look at other options.

References

[Buckland 02] M. Buckland. *AI Techniques for Game Programming*. Cincinnati, OH: Premier Press, 2002, pp. 233–274.

[Manslow 01] J. Manslow. *Game Programming Gems 2: Using a Neural Network in a Game: A Concrete Example*. Hingham, MA: Charles River Media, 2001, pp. 351–357.

[Millington 09] I. Millington and J. Funge. *Artificial Intelligence for Games*. Burlington, MA: Morgan Kaufmann, 2009, pp. 646–665.

6

Looking for Trouble
Making NPCs Search Realistically

Rich Welsh

6.1 Introduction

Searching is so second nature to us that apart from the inconvenience of having misplaced something, we're naturally able to effectively track down missing items. What thought processes do we go through while we're searching? How can we take these and apply them to our nonplayer characters (NPCs) in order to make them appear more realistic when they're searching? If you're searching for answers to these questions, then look no further!

6.2 Types of Searching

The main focus of this chapter is to outline the way in which NPCs search for hostile targets in a title that I am unable to name. Since the target in this game is a player character, the target will be referred to as "the player"; however, in terms of implementation, this could be any target that is hostile to the NPC. The assumption is also made that the player is actively hiding from hostile NPCs. Despite these assumptions, a lot of the principles described here are suitable for almost any type of search. With that in mind, there are two main types of search that can occur in the game.

6.2.1 Cautious Search

A cautious style of searching is one in which the NPC has been alerted, but does not know whether their target is hostile. This style of searching is generally used when the NPC has been alerted by a stimulus without any knowledge of the source, for example, if a player throws a bottle to draw attention and lure an NPC. While the NPC is aware of the noise, they are unaware of whether the source is a friend or foe.

6.2.2 Aggressive Search

An aggressive search is one where the NPC knows about the target they are searching for and, at the very least, that their target is a hostile one. In most cases, the NPC will have previously seen the player and the player will have successfully evaded the NPC. However, any NPC that has knowledge of their target should employ this style of search—this includes reinforcement NPCs who have just entered the engagement or NPCs who have been informed of their hostile target by an ally.

6.3 Triggering a Search

The first key to making a search seem realistic is triggering it at the right time and telegraphing that transition to the player. Since the player is usually still nearby when the search is triggered, it is likely that they are still able to see or hear the NPCs who are about to hunt for them. Therefore, a poor decision on starting the search will be obvious to the player.

While it may not seem as important as the search itself, telegraphing the transition into a searching state to the player is vital to get right in order for players to be able to identify what will and will not cause NPCs to react. In most games, this transition is signaled by some dialogue and occasionally an accompanying animation.

6.3.1 Initial Stimulus-Based Trigger

An initial stimulus-based trigger is one in which the NPC goes from an unaware state into a searching state due to an indirect stimulus such as a sound. If the NPC is able to see the target directly, then they would enter a combat state rather than search, so in this situation the player must have created some kind of stimulus that was sensed without a direct line of sight to the player.

Stimuli received by NPCs can be divided into two categories. *Hostile stimuli*, such as gunfire and explosions, will trigger an aggressive search response. Although the target isn't known, it is assumed to be hostile from the type of stimulus received. *Distraction stimuli* on the other hand, for example, a bottle being thrown or a prop being knocked over, will trigger a cautious search.

6.3.2 Losing a Target

This method of triggering a search is one in which the NPCs had a direct line of sight to the target at some point—whether the player just briefly dashed across the NPC's field of view or ran away when spotted or actively engaged in combat. When losing sight of a target, NPCs have knowledge of the last position and direction in which they were moving. Normally, if it were a person watching a target leave, they would be able to estimate the location of the target after losing sight. Simply using the target's last known velocity to estimate a current position after a time can cause problems however, as characters (especially players) don't move in perfectly straight lines.

One common problem with extrapolating a position in this manner arises when trying to then map that extrapolated position to a navigable position. Without testing against navigable surfaces (which can range from being a simple navmesh raycast through to a full-blown physics request), it is impossible to guarantee that such a naïve method won't have generated a position inside a prop or outside of the world. A far simpler solution to this problem is to simply allow the NPC to "know" the position of their target for a few seconds after losing sight of them—the exact number can be tweaked to suit the feel of the game, but around 2–3 s gives a reasonably realistic feel. This is both a cheap and effective way of giving the AI a human sense of "intuition" and has been used in a number of high-profile titles, including the *Halo*, *Crysis*, and *Crackdown* series of games.

6.4 Phases of Searching

When performing the actual search in the game, both the cautious and aggressive searches follow the same phases. The differences between the two come from the speed at which the character moves, the animations that they play, and the rate at which they abandon the search (see Table 6.1 for a summary of the differences).

6.4.1 Phase 1

When you're searching for something, the most sensible place to start looking is the last place that you saw it. The same principle should be applied here when NPCs are searching for their target. Whether it's a cautious or an aggressive search, the first phase should be to check the last known position in what can be described as a "narrow" search.

It is worth noting that while implementing phase 1, it is important to consider how many NPCs should be able to simultaneously investigate the search location. This also may vary between a cautious style and an aggressive style of searching.

6.4.1.1 Cautious

In the case of a stimulus that has drawn the NPC's attention, the NPC should either move up until they have line of sight with the stimulus position or move as close to the position as possible. A suitable animation (such as an animation that makes the character look around or report the incident over a radio) can then be played. Often with a cautious search, once the initial position of the stimulus has been investigated, there is no further need to progress into the second search phase.

In a cautious first phase, limiting the number of NPCs who move to investigate can dramatically change the feel of your game. By allowing only a single NPC, it gives the player the option to peel targets away from a group in order to take them out separately

Table 6.1 Differences between Cautious and Aggressive Searching Modes

	Cautious	Aggressive
Movement speed	Walk	Run
Animations	Slow, glancing around	Weapon raised, more alert
Abandon search	After initial location searched (phase 1 only)	After all locations searched or time limit reached (phases 1 and 2)

or sneak past them more easily. This also makes it possible for emergent interactions between the NPCs to take place—for example, the NPC going to investigate could play an audio clip to any nearby allies saying that he's going to check out the disturbance, and they could reply with an acknowledgment. If that character doesn't return within a certain time, a new stimulus could be generated at his position that attracts allies to see why he hasn't returned.

Any NPCs who weren't allowed to investigate the source should lose interest in the search and return to their standard behaviors.

6.4.1.2 Aggressive

When searching aggressively, NPCs know that they are engaging a hostile target; thus, they should be much more alert as they approach and their movement should reflect that. For example, they might run until they're able to establish a line of sight with the target's estimated position and then slow to walk more cautiously up to that position. This gives the appearance that while they are trying to track their target down, they are also aware of the potential danger that they're facing.

Unlike the cautious first phase, all NPCs who are involved in this search should stay in the first phase until either the search is completed or phase 2 is started. These NPCs should look as if they're assisting without starting to sweep—this can be achieved by having them cover their colleagues by aiming their weapons, moving into cover or more tactical positions nearer to the search target's last known position, or just playing suitable animations.

In the aggressive first phase, allowing multiple NPCs to all investigate simultaneously can allow the characters to appear more coordinated—however, a limit should still be placed to prevent every NPC from clustering at the same point (a limit of 2 or 3 characters searching simultaneously works well). Upon reaching their target destination, suitable animations and audio can be played, and all other NPCs who are participating in the search should be informed that the phase will now be advanced.

6.4.2 Phase 2

The second phase is a much broader search, with characters sweeping the area to try and locate the target after the first phase failed to locate them. This doesn't really apply for the cautious search, as after investigating the initial position of the stimuli, the search should finish (however, this is ultimately a design decision to be made to best suit your game).

It is important in this phase to have some kind of search coordinator that NPCs register with, as the search needs to be performed as a group. Each participant in the second phase of a search will request a new search spot to investigate from the coordinator and move until either they reach that position or have a clear line of sight to it. This behavior will be repeated until the search coordinator runs out of search spots or reaches a time limit.

6.4.2.1 Generation of Search Spots

These searching behaviors were originally designed to work with the CryENGINE AI system, which utilizes a tactical point system (TPS) [Jack 13]. The behaviors operate on a set of discrete points. Although there are other systems that can be used to describe search areas within the game (such as occupancy maps [Isla 06]), these data can always be reduced to a set of points on which these behaviors will operate.

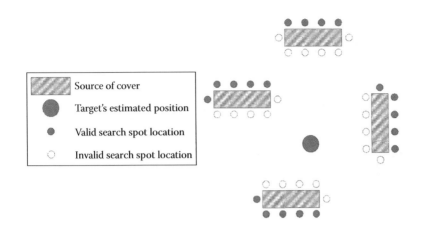

Figure 6.1

Search spot generation.

As soon as an aggressive style search is initiated, the search coordinator should start building up a list of search spots. A search spot is a location that could potentially be hiding the player and as such will need to be investigated.

Commonly, a location that provides cover for a character also obscures that character from sight. This allows cover positions to be used as a basis for generating search spots. Similarly, a system such as a TPS could be used to generate locations in a radius around the target's last known position that would obscure the target from view.

An example of search spot generation can be seen in Figure 6.1. In this example, cover is used as the basis for generating search spots. Any cover that is obscured from the target's estimated position is used to create a search spot. If there aren't enough points generated by using cover, then random positions on the navigation mesh that are hidden from the estimated position can be used to increase the number of search spots, for example, adding points that are around corners or in alleys.

6.4.2.2 Performing the Search

After the search spots have been generated and the search coordinator has a list of them, it's time for the NPCs to begin their broad phase 2 search. This works as follows:

A new search spot should be requested from the search coordinator. If the coordinator does not return a search spot (this could be because there are no more spots available or because a time limit has been reached), then the character should return to their regular behavior. If a spot is available, then the coordinator should calculate the best spot for the search, mark that spot as being "in progress," and return it to the NPC. The character should then move toward the spot with their weapon raised, playing alerted "glancing around" animations.

As the NPC is moving, line of sight checks should be done to all unsearched spots that are within its field of view (including the current target search spot). By having all searching NPCs test against all unsearched spots that they can potentially see, spots are quickly removed from the coordinator. This prevents different characters from searching an area that has already been swept, as in Figure 6.2.

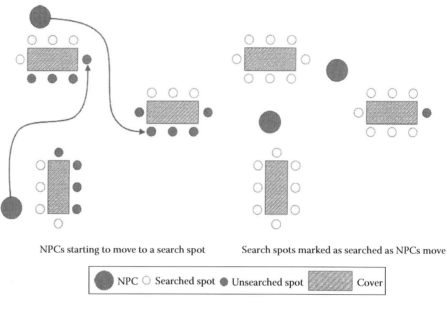

NPCs starting to move to a search spot Search spots marked as searched as NPCs move

● NPC ○ Searched spot ● Unsearched spot ▨ Cover

Figure 6.2

Search spots becoming marked as searched as NPCs move.

There are two issues with this approach that need to be addressed, however. First, raycasts are expensive. To address this issue, deferring or timeslicing these raycasts is a good option. Unless the characters are moving extremely fast, a raycast every 1 or 2 s to each unsearched spot will be enough to invalidate any that the character passively searches while moving toward their target spot.

The second issue that can arise with this method is that the coordinator's pool of search spots can be depleted very quickly if a lot of spots are in areas visible to characters. Rather than allow multiple NPCs to search the same spot, the best way to solve this problem is to ensure that the initial pool of spots is large enough to accommodate a suitably lengthy search. Alternatively, if the search needs to continue but all spots have been marked as searched, the coordinator could mark the oldest "searched" points as unsearched once more and allow the search to continue or increase the search radius and rerun the generation step once more to provide a new, larger pool of search spots.

6.4.2.3 Selecting the Best Search Spot

When the coordinator is asked to select the best search spot to return for an NPC, it first needs to check whether any of the search spots that it has stored in the search list are currently free to be searched. Any spots that are in progress are no good, since that would lead to two NPCs moving to the same spot at the same time. Similarly, any spots that have been marked as already searched should be ignored.

Once the unavailable spots have been eliminated, the remaining spots should be scored and the most suitable for the requesting NPC returned. This scoring of potential points is often used in AI systems for tactical positioning in order to help determine which potential position will be the most attractive option for an AI. A good example of how to score points can be seen in *Killzone's* Tactical Positioning system [Straatman 05]. If no spots are available or if the search has exceeded it's time limit, then the system returns NULL and the NPC should abandon the search.

When scoring the spots, the most important two weights should be the distance of the spot from the target's estimated position and the distance of the spot from the NPC's current location. However, as several NPCs will be drawing from the same pool of points, this leads to characters favoring search spots in areas localized around themselves. By adding an extra weight for the distance of the search spot from the player's actual current position, it gives the AI the illusion of human intuition and shapes the search pattern gently in the correct direction. The weighting for distance to target actual location should be quite subtle compared to the other two weights, so as not to make the NPCs all immediately flock to the target. This would both break the illusion of intuition and make the game feel unfairly stacked against the player.

6.4.3 Improving Phase 2 Search: Gap Detection

While moving toward their target search spot, it is important to keep the characters animated in order to keep them looking as if they are actively searching an area—not just mindlessly pathing from point to point.

The obvious way to handle this is simply to layer sweeping or glancing animations on top of the movement. This can result in glances that seem random or unmotivated, however. The realism of the NPCs and the effectiveness of their search can both be increased by adding gap or corner detection to their searching movement, as shown in Figure 6.3. By using long raycasts both perpendicular to the character's path direction and slightly ahead of the character, upcoming gaps can be detected on either side of the path. The character then has the option to turn and look into the gap, which will potentially invalidate search spots that would otherwise require further investigation. The character can pick

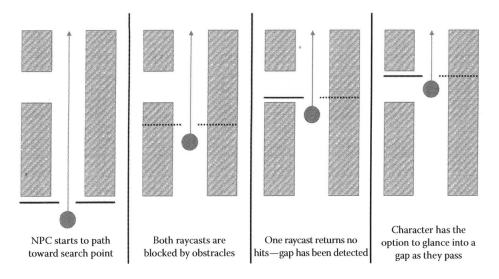

| NPC starts to path toward search point | Both raycasts are blocked by obstracles | One raycast returns no hits—gap has been detected | Character has the option to glance into a gap as they pass |

Figure 6.3

Gap detection.

randomly between going over to look, an animated turn, and a head-only glance, so that not every character passing by a gap will react in the same way.

6.4.4 Ending the Search

There are two ways that a search can end: either the target is successfully located by an NPC or the search is called off and the target is considered lost. With the latter, it will ultimately be the decision of the search coordinator as to whether the search should stop. When either no more search spots are valid to be searched or a time limit is reached, NPCs should naturally filter back to their regular behaviors in their own time. Although they are operating as a group, stopping all NPCs simultaneously looks very strange, giving the impression that they are operating under one hive mind.

6.5 Conclusion

This chapter examined the subtleties of NPC searching. First, the type of searching must be determined, either as a cautious search or an aggressive search, based on the triggering event. Then the search proceeds in two phases. The first phase attempts to find the source of the triggering event directly by going to its last known position. Once successfully investigated, a cautious search will complete, while an aggressive search will proceed to phase 2. In phase 2, new search spots will be generated and investigated, with NPCs sharing information over recently searched spots. If the player was not uncovered during these searches, then the NPCs should naturally return back to their previous tasks.

As a practical matter of effectiveness, there were several key tricks introduced that make the search behavior look more natural. First, if the NPC loses sight of the target, it should cheat and continue to know the target's position for 2–3 s, as if continuing to pursue by intuition. Second, within phase 2, it's important to generate enough search spots so that the search doesn't end prematurely. Lastly, the search behavior will appear much more natural if you implement gap detection and have the NPCs exhibit various glancing animations.

References

[Isla 06] Isla, D. 2006. Probabilistic target tracking and search using occupancy maps. In *AI Game Programming Wisdom 3*, ed. S. Rabin. Hingham, MA: Charles River Media.

[Jack 13] Jack, M. 2013. Tactical position selection: An architecture and query language. In *Game AI Pro: Collected Wisdom of Game AI Professionals*, ed. S. Rabin. New York: A K Peters/CRC Press.

[Straatman 05] Straatman, R. and Beij, A. 2005. Killzone's AI: Dynamic procedural tactics. http://www.cgf-ai.com/docs/straatman_remco_killzone_ai.pdf (accessed September 10, 2014).

7

Modeling Perception and Awareness in *Tom Clancy's Splinter Cell Blacklist*

Martin Walsh

7.1 Introduction

With many games incorporating stealth elements and generally trying to increase fidelity, having solid perception and awareness models for nonplayer characters (NPCs) is becoming increasingly important. This chapter discusses four types of perception and awareness that were modeled in *Tom Clancy's Splinter Cell Blacklist*: visual, auditory, environmental, and social/contextual. Before jumping in, we'll present the four characteristics that we believe these models need to display to be successful: fairness, consistency, good feedback, and intelligence.

7.1.1 Fairness

In a game with stealth, getting detected can be the difference between success and the player throwing their controller across the room, especially if it felt unfair. Having models that *feel* fair is key, it is also one of the most difficult things to achieve since both the models themselves and how fair they are in a given situation are extremely subjective.

7.1.2 Consistency

As a player, you need to have some idea of what the AI will perceive and how they will react so you as the player can strategize and improve; so the AI's behavior needs to be somewhat predictable. This is in contrast to actual humans who vary in terms of what they perceive and how they react and, as a result, tend to be very unpredictable. Note that predictability does not mean repetitiveness; we need, for example, to get similar distances and timing for reactions every time, but the animations and barks (short vocal clips) need to be different; otherwise, immersion is broken very quickly.

7.1.3 Good Feedback

While consistency is essential, good feedback is also required to help the player understand the AI's behavior. The player must be able to "read" or understand what the AI is doing and why they are doing it. Similar to what is mentioned earlier, it's a difficult balance between readable feedback and something that looks and feels human. Getting the right barks and animations is important, as well as having enough variety.

7.1.4 Intelligence

Finally, if your opponents feel dumb, it isn't satisfying to beat them. But not being dumb does not necessarily mean being smart; it means always being plausible.

Now that we've covered the four key components for success, let's examine the models themselves.

7.2 Visual Perception

Any game where the player can hide, or break line of sight (LOS), requires some type of visual perception model. Commonly, we refer to this as a vision cone, and while a cone does a good job of modeling what the NPC can see directly in front of him, it does a poor job of modeling many other aspects of vision. The two most glaring examples are peripheral vision and vision at a distance. It's pretty obvious why a cone doesn't model peripheral vision well, but for vision at a distance, we need to dive a bit deeper.

Before we do, we will examine the difference between perception and awareness. On *Splinter Cell*, we used the following definition of awareness and perception: awareness is a set of discreet mental states (levels of awareness) that represent an increasingly more detailed understanding of the thing being perceived and that can be reached progressively over time through sensory perception.

When you first perceive something, you only start to become aware of it. In other words, if you see something moving in the distance, all you can really say is, "I see *something* over there." What's key here is you don't know exactly what you see; that potentially takes more time and depends on many factors such as what you expect to see, lighting, and the amount of time you see it for. Many games, including *Blacklist*, abstract all of that into a progress bar that, while analog in nature, only represents two binary states for the NPC: "I don't see anything suspicious" or "that's enemy #1 over there!" Some games (including *Splinter Cell*) include a third, intermediate, state where the NPC knows he saw something and will go to investigate (usually at some percentage of the progress bar). See Figures 7.1 through 7.3 for a description of how we did this on *Blacklist*.

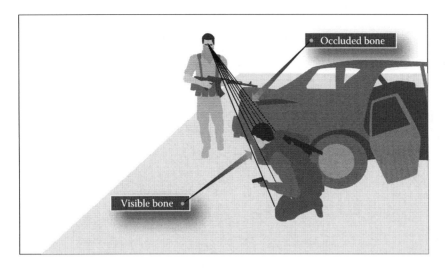

Figure 7.1

On *Blacklist*, we raycast to eight different bones on the player's body. Depending on the stance, it takes a certain number of visible bones to kick off detection. In this case, the player stance is "in cover" that requires more than the two bones that are currently visible so detection has not yet begun.

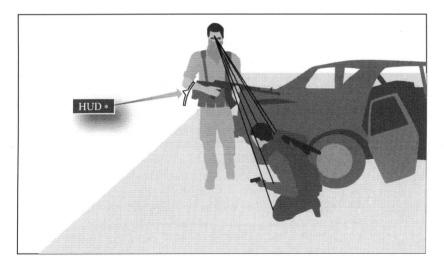

Figure 7.2

Once enough bones are visible to the NPC, the detection process starts and a timer kicks off. The full range of the timer is defined by the detection shape the player is in (Figure 7.3), and the actual value used is arrived at by scaling linearly inside that range based on the current distance to the player. The timer is represented by the growing HUD element that provides feedback to the player that defines his window of opportunity to break LOS or kill the NPC to avoid detection. Once the detection HUD is full, the player is detected.

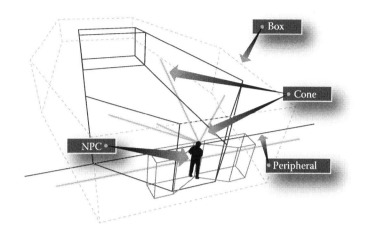

Figure 7.3

This debug drawing represents the detection shapes in *Blacklist*. The coffin-shaped box can be seen, as well as the standard vision cone that defines the area directly in front of the NPC where the player should get detected quickly. The most inclusive shape the player is in defines the range of the detection timer.

The point is that AI developers try to combine the concepts of seeing something and being aware of what we see into a single concept modeled essentially using vision shapes and a timer. On *Blacklist*, when the player is inside of a vision shape of the NPC, unobstructed and lit, a timer kicks off, which is scaled based on the distance to the player, lightness of the player, NPC state, etc., and when that timer reaches 0 (or the progress bar is full), the NPC immediately does two things: he *perceives* the player and becomes *aware* of him as a threat. This abstraction forces us to compromise: we need to define the area where the NPC should perceive *and* become aware of the player within some reasonable time.

Getting back to the vision cone, the reason a cone doesn't model vision at a distance well is that a cone expands as it moves away from the NPC, which implies that as things get further away from the NPC in the direction he is looking, he tends to perceive, and become aware of, things that are laterally farther away. Up to a certain distance that is plausible, but past that distance, it doesn't provide reasonable behavior. If the player is far enough away and off to one side, we don't want the NPCs to become aware of them at all, even though it seems they should still be perceiving him within their field of view. This insight caused us to first replace cones with boxes for vision at a distance; this is the solution we used on *Splinter Cell Conviction*. On *Blacklist*, we refined it further and replaced our standard boxes with coffin-shaped boxes (Figure 7.3) that expand up to a point like a cone and then start to contract as they continue to move further away from the NPC, which gives us the effect we want.

It's important to note that no solution is perfect. All of the variations described have a threshold (the edge of the vision shape). If the player is 1 cm outside of that threshold, then the NPC will stand there forever without seeing the player. One centimeter inside and the player will be detected within a couple of seconds at most. This is a direct result of the way the model is abstracted and the need to match the NPC state to the feedback we display to the player (in this case the detection HUD).

On *Splinter Cell*, we arrived at our solution through many hours of playtesting and designer tweaking. For different games, the right solution may be different and it's impossible to have a single solution that gives the expected results for everyone all the time. Even if we had a perfect model of vision, a player may feel that in a certain case, an NPC should have seen him when he didn't and vice versa. This is not fixable since even in real life we can be surprised when we think someone is looking right at something and doesn't see it (anyone who watches sports with referees can attest to that). What's important is to provide a consistent model, with good feedback, that fits the expectations of the players of your game.

7.3 Environmental Awareness

Environmental awareness is a broad term. At the very basic level, the navmesh or navigation graph provides environmental awareness. It tells the NPC which parts of the environment are walkable and whether two parts of the environment are connected. Other common parts of the model include cover representation and interactive objects like doors or switches. All of these give the NPC some knowledge about his environment that helps him interact with it better and appear more intelligent because of this. The two things we focused on modeling beyond these basics in SC were changes to objects in the environment and the connectivity of the environment.

7.3.1 Connectivity

In the first *Splinter Cell* games, there were very few active NPCs. This meant that, once in combat, finding a cover that (when peeked out) gave LOS on the player was relatively easy and taking that cover was enough to give the impression that NPCs were aware of their environment on a basic level. Starting with *Conviction*, we had 12 active NPCs and some very tight areas. This meant that often many NPCs could not find cover with LOS on the player because in many situations there were more NPCs than available covers. These NPCs ended up staring at the player through walls since they couldn't get a direct LOS but had nothing better to look at.

To solve this problem, we initially thought about pathfinding to the player and having the NPC look at some visible point along that path to give the impression that he is looking at where the player may be coming from instead of staring at a wall. While this could work in some cases, it has a couple of major drawbacks: it's often hard to find the right point to look at, and in our game the player could take paths that were not walkable or accessible to NPCs. For example, if the area the NPC is in is only directly connected to the player's area by a window, the pathfinding solution would have him staring in the wrong direction since it would not take that window into account. And even if it did, there could be multiple windows or doors; so picking the one along the shortest path would have all NPCs in that area covering the same choke point, which is not what we wanted. We realized that what we needed was a way to model the connectivity of the environment (i.e., which areas, or rooms, are connected to which other areas through which choke points).

It is important to note that this model maps better to an indoor environment with well-defined areas and choke points than it does to wide open spaces. However, in practice, even our outdoor environments could be broken down into areas separated by choke points although defining those areas and chokes is less obvious outdoors.

To achieve this we created a model we called Tactical Environment Awareness System (TEAS) (Figure 7.4). This system subdivided the world into areas (defined by subnavmesh areas) and defined the connections between those areas. So, for example, if two rooms are connected by a door and a window, each room would have its own *subnavmesh* (essentially a subset of the triangles of the navmesh), and these would be connected to each other by two choke nodes: one representing the window and the other the door.

One question that should immediately come to mind is, "How are these areas and connections generated?" This process on *Conviction* worked as follows. First, the level designer (LD) would subdivide the navmesh into subnavmeshes by tagging the triangles for each area using our navmesh tool (every triangle had to belong to at least one sub-navmesh). Note that the LD could tag triangles directly since our "base navmesh" was hand-authored to precisely fit to the contours of the structural geometry (all static props and dynamic objects would then automatically cut the navmesh). He would then create special overlap triangles to define the choke area (if it was walkable, like a door). These triangles were members of both subnavmeshes. Finally, the LD would place the choke nodes above the overlap triangles in the walkable case and above an area with no navmesh (like in a window) in the nonwalkable case. These choke nodes came with a red and a blue position node attached. The LD would place one of the position nodes above navmesh in area A and one in area B. This was sufficient to tell the system that area A is connected to area B through the choke node. There could be multiple choke nodes

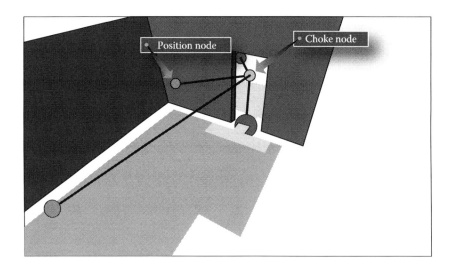

Figure 7.4

An example of TEAS in *Blacklist*. Assume we are looking at a door that leads from a hallway to a room. You can see the position node outside the room connected to the choke node, which is connected to the position node inside the room. This indicates that the area outside the room is connected to the area inside through the choke (a door in this case). You can also see the second position node attached to the choke node that can be used as a fallback position.

connecting two areas, one for each distinct choke point. Additionally, the LD had the option of adding multiple red or blue position nodes. The reason for this was that position nodes served two purposes. On top of defining which area was linked to the choke node, they also served as backup positions for covering that choke, so their position was important. If the NPC could not find suitable cover with LOS on the choke node, he knew he could always fall back to a position node that was a good open position with LOS. Finally, the LD would place an area property node above a triangle in the area. This node contained metadata for the area including the size of the area, the number of NPCs that should enter that area for search or combat, and the type of area (open balcony or closed room).

This system added substantial depth to our NPC tactics. They could now reason about player location with respect to the environment and act accordingly. For example, they could know that the player was hiding in a small room that is a dead end and cover the only way out instead of rushing in to their death. In the case with two rooms (areas A and B) connected by a door and a window, it meant that NPCs in area A who couldn't get LOS on the player in area B and didn't want to enter his area could intelligently cover the door and window leading to the player's area. In other words, NPCs who couldn't get LOS on the player always had something intelligent to do, which was important for our game since the player could outflank the NPCs in combat and see them through walls using his goggles. There is nothing worse than feeling smart by outflanking an NPC just to realize that he's just sitting there staring at a wall.

We made a lot of improvements to this system on *Blacklist* including autogenerating choke nodes and the special overlap triangles and adding a bunch of error checking in the editor to try to determine if the LD missed some linking opportunities or had linked two areas improperly. One thing we could have done but never got around to was autogenerating the subnavmesh areas themselves. We could have done this by allowing the LDs to place choke nodes where we couldn't autogenerate them first (i.e., narrow areas with no door objects), then generating the overlap triangles, and finally using flood fill to tag all the remaining triangles.

7.3.2 Changed Objects

The system we used for detecting and reacting to changes in environmental objects (doors, windows, lights, etc.) was very simple, but it is worth mentioning since it gave us more bang for our buck than any other system. In fact, a few of the reviews for the game brought up the fact that NPCs noticed doors that had been opened or light switches that turned off [Metro 13].

In *Splinter Cell*, when an object changed state from its previously known state, it would create an event with a lifetime. The first NPC to witness that event would claim it and potentially do a minor investigation depending on his state and other factors. Theoretically, the player could use this tactically to distract the NPC, but mostly it was there to give the impression of intelligence. Obviously, the key to making something like this work is selling the reaction with good feedback. If the NPC just looks like he randomly walked to the door the player left open, you get no sense of the fact that he noticed an open door; so the NPC needs to announce it, but in a way that feels realistic. We did this by having very obvious reaction animations where the NPC would stop and look at the area around the door, combined with more subtle barks where the NPC would ask introspectively, "Did I leave that door open?" after which he would walk through the door playing a "sweep" (look left–right) animation. This works very well but can lead to problems with immersion: the more specific a dialog line is, the more memorable it is, and the more immersion breaking it is when you hear that line repeated.

On *Blacklist* we did a major overhaul of our barks system, and one thing we did to address this issue was to create a three-tiered bark system that worked as follows: tier 1 barks were the very specific barks like the one mentioned earlier, tier 2 barks were more generic (e.g., "Did I leave that open?") that could apply to a door or window, and tier 3 barks were completely generic (e.g., "Huh?"). The idea was that we would cycle through the tier 1 barks first so the player would get the specific barks the first few times something happened, then we would drop to tier 2 and finally tier 3, so as the player got used to the NPC behavior and didn't need the specific barks, he would get the generic ones (which had a larger pool) and never hear the same memorable line twice.

7.4 Auditory Perception

Auditory perception for us is pretty simple: every audio event has a radius and priority; if an NPC is in range of the event, he will hear it and react differently based on the event, who else is in range, and his current state. On *Conviction*, we had two major problems with our auditory events: the first was accurately calculating the audio distance and the second had to do with the fairness of getting detected by NPCs you don't see because of events you don't directly control (details in the next section).

7.4.1 Calculating Audio Distance

In a game where creating sounds (e.g., by running) can get you detected, it is important to accurately calculate the audio distance of events. Using Euclidian distance is obviously not good enough since that would mean the player would be heard through walls. Initially, we used our sound engine, but it was not optimized for calculating arbitrary sound distance, and some calls were insanely expensive. A second issue with using the sound engine was that if the audio data weren't built (which happened often), it created all kinds of false detection bugs, which made testing difficult. The solution we ended up with made use of TEAS described earlier. Remember that TEAS is a connectivity graph that represents areas connected through choke points.

To calculate sound distance, we would get the "area path" from the source (event location) to the destination (NPC location). This would give us a shortest path represented by a series of areas (let's call it list A with n areas $A_0 \ldots A_{n-1}$) starting with the room containing the source and ending with the room containing the destination. In the trivial case where the source and destination are in the same room, we just used Euclidian distance; otherwise, we used the following equation:

$$\text{Total distance} = \text{dist}\left(\text{source, closest choke leading to } A_1\right)$$

$$+ \text{dist}\left(\text{closest choke leading to } A_1, \text{closest choke leading to } A_2\right)$$

$$+ \cdots + \text{dist}(\text{closest choke leading to } A_{n-1}, \text{destination}) \tag{7.1}$$

Now let's say the sound was made in area A and the NPC is in area D and those areas are connected in the following way: area A is connected by *window1* to area B, area B is connected by *door2* and *window2* to area C, and area C is connected by *door3* to area D, with the extra information that *window1* is closer to *door2* than *window2*. Then the total distance would be

$$\text{dist}(source, window1) + \text{dist}(window1, door2) + \text{dist}(door2, door3) + \text{dist}(door3, destination).$$

Although this is clearly a rough approximation, in practice, the results were accurate enough that we made the switch and never looked back.

7.4.2 Auditory Detection Fairness

The second problem we faced with auditory events is actually a general problem: it can feel unfair to be creating events that get noticed by guards you can't see, especially if you don't know that they are reacting to an event you created. This problem occurred often in internal reviews. Our creative director would often complain about being detected for no reason. For example, he'd be running down a hallway with no NPC in sight and all of a sudden hear an NPC say, "Hey, who's there!?!" Sometimes it was due to a bug, but often if we paused and used the free cam to show him where the NPC who heard him was, it usually made sense to him why he got detected. However, that didn't stop him from complaining the next time, and he was right to complain because ultimately it's irrelevant what the NPC *should* be able to hear. The player can't pause the game and free-cam, so it just ends up feeling unfair.

One important thing we learned here, as with tuning vision, is that it's only important what's plausible from the player's point of view—it really doesn't matter what the NPC *should* see or hear; it's what the player *thinks* the NPC can see and hear. This is a really important distinction. It implies that in the case of player perception versus simulation accuracy, player perception should win. This is not an absolute statement, however, and in the solution we will present, we'll show how this is actually limited by plausibility. However, first, let's look at a solution that we rejected.

To solve the fairness issue, we could have gone with the brute force solution of tuning down auditory event distances to make them more forgiving. This would have solved the unfairness problem but would have led to other issues: namely, it would feel ridiculous if you can see a guard in front of you, and you're sprinting toward him, but he can't hear your footsteps until you're very close. Not only would that make him seem unresponsive, but in our case, it would actually break the game since we had "insta-kill takedowns" if you got the jump on an NPC; so a player could just sprint through the map stabbing everyone in the back.

There's actually a big problem that we're trying to solve here: for two NPCs at the same distance from you (with one just around the corner), it can feel fair getting detected by the one that you see and unfair by the one you don't. To solve this problem, we considered having some HUD feedback for sound, which may have helped, but design wanted minimal HUD, so in the end we solved this in two ways.

The first thing we did was that NPCs that are offscreen, but far enough away from the player that it was plausible they didn't hear him, have their hearing reduced for certain events by ½. The result was that the game instantly became more fun and our creative director stopped complaining. We ended up applying this to some indirect visual events as well, such as seeing an NPC get shot. This is actually a good example of balancing plausibility versus fairness. Imagine the case where you are on one side of a corner and an NPC is right around the corner (a few feet from you). If you run and make noise, it still feels unfair if you get detected by the NPC you don't see, *but* if he didn't react and then you rounded the corner, it would feel ridiculous that he didn't hear you! Therefore, we still needed to pick a distance where this case leads to a plausible result even if it may feel unfair to the player (at least until he realizes where the NPC is), which is why we couldn't just reduce hearing completely for all offscreen NPCs.

The second thing we did was to provide better feedback to the player. We mentioned earlier how we overhauled our barks system with the "three-tiered" strategy, and this is one area where that had a big impact. We created a lot of very specific barks to put in tier 1 (like "I think I heard footsteps"); tier 2 had more generic barks like "I think I heard someone over there," down to tier 3's "I think someone's over there." The results, again, were that the player got the feedback they needed the first few times they were heard (so in this case, they realized that running created footstep noise) and then got the more generic versions to avoid repetition when the explicit ones were no longer necessary.

7.5 Social/Contextual Awareness

The last type of awareness I want to discuss is social and contextual. We've lumped these two together for a couple of reasons. First, the idea behind them is similar. You want the NPCs to appear aware of social and contextual events that are happening around them, and you want future NPC behavior to be affected by past events. Second, we'll look at these together because we didn't really have an overarching model for either of these. We did have a group behavior system that made modeling social awareness easier, but in general, the awareness came through in the design of the group behaviors themselves, not as a direct result of the system, and the rest was done with some clever tricks. So this section will be more like a "tips and tricks for giving the impression of social and contextual awareness" as opposed to a detailed description of a model.

Before presenting the tricks we used, we'd like to define what we mean by "contextual event" and give a couple of reasons for actually trying to model this in the first place since many games don't do this at all.

A contextual event is an event whose meaning changes based on context. So, for example, in *Splinter Cell*, if a searching NPC spots a dead body for the first time, he will get very agitated and call for help. On the other hand, if that same NPC spots a dead body in the middle of a war zone, he will ignore it. The event is the same ("see dead body"), but the context is different. Another example described in the following section is seeing the player. On *Splinter Cell*, seeing the player in the open was different from seeing the player in an unreachable area (like a rooftop) or seeing him in a dead end. Again, the event is the same ("see player"), but the reactions, barks, and behaviors are different. Perhaps more to the point, seeing a player on a rooftop for the first time is different from seeing him on that same rooftop again after he massacred five NPCs from there last time he was seen. In this case, the reactions and behaviors will be completely different (the NPCs will call out that he's back on the roof and immediately run to safety instead of trying to engage). So the event "see player" is actually interpreted as "see player again on rooftop after massacre" due to the context.

Social awareness is a subset of contextual awareness; if an NPC is engaged in a conversation with someone or waiting for someone to return, he will treat certain events (e.g., or lack of events—if he's expecting a response) very differently from the situation where he is just in the proximity of another NPC.

On *Splinter Cell*, we modeled this for two reasons:

1. To make NPCs seem more intelligent (you spend more time observing them than in most games)
2. To create antiexploits in the form of group behaviors

We'll give two examples that use group behaviors followed by a trick we used to solve a common social/contextual awareness problem: the disappearing NPC problem.

7.5.1 Social Awareness: Conversation

In most games, if you interrupt two NPCs talking, either it breaks the conversation or the conversation restarts robotically. On *Blacklist*, when NPCs are in a conversation, they are actually in a group behavior. The group behavior system takes control of all NPCs involved and gets to be first to handle any event received by any of those NPCs; so, for example, when a minor event occurs, the behavior gets the opportunity to handle it. In this case, it can pause itself and have the NPCs branch into a group investigation with the possibility of resuming the conversation after the investigation is complete. This allows us to do some interesting stuff, like having the NPC discuss the event received in context before investigating, maintain awareness of each other during the investigation, and branch seamlessly back into the conversation if the investigation does not yield anything. This was made possible by the fact that, for every conversation, our dialog writers wrote custom breakout and rejoin lines and also blocked out each conversation. When restarted, the rejoin line would be played and then the conversation would resume at the beginning of the current dialog block.

Here is an example of how a conversation that's interrupted by a minor event plays out in *Blacklist*:

1. The NPCs are discussing a football match on TV.
2. The player creates a minor event (footsteps, whistle, etc.).
3. The NPCs hear the event.
4. The system handles the event and branches to the "ignore minor event" behavior, with the lines:
   a. "Hey, did you hear that?"
   b. "Yeah, must've been the TV, now what were you saying…" (custom rejoin line)
5. The system then resumes the conversation only to be interrupted by a second event.
6. "Hey that wasn't the TV; you better go check it out!"

At this point the NPCs branch into a two-man investigation with the conversation on pause. Note how they delivered their lines in context and demonstrated awareness of what activity they are engaged in and what happened previously.

There are two possible outcomes to this investigation that could cause this scenario to continue: either the NPC finds nothing and they return to the conversation with a line like "Guess it was nothing. So what were you saying?" or the NPC gets killed silently during the investigation. In that case, the group behavior system receives the "NPC died" event that allows it to handle the event in context. The result is that the behavior waits a bit and then sends an investigation event to the NPC who's still alive near the location where the NPC was killed. He will branch into this second investigation with a line like "Hey, are you ok over there? Talk to me!" at which point the group behavior will end and he will do a systemic investigation at that location.

All of this really gives the impression that the NPCs are aware of their current situation and have some model of what has happened in the recent past and also who is around them and what they might be doing.

7.5.2 Contextual Awareness: Unreachable Area

Depending on where the player is, and what the situation is, the AI may not be able to, or want to, engage in direct combat. In this example I'll describe a situation that arises frequently in *Blacklist* (the player in an unreachable area) and how we deal with it. First, note that this situation can easily become an exploit; so when we deal with it, we are actually trying to solve two problems:

1. Remove the exploit. We don't want the player to be able to sit on a rooftop and shoot the AI like fish in a barrel.
2. React in a believable and readable way. We want the player to understand what the AI is doing and why. This makes them seem more intelligent for understanding the situation and also allows the player to adapt.

This is actually a situation that arises in many games: the player finds a spot where he has a big tactical advantage. This is exacerbated when the player has traversal moves the AI doesn't and can reach areas the AI can't get to. In *Splinter Cell*, there are really only three things the AI can do to deal with the player in this scenario: shoot back (which is not a good option since the player has the advantage), throw a grenade (this is not always easy to pull off since they have to land the grenade in a hard to reach area, but it's very effective when it works), and fall back (this is effective as an antiexploit but can be frustrating to the player if it's not called out).

To tackle this scenario, we used a combination of the group behavior system and TEAS. TEAS allows us to reason about the environment; so we know that the player is in an unreachable area (no valid area paths to the player) and what type of area it is, thanks to the markup in the area node. Therefore, in the scenario being described, TEAS allows us to know that the player is on a small, unreachable rooftop. The group behavior system then selects the appropriate behavior to kick off, in this case the "unreachable above" behavior. The mechanism for this selection works as follows: when no group behavior is running, the group behavior system is constantly looking for a trigger to kick off the most appropriate group behavior. The event "player seen" gets mapped to the event "player seen on unreachable rooftop" based on the criteria mentioned earlier. This event and some other checks (e.g., certain group behaviors should not be repeated) cause the group behavior system to select the most appropriate group behavior (which is mapped to its respective contextual event, "player seen on unreachable rooftop" in this case). The scenario proceeds as follows:

1. The player starts shooting at the AI from the unreachable rooftop.
2. Once his location is known, we kick off the "unreachable above" group behavior.
3. NPC A: "He's hiding up there! Toss a frag and flush him out!"
4. NPC B: "I'm on it! Give me cover fire!"
5. NPC A and other NPCs cover fire and NPC B throws the frag.

At this point, a few different things could happen, but we'll describe two of them. In the first case, the player gets off of the roof undetected and something similar to the following plays out after a few seconds:

1. NPC A: "Do you think he's still up there?"
2. NPC B: "I doubt it. Let's spread out and search the area!"
3. NPCs transition to search.

If the grenade throw is not successful and the player starts firing back and killing them, the following proceeds:

1. NPC A: "Forget it! Fall back! Fall back!"
2. NPC A covers fires while the other NPCs run for protective cover.
3. NPC B provides cover while NPC A falls back.

So you can see that we've been able to deal with this exploit in a way that preserves the lives of the NPCs, makes them seem aware, and gives the player the feedback they need. One important thing to note is that the dialog lines aren't callouts but a discussion. This has the effect of making the behavior seem much more natural as opposed to just being a means of giving information to the player [Orkin 06, Orkin 15].

7.5.3 Disappearing NPC Problem

We'll conclude this section by discussing our solution to a common problem: the disappearing NPC problem. The problem goes something like this: there are a bunch of NPCs guarding an area. The player starts stealthily taking them out one by one. At the end, there are only a couple of NPCs left, and unless they find a dead body, they are oblivious to the fact that an area that was crawling with their buddies is now an empty wasteland.

As mentioned earlier, we have a solution for the specific case when the NPCs are currently engaged in a conversation, but what about the general case where they are just near each other? Before discussing our solution, it's interesting to think about what we're trying to model. The idea here is that NPCs should be aware of the presence of other NPCs because they are seeing or hearing them at regular intervals. They should then become aware of the fact that they are no longer seeing and hearing those NPCs, get suspicious, and investigate. Trying to model this directly would be a lot of work for not a lot of gain. You'd have to create events for hearing and seeing NPCs, store a history of those events per NPC, and then detect the fact that the NPC is no longer receiving those events.

We chose a much simpler and cheaper solution. If NPC A has been in earshot (sound distance-wise) of NPC B for 10 seconds and then for 5 more seconds after he stops making noise (i.e., once he's dead), then we generate an investigation event. This event has a pretty long cooldown to avoid repetition and exploits. This gives us the result we want: if two NPCs are in the same general area and you kill one of them and if the other NPC is still in that area after a few seconds, he will become suspicious because he is no longer hearing/seeing the NPC that was just in his vicinity.

7.6 Conclusion

As you can see, the success of these models depends largely on a combination of picking the right abstraction and clever design. The goal is not so much to get an accurate model as it is to get one that feels fair to the player and allows you to provide good, consistent feedback, all while maintaining the illusion that the NPCs are human (plausibility). It's a difficult balance that requires a lot of playtesting, iterations, and working closely with design, animation, and dialogue. Hopefully, this chapter has brought those points home and given you some useful tips and tricks, which we arrived at through many hours of playtesting and iterating, that you can apply to your project.

References

[Metro 13] Metro.co.uk. 2013. Splinter cell: Blacklist—Sneaky compromise. http://metro.co.uk/2013/08/15/splinter-cell-blacklist-review-sneaky-compromise-3925136/ (accessed July 11, 2014).

[Orkin 06] Orkin, J. 2006. 3 States and a plan: The AI of F.E.A.R. *Game Developers Conference*, San Jose, CA.

[Orkin 15] Orkin, J. 2015. Combat dialogue in F.E.A.R.: The illusion of communication. In *Game AI Pro²: Collected Wisdom of Game AI Professionals*, ed. S. Rabin. A K Peters/CRC Press, Boca Raton, FL.

8

Escaping the Grid
Infinite-Resolution Influence Mapping

Mike Lewis

8.1 Introduction

One of the central elements of any robust AI system is *knowledge representation*. This encompasses a wide variety of techniques and mechanisms for storing and accessing information about an AI agent's perception of the world around it. The more powerful the knowledge representation, the more effective the AI can be.

A common form of knowledge representation involves measurable (or computable) quantities that vary throughout a region of space. The set of techniques for handling this sort of information is generally referred to as *spatial analysis* or *spatial reasoning*. One of the many powerful tools used in spatial reasoning is the *influence map*.

This chapter will look at the limitations with a traditional 2D influence map and introduce the concept of an infinite-resolution influence map. With this new representation, we'll then explore the issues of propagation, queries, handling of obstacles, and the third dimension.

8.2 Influence Mapping

To construct and use an influence map, three elements are typically involved. First, there must be some kind of *value* that varies throughout a spatial environment. Second, there is sometimes a *propagation method* by which these values change through space and/or time. Finally, there must be a *query mechanism*, which allows the AI system to examine and reason about the values stored in the influence map.

Classical influence mapping is generally performed on a regular 2D grid; more complex variants can also use arbitrary graphs, such as a navigation mesh (navmesh). In either case, the important element is not the representation of space, but the fact that space exists and is relevant to determining some value.

Propagation methods vary by application. For instance, a map used to represent the probability of an enemy occupying a given area (occupancy map) might use a simple combination of setting high values when an enemy is spotted and allowing values to decay and "spread outward" to nearby points over time. A more complex example is a visibility map, wherein the value of the map changes based on how well each point can be "seen" by a particular agent.

Some applications need not perform any propagation at all, such as tactical maps that store the instantaneous locations of various agents. Such maps can be queried directly for as long as their information is deemed up to date, and when the map becomes stale, it can simply be wiped and recomputed from scratch.

In any case, propagation generally consists of two elements: *placement* and *diffusion*. Placement is the mechanism by which new, known values are stored in the influence map. Diffusion is the process that allows influence to spread out, blur, smear, or otherwise travel across the influence map. Diffusion may occur over time or range smoothly across some distance from the nearest "placed" value, and so on.

See Figure 8.1 for an example of an influence map representing the AI's "guess" at the probability of a player being in a particular grid cell. Note that each cell contains a value from 0 to 9 and that these values increase toward areas where the player was last seen. Observe how the obstacles (dark squares) interact with the propagation of the influence.

Queries of the influence map are typically straightforward. Given a point in space (or a relevant point in the representational graph), determine the value of the influence quantity at that point. There may be some value in retaining historical data, so an agent can appear to "remember" recent influence states. A similar but more difficult trick is predicting future influence states, usually by simulating additional time-based propagation.

One final technique worth mentioning is *breadcrumbing*. In this mode, influence is deposited and diffused across the map in an ordinary fashion. When the map is updated, rather than resetting the values and recalculating them based on the relevant placement and diffusion rules, the old values are *decayed* by a given proportion. The new influence values are then added "on top of" the old values. This yields a sort of historical heat map. For example, rather than showing where agents are located *right now*, a bread-crumbed influence map can show where agents have generally tended to concentrate or travel routinely over a given span of time.

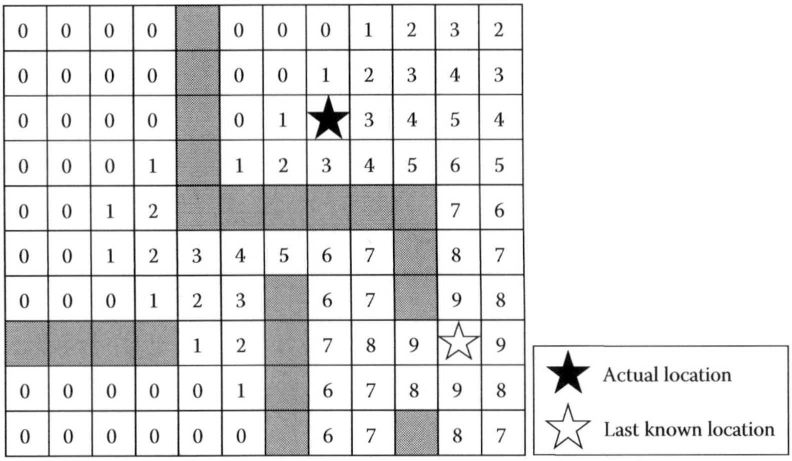

0	0	0	0	▓	0	0	0	1	2	3	2
0	0	0	0	▓	0	0	1	2	3	4	3
0	0	0	0	▓	0	1	★	3	4	5	4
0	0	0	1	▓	1	2	3	4	5	6	5
0	0	1	2	▓	▓	▓	▓	▓	▓	7	6
0	0	1	2	3	4	5	6	7	▓	8	7
0	0	0	1	2	3	▓	6	7	▓	9	8
▓	▓	▓	1	2	▓	7	8	9	☆	9	
0	0	0	0	0	1	▓	6	7	8	9	8
0	0	0	0	0	0	▓	6	7	▓	8	7

★ Actual location
☆ Last known location

Figure 8.1

This map illustrates the AI's best guesses about the player's location.

8.3 Limitations

Representing a large, finely detailed world as a grid is often cost prohibitive. A graph might help, but even then, the trade-off between resolution and performance must be carefully examined. In many cases, the difficulty of using a graph is not justified, given that they do not solve the resolution issue, and can even compound the performance problems if not managed carefully, due to the need for nontrivial mappings between points in space and nodes in the graph.

Not only are large grids expensive in terms of memory, but they can also consume a vast amount of CPU time during propagation. Each cell must be updated with *at least* the surrounding eight cells worth of influence value, and even more cells become necessary if propagation must reach beyond a point's immediate neighbors. For many applications, this might entail processing hundreds of cells each time a single cell is updated. Even though grid lookups are constant-time operations, the propagation phase can easily become an issue.

One potential approach to mitigate this problem is to use subgrids to minimize the number of cells involved; this can be done in a few flavors. For instance, a quadtree can be established, and empty nodes of the tree can have no associated grid. Another technique is to store small grids local to relevant AI agents or other influence-generating points in the world.

Unfortunately, the quadtree approach requires constantly allocating and freeing grids as influence sources move about. Localized grids can avoid this problem, but at the cost of making propagation and lookups substantially trickier. Both techniques perform worse than a giant, fixed grid when influence must be tracked uniformly across a very large area, for example, due to having agents covering an entire map.

8.4 Point-Based Influence

Consider that most influence sources can be considered point based. They deposit a defined amount of influence onto the map at their origin point and then potentially "radiate" influence outward over a limited range. This spread of influence can occur instantaneously, or over time, or both. For instantaneous propagation of influence, a simple *falloff function* is sufficient to describe the influence value contributed by the influence source at a given location on the influence map.

If the falloff function for a point is well defined, there is no need to represent the influence of that source in a discretized grid. Instead, influence at a *query point* on the influence map is simply equal to the value of the falloff function. Suppose the falloff function is a simple linear decay out to radius r, as described in the following equation:

$$f(x) = 1 - \frac{x}{r} \quad \text{for } x \leq r \tag{8.1}$$

The influence value ranges smoothly from 1 to 0 as the distance from the origin increases. For a 2D influence map, the equivalent falloff function is expressed in Equation 8.2, based on an influence source at the point (x_0, y_0):

$$f(x,y) = \max\left(1 - \frac{\sqrt{(x-x_0)^2 + (y-y_0)^2}}{r}, 0\right) \tag{8.2}$$

Naturally, influence maps with only one influence source are rather boring. On the plus side, adding in multiple influence sources is trivial: just add the values of the falloff functions. In formal notation, the computation looks like the following equation:

$$g(x,y) = \sum_i f_i(x,y) = \sum_i \max\left(1 - \frac{\sqrt{(x-x_i)^2 + (y-y_i)^2}}{r_i}, 0\right) \tag{8.3}$$

One highly useful observation is that the influence falloff function need not be trivial and linear; any differentiable function will suffice. (The importance of the ability to compute well-defined partial derivatives of the falloff function will be explored in a later section.) In fact, each individual influence source can use any falloff function desired; the value of the influence at a point remains the sum of the falloff functions for each individual influence source.

Another useful addition to this recipe is the ability to scale individual influence sources so that they do not all contribute the exact same maximum value (of 1, in this case). This is easily demonstrated in the linear falloff model as shown in the following equation:

$$g(x,y) = \sum_i \max\left(s_i \left(1 - \frac{\sqrt{(x-x_i)^2 + (y-y_i)^2}}{r_i} \right), 0 \right) \tag{8.4}$$

Given this set of tools, it is possible to replicate and even improve upon the discretized mechanisms typically used for influence mapping. Note that the value of the influence map can be queried at any arbitrary point with unlimited resolution; there is no loss of detail due to plotting the influence value onto a grid. Further, memory requirements are linear in the number of influence sources rather than increasing quadratically with the size and resolution of the grid itself.

Nothing comes for free, though; in this case, the cost of performing a query increases dramatically from $O(1)$ to $O(n)$ in the number of influence sources. Dealing with non-trivial topologies and obstacles is also significantly trickier, although, as will be explored later, some effective solutions do exist. There is also the matter of performing believable time-based propagation of influence, which is not immediately supported by the falloff function model as described. Last but not least, only one type of query has been detailed thus far; queries such as "find the point in a given area with the lowest (or highest) influence value" have not been considered.

Thankfully, all of these issues can be addressed well enough for practical purposes. Together with some optimizations and some mathematical tricks, this elimination of grids yields *infinite-resolution influence mapping.*

8.5 Making Queries Fast

Perhaps the most worrisome of the limitations of the influence mapping model described thus far is the need for comparatively expensive calculations for each query. Fixing this shortcoming is straightforward but takes some careful effort.

A key observation is that, in most practical cases, the vast majority of influence sources will not be contributing any value at an arbitrary query point. In other words, most of the influence sources can be completely ignored, drastically reducing the cost of a query.

The general idea is to use a *spatial partitioning structure* to make it possible to trivially reject influence sources that cannot possibly have an impact on a particular query. From among the many different partitioning schemes that have been developed, there are a few that seem particularly promising.

Voronoi diagrams are an appealing candidate. Constructing a Voronoi diagram optimally costs $O(n\log n)$ time in the number of influence sources, using the canonical *Fortune's algorithm* [Fortune 86]. The difficulty here is that it is often important for multiple influence sources to *overlap* each other, which fundamentally contradicts the purpose of a Voronoi diagram (i.e., to separate the search space such that each source is in exactly one *cell*).

Search trees are another category of techniques with great potential. Quadtrees are perhaps the most popular of these methods, but there is an even better option available: the *k*-d tree [Bentley 75].

Intuitively, a *k*-d tree is fairly simple. Each node in the tree has a *splitting axis*, a *left-hand branch*, and a *right-hand branch*. The splitting axis determines how the descendants of the tree node are organized. If the splitting axis is *x*, for example, all points in the left-hand branch have an *x* coordinate less than the parent node, and all points in the right-hand branch have an *x* coordinate, which is greater than that of the parent node.

A *k*-d tree is considered *balanced* if it has a (roughly) equal number of nodes in the left-hand branch as in the right-hand branch. Constructing a balanced *k*-d tree is relatively easy. Given a set of points, recursively perform the following procedure:

1. Pick an axis for the splitting axis.
2. Sort all of the input points along this axis.
3. Select the median of the input points from the sorted list.
4. This median node is now considered a *k*-d tree node.
5. Recursively apply this method to all points in the first half of the sorted list.
6. The resulting node becomes the left-hand node of the parent found in step 4.
7. Recursively apply this method to all points in the latter half of the sorted list.
8. The resulting node becomes the right-hand node of the parent found in step 4.

The splitting axis generally alternates between levels of the tree; if a given node is split on the *x*-axis, its two children will be split on *y*, and so on. Other methods for selecting a splitting axis exist but are generally most useful in fairly extreme cases. Experimentation is always encouraged, but for most uses, a simple alternation scheme is more than sufficient. A very simple *k*-d tree constructed in this manner is illustrated in Figure 8.2. The corresponding tree-style arrangement is shown in Figure 8.3.

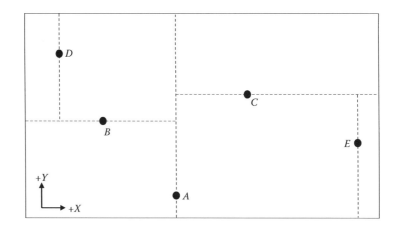

Figure 8.2

The points in this space have been partitioned into a *k*-d tree.

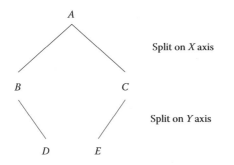

Figure 8.3

This is the same *k*-d tree as Figure 8.2, visualized as a tree structure.

Using this structure, the worst-case search time for points lying in a given range is known to be $O\left(2\sqrt{n}\right)$ for 2D *k*-d trees with *n* points [Lee 77]. The lower bound on search time is $O(\log n)$ given that *k*-d trees are fundamentally binary trees.

With these characteristics, the application of a *k*-d tree can substantially increase the performance of the infinite-resolution influence map. However, constructing the *k*-d tree represents a nonzero overhead, largely due to the need for sorting points along each axis. The number of queries desired, frequency of influence source position updates, and number of influence sources must all be carefully considered to determine if this data structure is a net win. As always, performance profiling should be conducted rigorously during such evaluations.

Once the influence source points are partitioned into a *k*-d tree, it is necessary to perform a *range query* on the tree to find influence sources that can potentially affect a given location of interest. The implementation of a range query is simple but has a few subtleties that merit careful investigation.

A range query begins at the root node of the *k*-d tree and recursively walks the branches. If the query region lies in the negative direction (i.e., left or down) from the *k*-d tree node's associated influence source point, the *left* branch of the tree is explored. If the region lies in the positive direction (i.e., right or up), the *right* branch is explored. If at any time the space bounded by a branch cannot possibly overlap the query area, the entire branch and all of its descendants can be ignored. A sample implementation is provided in Listing 8.1.

Note that it is not sufficient to check if the query location lies closer to the left or right branch. Due to the potential for the query area to overlap the splitting axis represented by the *k*-d tree node, it is important to include branches of the tree that *might* intersect the query area. The final two `if` checks in Listing 8.1 represent this logic; since they are not mutually exclusive conditions, no `else` is present.

8.6 Temporal Influence Propagation

An interesting characteristic of traditional influence maps is the ability to propagate influence values through the map over time. This behavior can be replicated in the infinite-resolution approach. Once again, the cost comparison between a grid-based propagation method and the infinite-resolution method will vary widely depending on the application.

Listing 8.1. Example C# implementation of a k-d tree range query.

```csharp
void FindPointsInRadius (
    KdTreeNode node,
    float x,
    float y,
    float radius,
    ref List<KdTreeNode> outpoints
) {
    if (node == null)
        return;

    float dx = x - node.x;
    float dy = y - node.y;
    float rsq = (dx * dx) + (dy * dy);
    if (rsq < (radius * radius))
        outpoints.Add(node);

    float axisdelta;
    if (node.SplitAxis == SplitAxis.X)
        axisdelta = node.x - x;
    else
        axisdelta = node.y - y;

    if (axisdelta > -radius) {
        FindPointsInRadius(
            node.Left, x, y, radius, ref outpoints
        );
    }

    if (axisdelta < radius) {
        FindPointsInRadius(
            node.Right, x, y, radius, ref outpoints
        );
    }
}
```

The number of influence sources, relative density, complexity of obstacles on the map, and so on will all contribute to the performance differences. While temporal propagation is certainly possible in the grid-free design, it is not always an immediate performance win.

To accomplish propagation of influence over time, two passes are needed. In the first stage, new influence sources are generated based on each existing source. These are generally organized in a circle around each original source, to represent spatial "smearing" of the values. A decay function is applied to the old source, and influence is spread evenly among the new sources, to represent falloff occurring over time and conservation of influence as it radiates outward, respectively.

On subsequent timesteps, this procedure is repeated, causing each point to split into a further "ring" of influence sources. If splitting a source would cause its contribution to the influence map to drop below a tuned threshold, the entire point is considered to have *expired* and the source is removed from the map completely.

It is possible to approximate this result by adjusting the falloff function, for example, to a Gaussian distribution function centered on the influence source point. This reduces the number of sources involved but introduces a complication that will be important later on when considering obstacles.

Once influence sources have been added, a simplification step is performed. The goal of this step is to minimize the number of k-d tree nodes required to represent the influence present on the map. It must be emphasized that this simplification is *lossy,* that is, it will introduce subtle changes in the values of the influence map. However, these changes are generally very minor and can be tuned arbitrarily at the cost of a little bit of performance.

Simplification is accomplished by looking at each node in the k-d tree in turn. For each node, the number of nearby nodes is queried. A *neighbor* is a node close enough to the test node to contribute influence, based on the limiting radius of the applicable falloff function. If too few neighbors exist, the test node is allowed to exist unmodified.

However, if more than a certain number of neighbors are found, their *centroid* is computed by independently averaging the x and y coordinates of each neighbor. The total influence at the centroid is then sampled. If this value is sufficiently large, all of the neighbors (and the test node) are pruned from the k-d tree and replaced by a *new* influence source node that attempts to replicate the contributions of the neighbors.

The net effect of this procedure is that tightly clustered groups of nodes can be replaced by smaller numbers of nodes without *excessively* disturbing the overall values in the map. (Note again that some loss is inevitable, although for some use cases, this simplification method can actually produce very pleasing effects.)

8.7 Handling Obstacles and Nontrivial Topologies

While this method works nicely on plain, flat, empty geometry, it lacks a critical component for dealing with *obstacles*, that is, areas of the influence map where values should not propagate. There is also no consideration of more interesting topologies, for instance, where the influence propagation distance is not strictly linear.

As described, things quickly break down when considering influence propagation, because it is important to conserve "energy" as influence spreads outward. Influence that hits an obstacle should not simply vanish, but rather "bounce off" and appear to flow *around* the boundary of the obstruction.

Fortunately, a pretty convincing effect can be implemented with relatively minor adjustments to the propagation/simplification technique. During propagation, before placing a new influence source, the new point is queried to determine if that point is obstructed. If not, the point is placed as normal. If so, the point is not placed at all. Once the set of valid points is established, each one is given a fraction of the original influence source's energy, based on the number of points that were ultimately placed.

This allows influence propagation to flow smoothly through narrow corridors, for example. The result closely resembles something from a fluid dynamics simulation, where tighter constraints cause influence to move faster and farther, as if under higher pressure. By splitting influence points explicitly into new sources, it is possible to guide this "flow" through unobstructed regions of geometry, rather than uniformly outward, as would occur if the falloff function were simply replaced with a Gaussian distribution or similar function.

Another way to visualize this procedure is to consider an influence source as a cellular automaton. In the propagation step, the automaton distributes the energy it carries into a

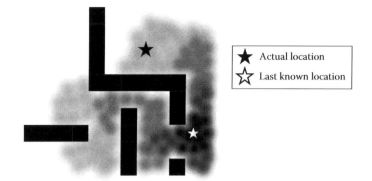

Figure 8.4

This map illustrates grid free, obstacle-aware influence propagation.

number of descendants in the surrounding (nonoccluded) space. During the simplification step, automata are resampled so that those sharing a sufficient amount of space in the world are collapsed into a single "cell." Additionally, automata that have lost too much energy due to decay or splitting are considered to have gone extinct.

If this cellular automata concept is plotted onto a grid, the result looks remarkably similar to that illustrated earlier in Figure 8.1. Allowing the influence sources to move freely rather than being truly cell based yields the effect shown in Figure 8.4, which offers a snapshot view of how infinite-resolution influence mapping handles obstacles during propagation.

Each influence source in this image is propagating a short, linear distance. However, *in totality*, the influence values will range smoothly and fluidly around obstacles, as the figure shows. By carefully controlling the placement of propagated influence nodes, it is possible to represent any spatial characteristics desired.

The methods leading to these results are directly inspired by similar techniques used in the computer graphics world, most notably *photon mapping* [Jensen 01]. In turn, more generalized statistical techniques such as *kernel density estimation* [Rosenblatt 56] are important ancestors of infinite-resolution influence mapping. These approaches provide both the foundations of the methods described in this article as well as ample opportunities for exploring the technique further.

Although it can initially seem limiting to use simple (even linear) falloff functions for representing influence sources, the vast body of prior research in the aforementioned areas should offer some reassurance that nontrivial problem spaces can be very effectively handled using such straightforward mathematical processes.

8.8 Optimization Queries

Influence mapping is valuable for far more than just acting as a mapping of spatial coordinates to arbitrary numbers. Besides just testing the value at a point, there are several other types of query that are commonly employed. In mathematical terms, these are all reducible to *local optimization queries*.

For instance, it might be useful to know the location (and value) of the point of lowest (or highest) influence, within a given area. Looking for such a lowest value is known as *local minimization*, and looking for the highest value is similarly referred to as *local maximization*. More generally, optimization within a restricted input domain is known as *constrained optimization*.

A tremendous volume of research has gone into optimization problems of various kinds. Fortunately, if the influence falloff function is carefully selected (i.e., continuously differentiable), the infinite-resolution influence map optimization problem becomes fairly straightforward.

For some types of optimization problems, there are known techniques for analytically finding an exact solution. Some require processes that are fairly difficult to automate, however. In practice, it is usually adequate to rely on *iterative* approximations to optimization queries, which are much easier to implement in the general case and typically more than fast enough for real-time use.

Specifically, the *gradient descent* optimization method [Cauchy 47] can yield local minima or maxima in a relatively short number of iterations, provided that the function being optimized is continuously differentiable. In essence, gradient descent is performed by looking at a random starting point and computing the slope of the function at that point. Based on that slope, the algorithm moves down (or up) the gradient defined by the function's curve or surface. This is repeated until further steps fail to yield improvements, indicating that a local optimum has been found.

There is a considerable tuning caveat to this technique, which is selecting the distance up (or down) the gradient to travel between steps. Different applications might find very different optimal values for this stepping. It is advisable to calibrate this value using a realistic sample set of influence sources. Optionally, the distance can be "guessed at" by examining the magnitude of the function at the current sample point and attempting to dynamically increase or decrease the step size accordingly.

Gradient descent in two dimensions simply requires partial differentiation of the candidate function and can also be generalized to three dimensions easily enough. The question is, what is the candidate function being optimized? In this case, the influence contribution function is defined again in the following equation:

$$g(x,y) = \sum_i \max\left(s_i \left(1 - \frac{\sqrt{(x-x_i)^2 + (y-y_i)^2}}{r_i} \right), 0 \right) \tag{8.5}$$

Recall that this boils down to adding up several individual functions. Conveniently, the derivative of such a summation is equal to the sum of the derivative of each function in turn. This can be succinctly expressed as in the following equation:

$$g'(x,y) = \sum_i f_i'(x,y) \tag{8.6}$$

So all that is necessary to compute the derivative of the influence map function itself is to sum up the derivatives of the influence functions for each contributing influence source.

The partial derivative of the influence function with respect to x is given by Equation 8.7. Similarly, the partial derivative with respect to y is given by Equation 8.8. The vector describing the slope of the influence function is then equal to Equation 8.9:

$$\frac{d}{dx} f_i(x,y) = \frac{-s_i(x - x_i)}{r_i \sqrt{(x - x_i)^2 + (y - y_i)^2}} \tag{8.7}$$

$$\frac{d}{dy} f_i(x,y) = \frac{-s_i(y - y_i)}{r_i \sqrt{(x - x_i)^2 + (y - y_i)^2}} \tag{8.8}$$

$$\left(\frac{d}{dx} f_i(x,y), \quad \frac{d}{dy} f_i(x,y) \right) \tag{8.9}$$

Note that the influence function is defined to fall off to 0 outside the effective radius of each influence source. This logic must also be included when computing the values of the partial derivatives. In this case, it is sufficient to check the distance from the test point to the influence source beforehand and simply skip the source if its contribution would be zero.

Once this slope at a point can be computed, the gradient descent algorithm can be used to find nearby local optima. Queries for local minima or maxima can be accomplished by performing gradient descent and constraining the distance from the query point to a given radius (or other area). The algorithm for minimization is demonstrated in Listing 8.2. Note that this is an approximation only and will not necessarily find the

Listing 8.2. A pseudocode implementation of gradient descent for a local minimum.

```
maxRadius = searchRadius + NODE_MAX_RADIUS
nodeList = FindNodesInRadius(searchPoint, maxRadius)
minimum = InfluenceAtPoint(searchPoint, nodeList)

for (STEP_LIMIT) {
    if (minimum <= 0.0)
        break;

    gradientXY = GradientAtPoint(searchPoint, nodeList)
    newSearchPoint = searchPoint - (gradientXY * SCALE)
    newSum = InfluenceAtPoint(newSearchPoint, nodeList)

    if (distance(newSearchPoint, originalPoint) > maxRadius)
        break;

    if (newSum < minimum) {
        searchPoint = newSearchPoint;
        minimum = newSum;
    }
}
minimumPoint = searchPoint;
```

true optimal point in a given range without some additional modifications. However, in practice, it works well enough for general use.

Modifying this code for maximization is straightforward: each search step should check for *increasing* values of influence, and the new search point should be found by adding the scaled gradient vector instead of subtracting it.

Of course, the provided equations work only for the linear falloff function defined earlier; again, though, any falloff function can be used provided that it is continuously differentiable. If doing a lot of manual calculus is not appealing, any suitable mathematics package (including several online web sites) can be used to find the partial derivatives of a substitute falloff function [Scherfgen 14]. It is worth noting that more complex falloff functions may be substantially more expensive to compute and differentiate than the linear model.

8.9 Traveling to the Third Dimension

Thus far, influence mapping has been considered only in the context of flat, 2D geometry. While influence maps can be applied to more complex terrain, they often struggle to cope efficiently with overlapping vertical areas, such as multiple floors in a building. Potential solutions for this problem include manually marking up horizontal regions of a map, thereby creating smaller influence maps on each floor of the building, for example.

It is not difficult to find "pathological" cases where 3D geometry simply does not lend itself well to grid-based influence mapping. For games utilizing a navigation mesh, the basic technique can be loosely applied to navmesh polygons instead of squares in a grid. However, this generally equates to a loss of resolution, and a measurably more expensive propagation phase, since mesh adjacency information must be used to spread out influence instead of trivial grid cell lookups. Moreover, if the environment does not lend itself to the use of a navmesh, influence mapping in a cube-based grid is even more problematic in terms of memory and computation time.

For the 2D case, removing grids and location-based networks has a number of advantages. In the 3D case, avoiding voxelization of the world space makes infinite-resolution influence mapping an intriguing possibility. However, it is important to note that the propagation techniques discussed earlier will become accordingly more expensive in three dimensions, due to the increased number of influence sources generated during each propagation step.

Getting the infinite-resolution technique to work in three dimensions is pretty simple. The k-d tree data structure generalizes to any number of dimensions—in fact, the name stands for "k-dimensional tree." Adding a third dimension is simply a matter of adding another splitting axis option when partitioning points into the tree.

Point-based influence is also simple to generalize to three dimensions. The linear, distance-based falloff function is adjusted to compute distance based on all three coordinates instead of only two. Summation of contributing influence sources works exactly as in two dimensions.

Temporal propagation can be appreciably more expensive due to the extra points needed to effectively spread influence out over time. However, aggressive simplification and careful tuning can mitigate this expense. For very geometrically sparse environments, one alternate option is to increase the radius of an influence source as it spreads, rather than adding new points. Note that this might complicate k-d tree construction and traversal, however, due to the increased maximum effective radius of any given influence source.

Last but not least, optimization queries can also be carried forward into the third dimension with relative ease. The partial derivative of the falloff function with respect to z follows the same pattern as the first two derivatives, and as with computing the influence value itself, computing the slope (or *gradient*) of the influence function is just a matter of summing up the partial derivatives for each axis.

8.10 Example Implementation

A complete implementation of the 2D form of infinite-resolution influence mapping can be found on this book's website (http://www.gameaipro.com/). The demo is written in C# for simplicity. While it should not be considered a performance benchmark, the speed is appreciable and illustrates the potential of the technique to provide a powerful alternative to grid-based approaches.

The demo is divided into two sections. One displays a raw influence map with a variable number of influence sources placed in a configurable pattern (or randomly). This view includes the ability to perform optimization queries (specifically minimization) against the generated influence map and can show the gradient descent algorithm in action. The second section of the demo shows how temporal propagation works, including moving influence around a simple set of obstacle regions.

All code in the demo is thoroughly commented and includes some tricks not covered in detail here. It is worth repeating that this example is written for clarity rather than performance, so an optimized C++ version may look substantially different.

While the influence mapping techniques illustrated are not (to the author's knowledge) presently in use in games, the foundational mathematics is certainly highly proven in other spheres, again notably including computer graphics in the form of photon mapping. Examination of the demo code is strongly encouraged, as an animated visual demonstration is far more illustrative than simple descriptions in prose.

8.11 Suitability Considerations

Infinite-resolution influence mapping is not a drop-in improvement for standard grid-based techniques. Before applying it to a particular problem space, it is important to consider several factors that may heavily affect performance and suitability. Although there are no hard and fast rules for these considerations, careful planning up front can be invaluable.

8.11.1 Influence Source Density

Due to the use of a k-d tree to store influence source points, the density of sources can be a major factor affecting performance. While having a few dozen points in close proximity is no issue, scaling to thousands or tens of thousands of overlapping influence sources would pose a significant challenge. Note that many thousands of sources are easily handled if they are spatially distributed such that most sources do not overlap; this allows the k-d tree to ignore a larger proportion of nodes that cannot possibly be relevant to a given query.

8.11.2 Query Point Density

If the locations of queries against the influence map are relatively well distributed and sparse, infinite-resolution techniques may be very well suited. However, as queries tend to cluster or repeatedly sample very small areas, the cost of recalculating the influence contributions (and, even more so, of performing optimization queries) can become prohibitive. Use cases that need to issue large numbers of queries in dense proximity are likely better served using a grid-based approach.

8.11.3 Update Frequency

One of the most expensive steps of the infinite-resolution method is rebuilding the k-d tree. When updates to the influence map can be batched and performed in a single pass, the cost of propagation, simplification, and k-d tree reconstruction can be significantly amortized. However, if updates need to occur very frequently, or in a series of many small, independent changes, the costs of keeping the data structures up to date may be come problematic.

8.11.4 Need for Precise or Extremely Accurate Results

Fundamentally speaking, infinite-resolution influence mapping works by discarding information and relying on statistical approximations. These approximations tend to lead to subtly less precise and less accurate results. For cases where the production of exact influence values is important, grid-based methods are almost certainly preferable.

8.12 Conclusion

Influence mapping is a remarkably effective tool for knowledge representation in game AI. Traditionally, it has been confined to 2D grids and relatively simple connected graphs, such as navigation meshes. Representing large, fine-grained, and/or 3D spaces is typically very difficult if not outright impractical for influence maps. Escaping these limitations is deeply appealing.

Truly 3D, freeform influence mapping can be a remarkably powerful tool. This power, as is often the case, comes at a cost. While the infinite-resolution method is certainly very efficient in terms of memory storage, it can become highly costly to query and update influence maps created in this fashion.

As with any such performance trade-off, there will be situations where infinite-resolution influence mapping is useful and other cases where it is not applicable at all. Care should be taken to measure the performance of both techniques within the context of a specific use case. Like all game AI techniques, this one has its limitations. Given the right circumstances, though, it can be a very powerful tool in any AI developer's arsenal.

References

[Bentley 75] Bentley, J. L. 1975. Multidimensional binary search trees used for associative searching. *Communications of the ACM* 18(9): 509.

[Cauchy 47] Cauchy, A. 1847. Méthode générale pour la résolution des systèmes d'équations simultanées. *Compte Rendu des Séances de L'Académie des Sciences XXV, Vol. Série A* 25: 536–538.

[Fortune 86] Fortune, S. 1986. A sweepline algorithm for Voronoi diagrams. In *Proceedings of the Second Annual Symposium on Computational Geometry*, Yorktown Heights, NY, pp. 313–322.

[Jensen 01] Jensen, H. W. 2001. *Realistic Image Synthesis Using Photon Mapping.* Natick, MA: A.K. Peters.

[Lee 77] Lee, D. T. and Wong, C. K. 1977. Worst-case analysis for region and partial region searches in multidimensional binary search trees and balanced quad trees. *Acta Informatica* 9(1): 23–29.

[Rosenblatt 56] Rosenblatt, M. 1956. Remarks on some nonparametric estimates of a density function. *The Annals of Mathematical Statistics* 27(3): 832.

[Scherfgen 14] Scherfgen, D. 2014. Online derivative calculator. http://www.derivative-calculator.net/ (accessed January 17, 2015).

9

Modular Tactical Influence Maps

Dave Mark

9.1 Introduction

A large portion of the believability of AI characters in shooter and role-playing games (RPGs) comes from how they act in their environment. This often goes beyond *what* the character elects to do and gets into *where* the character decides to do it. Certainly, technologies such as traditional pathfinding and automatic cover selection provide much of this illusion. However, there is another layer of "spatial awareness" that, by helping to inform the decision process, can provide even more of the appearance of intelligence in game characters. Much of this stems from the character not only being aware of the static environment around it (i.e., the fixed level geometry) but also being aware of the positioning of other characters—both enemy and ally—in their immediate area. This is often done through the use of influence maps.

Influence mapping is not a new technology. There have been many articles and lectures on the subject [Tozour 01, Woodcock 02]. This article does not give a complete overview of how to construct and use them. Instead, we present an architecture we developed for easily creating and manipulating influence maps in such a way that a variety of information can be extracted from them and used for things such as situation analysis, tactical positioning, and targeting of spells. Additionally, while influence maps can be used on a variety of scales for things such as strategic or ecological uses—for example, the positioning of armies on a map or guiding the habitats and migrations of creature—this article will primarily focus on their use in tactical situations—that is, positioning in individual or small group combat. Note that many of the techniques, however, can be adapted for use in higher level applications.

This architecture was originally developed for the prototypes of two large, online RPG games. However, it can apply to many types of games including first-person shooters, RPGs, or even strategy games where multiple agents need to appear aware of each other spatially and act in a cohesive manner in the game space.

The in-game results that we achieved from utilizing this architecture included the following:

- Positioning of "tank style" defenders between enemies and more vulnerable allies such as spellcasters
- Determining the relative threat that an agent was under at a given moment
- Determining safe locations to evade to or withdraw to
- Identifying and locating clusters of enemies for targeting of area of effect spells
- Identifying locations for placement of blocking spells between the caster and groups of enemies
- Maintaining spacing from allies to avoid agents "bunching up"
- Determining when there enough allies near a prospective target to avoid "piling on"

9.2 Influence Map Overview

Tactical influence maps are primarily used by individual agents to assist in making tactical and positional decisions in individual or small group combat. The influence map doesn't actually provide instruction—it only provides information that is used by the decision-making structures of the agents. One particular advantage to using influence maps is that they can represent information that all characters could potentially have knowledge of. By calculating and storing this information once for all characters, it prevents the expensive and possibly redundant calculation of information by each individual agent. For example, an influence map that represents where people are standing in a room is information that could potentially be common knowledge to those people. By calculating it once and storing it for all to access as needed, we save the time that would be involved in each agent processing that information on its own. An additional benefit is that, although the decisions are still being made by the individuals, by using shared information about the battlefield, some sense of emergent group behavior can result.

While a simple (x, y, z) coordinate is sufficient for describing the location of an object or agent in a space, an influence map gives a coherent way of describing how that object affects that space—either at that moment or possibly in the near future. It helps to answer questions such as the following:

- What could it hit?
- How far could it attack?
- Where could it move to in the next few seconds?
- What is its "personal space?"

While some of these seem like they could be answered with a simple direction vector (and they can), the advantages gained by the influence map are realized when multiple agents are affecting the space. Rather than dealing with the n^2 problem of calculating multiple distance vectors between agents, we can look at the influence map and determine where the combined influence is. Now we can ask group-based questions such as "what could *they* hit?" or "where is it crowded?"

Additionally, the questions needed by game agents are often not "where is this," but rather "where is this *not*." The questions now become

- Where can they *not* hit?
- Where can I *not* be reached in the next few seconds?
- Where will I *not* be too close to people?

The basic form of the influence map is to divide the space into sections—most often a grid—and assign values to the cells. The values of the cells can represent a wide variety of concepts such as "strength," "danger," "value," or anything else that can be measured. Typically, a value has a locus that the "influence" radiates out from. For example, an agent that has a certain strength in its local cell may radiate influence out to a certain radius with the influence declining as the distance from the agent increases (see Figure 9.1). In some

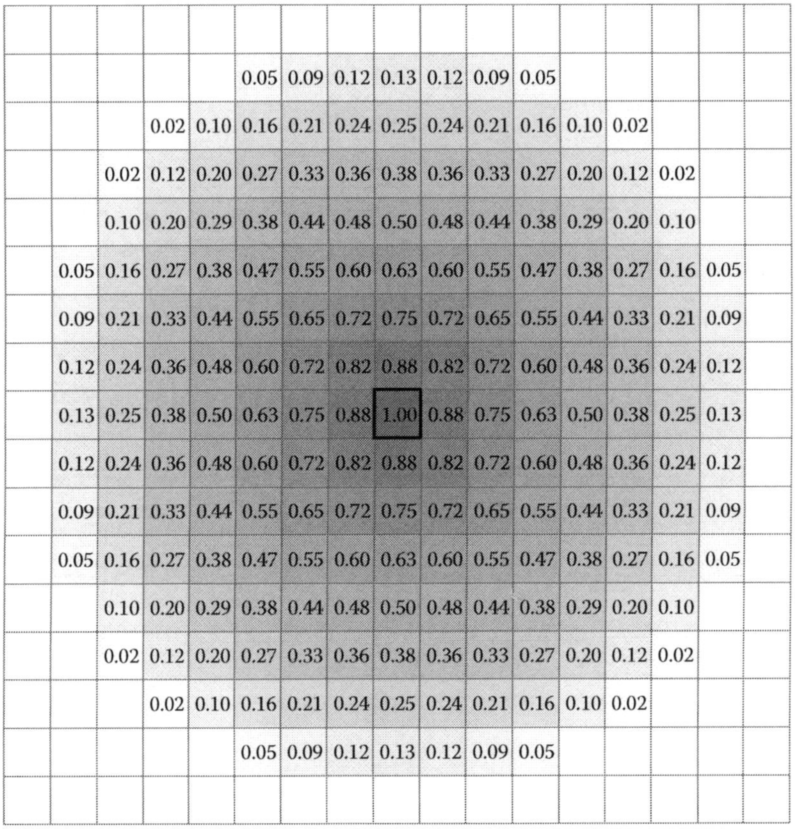

			0.05	0.09	0.12	0.13	0.12	0.09	0.05				
	0.02	0.10	0.16	0.21	0.24	0.25	0.24	0.21	0.16	0.10	0.02		
0.02	0.12	0.20	0.27	0.33	0.36	0.38	0.36	0.33	0.27	0.20	0.12	0.02	
0.10	0.20	0.29	0.38	0.44	0.48	0.50	0.48	0.44	0.38	0.29	0.20	0.10	
0.05	0.16	0.27	0.38	0.47	0.55	0.60	0.63	0.60	0.55	0.47	0.38	0.27	0.16	0.05
0.09	0.21	0.33	0.44	0.55	0.65	0.72	0.75	0.72	0.65	0.55	0.44	0.33	0.21	0.09
0.12	0.24	0.36	0.48	0.60	0.72	0.82	0.88	0.82	0.72	0.60	0.48	0.36	0.24	0.12
0.13	0.25	0.38	0.50	0.63	0.75	0.88	1.00	0.88	0.75	0.63	0.50	0.38	0.25	0.13
0.12	0.24	0.36	0.48	0.60	0.72	0.82	0.88	0.82	0.72	0.60	0.48	0.36	0.24	0.12
0.09	0.21	0.33	0.44	0.55	0.65	0.72	0.75	0.72	0.65	0.55	0.44	0.33	0.21	0.09
0.05	0.16	0.27	0.38	0.47	0.55	0.60	0.63	0.60	0.55	0.47	0.38	0.27	0.16	0.05
0.10	0.20	0.29	0.38	0.44	0.48	0.50	0.48	0.44	0.38	0.29	0.20	0.10		
0.02	0.12	0.20	0.27	0.33	0.36	0.38	0.36	0.33	0.27	0.20	0.12	0.02	
	0.02	0.10	0.16	0.21	0.24	0.25	0.24	0.21	0.16	0.10	0.02		
			0.05	0.09	0.12	0.13	0.12	0.09	0.05				

Figure 9.1

Influence radiating out from the location of a single agent to a radius of 8 units.

implementations, this is the result of influence propagation that takes place over time. In our system, we simply evaluate the influence of individual cells as a function of distance from the locus.

In many implementations, including ours, when multiple agents are placed in an area together, the values that they radiate are added together so that a combined influence is created. By looking at the values of the cells, we can determine how much *combined* influence is in any given location. If the agents are closer together, the influence between them is higher than if they are farther apart. Because the influence decreases over distance, as you move away from the agents, you will eventually arrive at a location where their influence is 0. In Figure 9.2, you can see two agents who are close enough together that their influence overlaps. Note that, while each agent has a maximum influence of 1.0 (as in Figure 9.1), the area where they overlap significantly shows influences greater than 1.0.

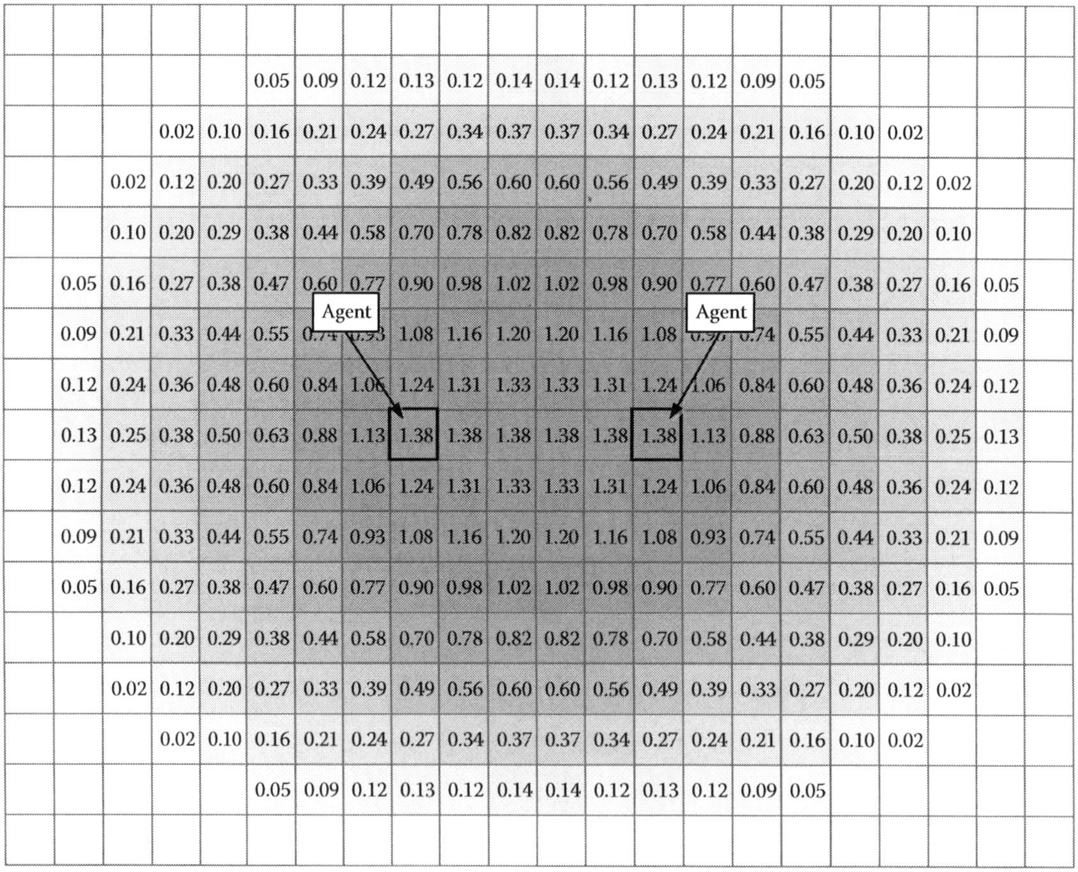
Agent
Agent
0.05 0.09 0.12 0.13 0.12 0.14 0.14 0.12 0.13 0.12 0.09 0.05
0.02 0.10 0.16 0.21 0.24 0.27 0.34 0.37 0.37 0.34 0.27 0.24 0.21 0.16 0.10 0.02
0.02 0.12 0.20 0.27 0.33 0.39 0.49 0.56 0.60 0.60 0.56 0.49 0.39 0.33 0.27 0.20 0.12 0.02
0.10 0.20 0.29 0.38 0.44 0.58 0.70 0.78 0.82 0.82 0.78 0.70 0.58 0.44 0.38 0.29 0.20 0.10
0.05 0.16 0.27 0.38 0.47 0.60 0.77 0.90 0.98 1.02 1.02 0.98 0.90 0.77 0.60 0.47 0.38 0.27 0.16 0.05
0.09 0.21 0.33 0.44 0.55 1.08 1.16 1.20 1.20 1.16 1.08 0.55 0.44 0.33 0.21 0.09
0.12 0.24 0.36 0.48 0.60 0.84 1.24 1.31 1.33 1.33 1.31 1.24 0.84 0.60 0.48 0.36 0.24 0.12
0.13 0.25 0.38 0.50 0.63 0.88 1.13 1.38 1.38 1.38 1.38 1.38 1.38 1.13 0.88 0.63 0.50 0.38 0.25 0.13
0.12 0.24 0.36 0.48 0.60 0.84 1.06 1.24 1.31 1.33 1.33 1.31 1.24 1.06 0.84 0.60 0.48 0.36 0.24 0.12
0.09 0.21 0.33 0.44 0.55 0.74 0.93 1.08 1.16 1.20 1.20 1.16 1.08 0.93 0.74 0.55 0.44 0.33 0.21 0.09
0.05 0.16 0.27 0.38 0.47 0.60 0.77 0.90 0.98 1.02 1.02 0.98 0.90 0.77 0.60 0.47 0.38 0.27 0.16 0.05
0.10 0.20 0.29 0.38 0.44 0.58 0.70 0.78 0.82 0.82 0.78 0.70 0.58 0.44 0.38 0.29 0.20 0.10
0.02 0.12 0.20 0.27 0.33 0.39 0.49 0.56 0.60 0.60 0.56 0.49 0.39 0.33 0.27 0.20 0.12 0.02
0.02 0.10 0.16 0.21 0.24 0.27 0.34 0.37 0.37 0.34 0.27 0.24 0.21 0.16 0.10 0.02
0.05 0.09 0.12 0.13 0.12 0.14 0.14 0.12 0.13 0.12 0.09 0.05

Figure 9.2

The combined influence from two agents can be greater than the influence of a single agent alone.

If the same process is performed for enemy agents and then inverted (i.e., allies are positive influence and enemies are negative), a topography is created that goes beyond a binary "ours" and "theirs." It can also express ranges from "strongly ours" to "weakly ours" based on the total value in cells. The resulting map, such as the one in Figure 9.3, can give a view of the state of any given location on the map as well as the orientation of the forces in an entire area. Behaviors can then be designed to take this information into account. For example, agents could be made to move toward the battlefront, stay out of conflict, or try to flank the enemy.

Other information can also be represented in influence maps. For example, environmental effects such as a dangerous area (e.g., due to a fire, a damaging spell, or a pending explosion) can be represented and taken into account by the game agents in the same way that they can process information about the location of other agents.

				0.05	0.09	0.12	0.13	0.12	0.04	-0.04	-0.12	-0.13	-0.12	-0.09	-0.05				
			0.02	0.10	0.16	0.21	0.24	0.23	0.14	0.05	-0.05	-0.14	-0.23	-0.24	-0.21	-0.16	-0.10	-0.02	
		0.02	0.12	0.20	0.27	0.33	0.34	0.26	0.16	0.06	-0.06	-0.16	-0.26	-0.34	-0.33	-0.27	-0.20	-0.12	-0.02
	0.10	0.20	0.29	0.38	0.44	0.39	0.30	0.19	0.07	-0.07	-0.19	-0.30	-0.39	-0.44	-0.38	-0.29	-0.20	-0.10	
0.05	0.16	0.27	0.38	0.47	Friendly agent		0.35	0.23	0.08	-0.08	-0.23	-0.3	Enemy agent		-0.47	-0.38	-0.27	-0.16	-0.05
0.09	0.21	0.33	0.44	0.55	0.56	0.51	0.42	0.28	0.10	-0.10	-0.28	-0.42	-0.51	-0.56	-0.55	-0.44	-0.33	-0.21	-0.09
0.12	0.24	0.36	0.48	0.60	0.60	0.58	0.51	0.34	0.12	-0.12	-0.34	-0.51	-0.58	-0.60	-0.60	-0.48	-0.36	-0.24	-0.12
0.13	0.25	0.38	0.50	0.63	0.63	0.63	0.63	0.38	0.13	-0.13	-0.38	-0.63	-0.63	-0.63	-0.63	-0.50	-0.38	-0.25	-0.13
0.12	0.24	0.36	0.48	0.60	0.60	0.58	0.51	0.34	0.12	-0.12	-0.34	-0.51	-0.58	-0.60	-0.60	-0.48	-0.36	-0.24	-0.12
0.09	0.21	0.33	0.44	0.55	0.56	0.51	0.42	0.28	0.10	-0.10	-0.28	-0.42	-0.51	-0.56	-0.55	-0.44	-0.33	-0.21	-0.09
0.05	0.16	0.27	0.38	0.47	0.50	0.44	0.35	0.23	0.08	-0.08	-0.23	-0.35	-0.44	-0.50	-0.47	-0.38	-0.27	-0.16	-0.05
	0.10	0.20	0.29	0.38	0.44	0.39	0.30	0.19	0.07	-0.07	-0.19	-0.30	-0.39	-0.44	-0.38	-0.29	-0.20	-0.10	
		0.02	0.12	0.20	0.27	0.33	0.34	0.26	0.16	0.06	-0.06	-0.16	-0.26	-0.34	-0.33	-0.27	-0.20	-0.12	-0.02
			0.02	0.10	0.16	0.21	0.24	0.23	0.14	0.05	-0.05	-0.14	-0.23	-0.24	-0.21	-0.16	-0.10	-0.02	
				0.05	0.09	0.12	0.13	0.12	0.04	-0.04	-0.12	-0.13	-0.12	-0.09	-0.05				

Figure 9.3

An allied agent spreading positive influence and an enemy one spreading negative influence can show a "neutral zone" where the influence crosses 0.0.

9.3 Propagation

As we have alluded to earlier, influence can be propagated into the map from each agent. One way of propagating influence into a map is to walk through the cells surrounding the agent. For each cell, the influence is determined by using the distance from the agent to the center of that cell passed through a response curve that defines the propagation decay of the distance. For example, the formula for linear propagation of influence is shown in the following equation:

$$\text{Influence} = \text{MaxValue} - \left(\text{MaxValue} \times \frac{\text{Distance}}{\text{MaxDistance}} \right) \tag{9.1}$$

Note that influence propagation does not have to be a linear formula. In fact, different types of influence propagation might be better represented by other response curves. Another common type is an inverse polynomial defined by a formula similar to the one shown in the following equation:

$$\text{Influence} = \text{MaxValue} - \left(\text{MaxValue} \times \frac{\text{Distance}}{\text{MaxDistance}} \right)^2 \tag{9.2}$$

Figure 9.4 shows the difference between linear propagation, the polynomial formula earlier, and a similar one with an exponent of 4 rather than 2. The graph in Figure 9.4 shows both the positive and negative sides of the equation in order to illustrate the "shape" of the influence circle around the agent that would result from the different formulas—specifically, the falloff of the values as the distance from the agent increases.

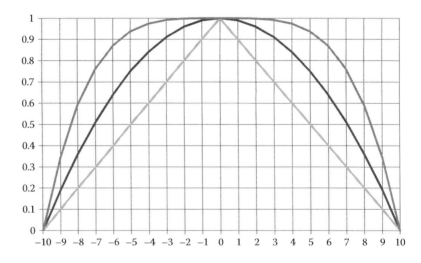

Figure 9.4

The shapes of a sample of propagation formulas centered on the agent: linear (inside) and two polynomial curves with exponents of 2 (middle) and 4 (outer).

The important thing to remember when selecting formulas is that the response curve simply shapes the propagation of the influence as it spreads away from the agent's location. Note that there is nothing stating that the value must be at its maximum at the location of the agent. For example, a catapult is fairly innocuous at close range but has a ring of influence that it projects at its firing range. An influence map designed to represent this threat would be at its highest point in a ring surrounding the catapult rather than at its actual location.

All of the aforementioned propagations of threat assume no barriers to sight or movement around the agent. Certainly, that is not the case in many game environments. In those cases, other methods of propagation need to be employed. If the influence that is being spread is entirely based on line of sight (such as the threat from a guard or someone with a direct fire weapon), it is often enough to simply not propagate influence to locations that cannot be seen by the agent.

If the influence is meant to represent the potential threat of where an agent could possibly move—for instance, "what could that tiger bite in the next 3 seconds?"—the path distance between the agent and the location in question could be used. This helps solve situations where, for example, the tiger is on the other side of fence. Yes, it is close to the target location, but it is not a threat because it would take a while for the tiger to move *around* the fence. The solution here is often simply to swap the linear distance calculation code with a call to the pathfinding system to return a distance. Since many such queries are likely to be made over the course of an influence map evaluation, a common solution is to precompute cell path-distances for a large set of cells using an undirected Dijkstra search starting from the agent's location. Either way, the costs in run-time performance and engineering effort alike are nonnegligible.

9.4 Architecture

There are different types of maps in our architecture. Some of them are the base maps for holding various types of information. Others are created at run time and stored for use in the repetitive task of populating the main maps. Still others are temporary in nature for use in combining the data into usable forms. The following sections describe each type of map.

9.4.1 Base Map Structure

The most important type of map structure is base map. The definition of this map is what determines the definitions of all the other maps to follow.

Maps are defined as rectangular areas so that they can be stored and accessed as a 2D array (or similar structure). The base map typically covers the entire level. In the case of maps where there are rigidly defined areas that are to be processed separately (e.g., the inside of a building), then a map could theoretically be smaller than the entire game level. It is often preferable, however, to attempt to simply combine maps into large areas due to complications of propagating influence from the edge of one map to an adjacent map. As you will see in the *working maps* section, it is usually easier to simply store the base map information in as large a chunk as possible.

Each map is a regular square grid. While the dimensions of the influence map are determined by the game map that it is to be used on, the cell granularity is more subject to adjustment. In general, they should be a size that would represent approximately the minimum granularity that you would want characters to position at, target at, etc. For example, if you want characters to "think in terms of" 1 m for where to stand, your cell sizes would be 1 m as well.

Because a small change in the granularity of cells can result in a massive change in the number of cells (and therefore the memory footprint and calculation time), a balance must be struck between the fidelity of the actions and the resources available to you. Suffice to say, there is no "right answer" for any of these values. They will have to be chosen based on the game design and the restrictions on processing power that might be in place.

9.4.2 Types of Base Maps

We use two types of base maps in our game. The first, and most common, is a map representing the physical location of characters—what we call a "proximity map," or simply "prox map." This map goes beyond showing the physical location at the moment—the influence radiated by the agents also shows where that agent could get to in a short period of time. Therefore, each agent's presence in the location map is represented by a circle, centered on their current location and spreading out in a circle of decreasing value until 0 is reached (see Section 9.4.3). A proximity map that contains multiple agents would show not only their current locations but also where those agents could reach in short order. The higher the value of a cell, the closer that cell is to one or more agents and the higher the likelihood of it being influenced by an agent.

The second type of map is the "threat map." This differs from the location map in that it represents not where an agent could go, but what it could potentially threaten. This may differ significantly depending on the game design. A game that involves only melee combat may have a significantly different set of demands for a threat map from a game involving gunfire with unlimited (or at least functionally unlimited) ranges. As we will see in the next section, the architecture supports different ranges of threat in the same game.

In the case of a melee unit, the threat map functions in a manner similar to the proximity map earlier, with the highest threat value propagated from the agent at the agent's location and with the threat decreasing with distance to zero. In the case of ranged units, the threat influence may take the form of a ring of influence surrounding the agent's location, as in the catapult example cited earlier. If a cell is being threatened by more than one agent, it is possible (even likely) that the threat value at that location will be greater than that generated by a single agent alone.

There will be one base map of each type (proximity and threat) for each faction in the game—often at least two factions (i.e., "us vs. them"). This allows us to pull information about either enemies or allies and combine them as necessary.

9.4.3 Templates

One problem with the calculation of influence propagation is the significant number of repetitive calculations that are needed. While they may seem trivial at first, we will soon realize that the calculations mount quickly as the number of agents increases. The most obvious fix is to limit the number of cells filled by only calculating cells in the square defined by our propagation radius. That is, if the radius of influence is 10 cells, only attempt to propagate into the cells that are within 10 vertically or horizontally from the agent—there's no point in iterating through the potentially hundreds or thousands of cells that are outside that range. However, the major stumbling block is that the distance calculations between cells—even in the small area—involve many repetitive square root calculations. When multiplied by dozens—or even hundreds—of characters, these calculations can be overwhelming.

The best optimization that eliminates the repetitive distance and response curve calculations is gained through the use of "templates." Templates are precalculated and stored maps that can be utilized by the influence map engine to "stamp" the influence for agents into the base map. We precalculate and store templates of various sizes at start-up. When it comes time to populate the map (see Section 9.5), we select the appropriate size and type of map and simply add the precalculated influence values in the template into the map at the appropriate location. Because the propagation has already been calculated in the template, we eliminate the repetitive distance and response curve calculations and replace them with addition of the value of the template cell into a corresponding cell on the base map.

As we alluded to earlier, this "stamp" method does not work when there are significant obstacles to movement in the area—particularly for proximity maps. For those situations, it would be necessary to calculate the path distance and then determine the influence value for that location.

The number and type of templates that we need depends on a number of factors:

- What does the base map represent?
- What is the possible range of values that we would use to look up the correct template?
- What is an acceptable granularity for that range of values?

As we go through the three types of templates, we will see how these values determine how many templates we need and what they represent.

Note that the influence in each of these templates is normalized—that is, the range of values is between 0 and 1. This is largely because we are defining the *shape* of the influence curve only at this point. When it comes to usage of the templates, we may often use these simple normalized curves. However, as we will explain shortly, we may want to multiply the "weight" of the influence that an agent has. By leaving the templates normalized, we can make that decision later as needed.

We utilize two different types of templates—one for proximity maps and one for threat maps. We use different templates because the propagation formula differs between them. If we were using the same formula, the templates would be identical and this differentiation would not be needed.

The first type of template is used for location maps. A location template represents what was discussed earlier in this article—where can the agent get to quickly? As mentioned in the propagation section earlier, the formula for location templates should be a linear gradient with a formula as shown in Equation 9.1.

If our map granularity was 1 m (meaning a cell was 1 m²), our maximum speed in the game was 10 m/s, and our refresh time on maps was 1 second, and our maximum map size would be a radius of 10 m. This allows us to propagate influence out to how far an agent could get in the amount of time between map updates (1 s). Therefore, our maximum template size would be a 21 × 21 grid (10 cells on either side of the center row or column).

In order to support agents that would move at slower speeds, we must create templates that radiate out to different ranges, however. If there was a slower agent that only moved at 5 m/s, we would need one for that speed. In an RPG where there could be many different types of characters with many different movement speeds, we may want to have 1 template for each integer speed from 1 to 10.

Constructing templates for threat maps—the second type of template—would be similar. However, there are a couple of changes. First, threat maps are best calculated with a polynomial formula that reflects that the threat is similar across most of the distance and only drops off as it reaches its furthest point. Equation 9.3 shows a formula that we often use for this—a polynomial with an exponent of 4:

$$\text{Influence} = \text{MaxValue} - \left(\text{MaxValue} \times \frac{\text{Distance}}{\text{MaxDistance}} \right)^4 \qquad (9.3)$$

The template is looked up by using the maximum range of the threat of the agent. An RPG character with a spell range of 30 m, for example, would need a map that was 61 × 61. On the other hand, a primarily melee character with a range of 2 m would use a significantly smaller map.

As with the speeds earlier, there needs to be a map that approximately matches the threat range of the agent in question. If you have only a small number of very specific characters and abilities, then certainly create templates to match. If there is a wider variety that would necessitate more sizes of maps, use discretion in how to create them. Because of the potentially great variety and differences between threat ranges, it might not be advisable to create one template for each measurement unit (in our example, each meter). Instead, templates can be created at specified intervals so as to give coverage adequate enough to provide a template that is at least roughly similar to the needs of the agent.

The third type of template is the personal interest map. Rather than being used to propagate influence into the base maps, these templates are specifically designed to apply to other maps in order to determine what an agent might be interested in. We will discuss the application of these maps later. As with location and threat templates, depending on the game design, it is often advisable to have multiple sizes of these maps as well so the appropriate size can be applied as needed without calculation.

9.4.4 Working Maps

Working maps are temporary maps that are used to assemble data from the main maps and templates. Working maps can be of any size but they are usually smaller than the main map because they only are used for the data directly relevant to a decision. They will always be as large as the largest template used for the decision. Most often, the working maps will be centered on the agent location (Figure 9.5).

The rationale behind working maps is that, when we are assembling combinations of map information, we will often be iterating over the relevant portions of the required maps to add or multiply their values. There is no point in iterating over the entire level if we are only interested in values that are close to the agent requesting the information. By creating a working map and copying the necessary values from

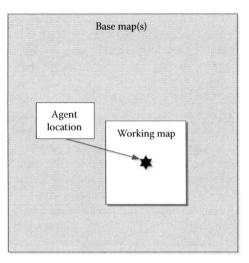

Figure 9.5

A working map is a temporary, small map centered on an agent used to assemble and process information from multiple maps in the local area.

the base maps into it (through addition or multiplication), we limit the iterations necessary and the memory footprint needed.

Because working maps are discarded immediately after use, in a single-threaded environment, there will only be one working map in existence at a time. In order to eliminate the issue of repeatedly creating and destroying these arrays often, it is often a good idea to create a single, larger, working map and preserve it for continual use.

9.5 Population of Map Data

Because the base maps must draw their information from the world data—namely, the positions and dispositions of the agents—they must be updated on a regular basis. For the games we have used this system on, we updated tactical influence maps once per second. However, any frequency can be selected based on the needs of the game, the period between think cycles for your agents, and the processing power available. For tactical movement, we would not recommend updating them any faster than 0.5 s (game characters will not need data much faster than that) or any less often than every 2 s (the data will get too stale between updates).

On each update, the map is first zeroed out—no data is carried over from one pass to the next. We then iterate through the population of the game world, and, for each agent, we apply—or "stamp"—their influence onto the appropriate maps for their faction based on their location. Assuming that we are using both proximity and threat maps, this means that each character is registering its influence on the two maps corresponding to its faction.

For the proximity map, we select the proximity template that most closely corresponds to the agent's maximum speed. That is, if an agent's maximum speed was 4 m/s, we would select the template that matched this. (If we had used integer speeds from 1–10, this would simply be the template for a speed of 4.) We then align the center of the template with the corresponding cell on the base map, offset by the size (in cells) of the template, and add the cell values from the template into the base map.

Looking up the appropriate threat template is similar to the process for the location templates earlier. As mentioned in the section on creating and storing templates, however, there may be more "slush" in selecting the correct sized template. Whether you round up or down is purely a game design decision. Rounding up to a larger threat template will cause their ranges to seem bigger than they are—possibly making attackers stay farther away. On the other hand, rounding down may cause attackers to seem that they don't realize the danger of the agent that is projecting the threat. Regardless, once the appropriate template is selected, the process of applying it into the base map is identical.

Note that in both cases, care must be taken along the edges of the map. If an agent is closer to the edge of map than the radius of its template, the addition process will attempt to apply the value of the template cell to a base map cell that does not exist. This is avoided simply by range checking on the bounds of the base map cells.

One possible addition to this process is that we may want different agents to exert different levels of influence into the map. For example, a weak character with a threat range of 10 needs to be represented differently than a strong character with an identical threat range. We need a representation that the area around the stronger character is more dangerous than around the weaker character.

Because the templates are normalized to 1.0, we can simply add a magnitude to the process of adding the influence to the map. If the stronger character was three times as powerful as the weaker character, we would simply need to pass a strength value of 3 into the function and the values in the template would be multiplied by 3 as it is stamped into the threat map. Therefore, the value of the influence of the stronger character would start at 3 and drop to 0 at the maximum range.

9.6 Information Retrieval

Once information is in the base maps, it can be retrieved in different ways depending on the needs at the time. While we will address specific use cases in the next section, the process is the same for most applications.

9.6.1 Values at a Point

The simplest form of information is retrieving the value of one map or a combination of maps at a specified point. For example, if an agent wanted to know the amount of enemy threat at its location, it could simply retrieve the value of the threat map cells for each faction that it considers an enemy. These are simply added together and returned to the agent for its consideration. Again, more use cases will be covered in the next section.

9.6.2 Combinations of Maps

Much as we applied templates into the base maps, we can lift information out of the base maps into working maps. The process is essentially the reverse of how we applied templates into the base map. We do this so that we can easily combine the map information for the area of interest without having to worry about processing the entire map.

In addition to simply passing the map into the functions to be modified, we also can pass in a modifier that dictates a magnitude for the modification. For example, rather than simply constructing a working map that consists of the values in MapA plus the values in MapB, we can specify that we want the values in MapA plus 0.5 times the values in MapB. The latter would yield a different output that might suit our purposes better at the time. In words, it would read "the influence of MapA plus *half* of the influence of MapB." By doing so, we can craft "recipes" for how an agent is looking at the world—including priorities of what is important to consider.

By including basic functions for adding and multiplying maps into the map class, we can construct a simple syntax that assists in building a working map that includes the information that we need. Each function takes a map and processes it into the working map according to its design and parameters if necessary. This is how we achieve the modularity to be able to construct a variety of outputs in an *ad hoc* manner.

For example, our code could look like the following:

```
WorkingMap.New(MyLocation);
WorkingMap.AddMap(EnemyLocationMap(MyLocation), 1.0f);
WorkingMap.AddMap(AllyLocationMap(MyLocation), -0.5f);
WorkingMap.MultiplyMap(InterestTemplate(MyLocation), 1.0f);
Location InterestingPlace = WorkingMap.GetHighestPoint();
```

We will see what can be done with these combinations in the next section.

9.6.3 Special Functions

There are a number of special functions that we must set up in order to make things easier for modular use later.

First, we can construct a general "normalization" function that takes a working map and normalizes its values to be between 0 and 1. The standard method of normalizing is to take the highest and lowest values present on the map and scale the contents such that they become 1.0 and 0.0, respectively. For instance, consider a map with a maximum value of 1.4 with a particular cell that had a value of 0.7. After normalization, the maximum value would be 1.0 (by definition) and the cell in question would now have a value of 0.5 (0.7/1.4).

The normalized map is convenient for times when we are interested in the general "terrain" of the map, but not its true values. We can then take that normalized map and combine it meaningfully with other normalized maps. We will investigate those further in the next section.

The other helper function is "inverse." In this case, we "flip the map contours upside down" in effect. This is done by subtracting the cell values in the map from 1.0. Therefore, an influence map of agents that would normally have high values at the points of greatest concentration and 0 values at the locations of no influence would now have a value of 1.0 at the places of no influence and its lowest points at the locations of the greatest influence.

The inverse function is helpful when combining maps from enemy factions. Instead of subtracting one faction's map from another, we can add one map to the inverse of the other. While, at first glance, this seems like it would yield the same result, the shift in values allows us to preserve convenient functions (such as retrieving the highest point) in our modular system.

9.7 Usage

The collection and storage of influence map data is useless without ways to use it. The power of the system is in how many ways the underlying data can be reassembled into usable forms. This information retrieval and processing can be divided into three general categories:

1. Gathering information about our location and the area around us
2. Targeting locations
3. Movement destinations

We address each of these in Sections 9.7.1 through 9.7.3.

9.7.1 Information

The most basic function that the influence map system can serve is providing information about a point in space. One function simply provides an answer to the simple question, "what is the status of this point?" The word "status" here could mean a wide variety of things depending on the combination of maps utilized in the query. However, other methods can query an entire area and answer the similar question, "what is the status of the (highest/lowest) point around me?" The latter can be done without specifying a point at all simply by looking at the surrounding area.

The first method—that of querying a specific point—is achieved by querying the value of a location through its associated influence map cell on one or more maps (Figure 9.6). For example, if we wanted to know the total threat from our enemies at the location we are standing, we would simply retrieve the value of the cell we are standing in from all of the threat maps that belong to enemy factions. Because the value that is returned represents the total threat at our location, it can be used in decisions such as when to relocate to a safer position. A similar query of the physical proximity map of our own faction would hint us as to whether or not we might need to move slightly to give space to our co-combatants. Note that this method does not require us to use a working map because we are only interested in the values of individual cells.

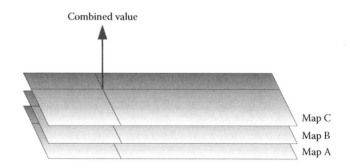

Figure 9.6

We can query a point on the map and retrieve data accumulated from a combination of maps at that point.

Another method for querying information is to look at the entire area surrounding us. For example, we may want to query the area to see if there are concentrations of enemies that are standing close together. To do this, we create a working map that is the same size as a personal interest template that, in this instance, might be how far we could attack in 1 s (our maximum threat range + our movement speed). We then populate that working map with the data from the proximity maps of our enemies. We then run a function that walks through the working map and returns the highest value (not the location). This value tells us what the maximum concentration of enemies is due to the fact that enemies closer together have their influence areas overlapping resulting in a higher sum as is shown in Figure 9.7. This might be useful in informing us that we might want to cast an area of effect spell. (Note that the location at which we would cast it is addressed in the next section.)

The usefulness of the modular nature of the map system becomes clear when we extend the aforementioned query to ask, "what is the highest concentration of all factions?" We could add all the factions together and find the highest value. Summing the enemy factions to the *inverse* of allied factions would give a number representing the highest concentration of enemies that isn't close to any allies. By mixing location and threat maps, we can extend the possible information we can get.

Often, it is good to prioritize information that is closer to the agent so that it doesn't make decisions that cause it to, perhaps, run past one threat to get to another. By multiplying the resulting working map by our personal interest template, we adjust the data so that closer cells are left relatively untouched, but cells on the periphery are reduced artificially—ultimately dropping to zero. In the example shown in Figure 9.8, the high point on the original map (a) is located at the edge of the personal interest map (b) surrounding the agent's location (dotted line). By multiplying the original map by the interest map, the resulting map (c) yields a different high point. While the *actual value* of this location is smaller than the high point in the original map, it is prioritized due to its proximity to the agent's actual location. Note that any points outside the radius of the personal interest map are reduced to 0 due to multiplying by 0. This is similar to the agent saying, "Yes, there is something interesting over there, but it is too far away for me to care."

9.7.2 Targeting

Another primary use for assembling information from combined influence maps is for use in targeting. In the aforementioned section, we mentioned that we could query the local area for the highest value. By using a similar process, we can acquire the actual location of the cell that produced that value. This is as simple as making a note of the cell in the working map that contains the highest value and then converting it back into a position in the world.

Possible uses for this include using the proximity maps for determining a location to cast an area of effect spell—a damaging one against enemies or a healing buff for allies. By finding the highest point on the working map, we know that it is the center of concentration of the forces of the faction we are checking. This means that the target will not be a character in the world but rather at a point that should be the "center of mass" of the group. Referring again to Figure 9.7, the "high point" identified on the map is the location of the highest concentration of agents.

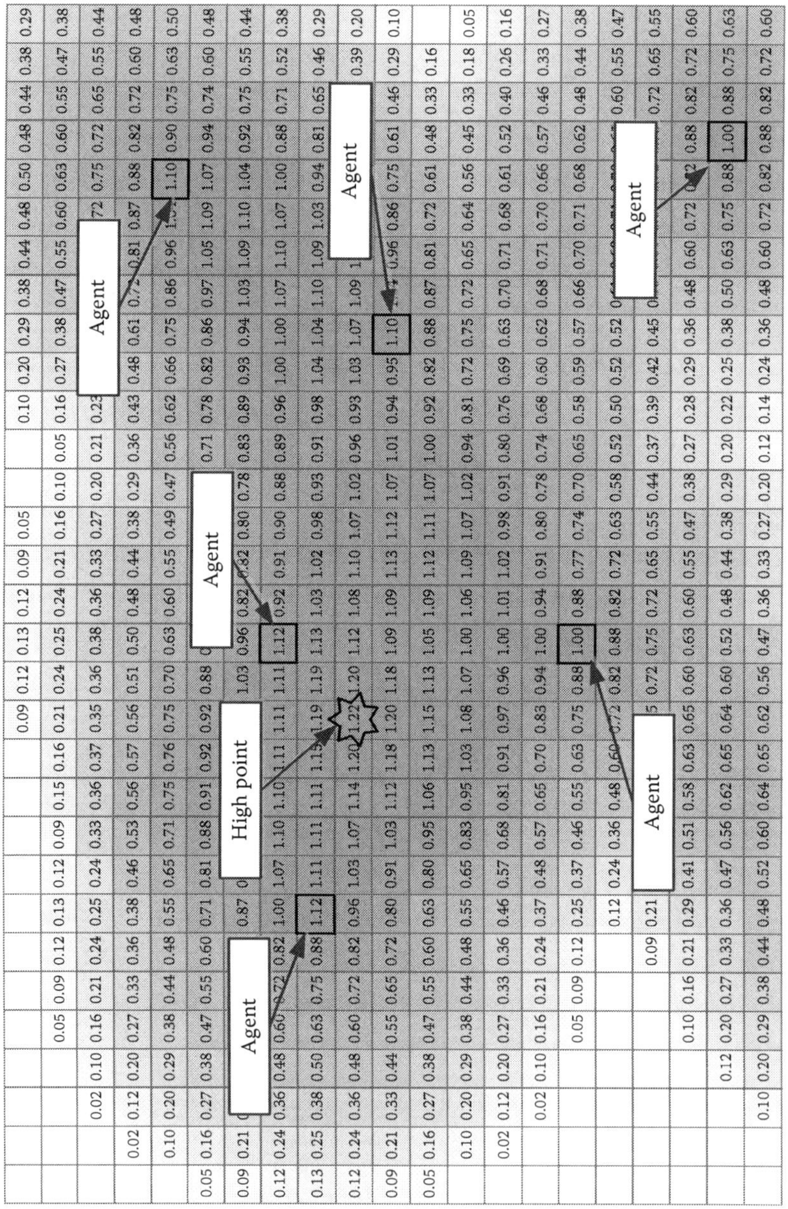

Figure 9.7
The "center of mass" of agents can be determined by finding the highest value on one or a combination of base maps.

9. Modular Tactical Influence Maps

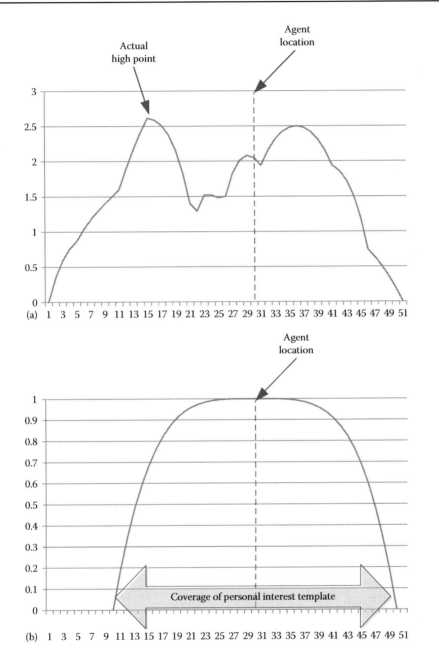

Figure 9.8

A complex influence map (a), when multiplied by a personal interest template (b),
(Continued)

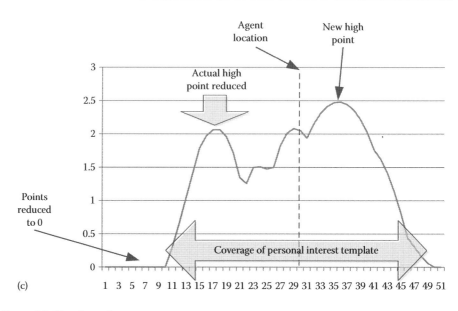

Figure 9.8 (*Continued*)

Might yield different high points (c).

Because of the modular nature of the system, we could add the enemy location maps together and then *subtract* the location maps for allies. The resulting high point would give a location of concentration enemies that is also *not near* allies. This might be useful in avoiding friendly fire, for example.

Another possible use would be identifying a position between the agent and the bulk of the enemies or even between the bulk of the agent's allies and the enemies. This might help identify where to place a blocking spell such as a wall of fire. This is accomplished by determining that point of the concentration of the enemies as we did earlier, but then using that as an endpoint for a line segment either between that point and the agent or that point and a corresponding one for the allies. In effect, this is determining the "threat axis" to be aware of. By selecting a location partway along that segment, you are able to identify a spot that would be good for a blocking spell (Figure 9.9) or for the positioning of forces, as we shall see in the next section.

9.7.3 Positioning

The third primary use for tactical influence maps is to inform movement commands. This is very similar to the use for targeting earlier. Upon deciding that it would like to perform some sort of movement (move toward a group, withdraw to a safe spot), the agent requests an appropriate destination location from the influence map system. As with the methods earlier, a working map is created and populated with data from the necessary maps, the personal interest template is applied (via multiplication), and the highest or lowest scoring location is returned.

Another use for positioning is to encourage spacing between agents—notably allied agents. By subtracting the location maps of the agent's faction—*and adding the agent's*

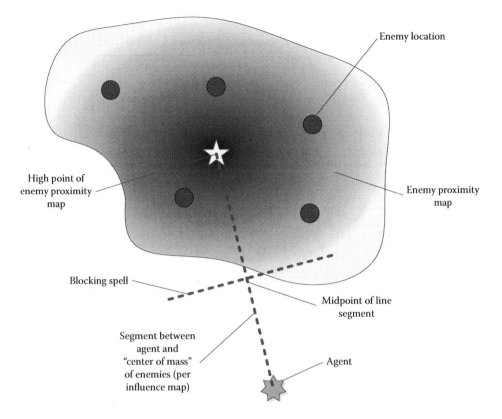

Figure 9.9

By determining the location of the high point of the enemy proximity map, we can select a location along the line between that point the agent to position a blocking spell, for instance.

own proximity template—the agent can adjust and take allied agents' positioning into account. This can be used on a stand-alone basis for a simple "spacing" maneuver (e.g., as part of an idle) or as a modifier to other positioning activities. At this point, the logic from the influence map request can be read as something similar to "find me a location that is away from enemy threats *but also spaced apart from my allies.*"

9.8 Examples

The following are some examples of modularly constructed influence maps that can be used for common behaviors. Note that this assumes only one enemy and one allied faction. A separate code could be written to assemble all relevant factions.

The examples are written in a simplified structure for brevity and clarity. The actual implementation of the functions referenced here would be more involved and would differ largely depending on your base implementation. However, the actual modular functions to access the data should be little more complicated than what is shown here.

9.8.1 Location for Area of Effect Attack

This identifies if there is a point that is worth casting an area of effect attack on and retrieves the location. The `MultiplyMap` function that applies the `InterestTemplate` (of a size determined by our movement speed) is used to prioritize locations that are closer to the agent similar to what is show in Figure 9.8.

```
WorkingMap.New(MyLocation);
WorkingMap.Add(LocationMap(MyLocation, ENEMY), 1.0f);
WorkingMap.Multiply(InterestTemplate(MySpeed), 1.0f);

return WorkingMap.GetHighestLocation();
```

Note that to change the aforementioned code to find a position for an area of effect spell for allies (such as a group buff spell), we only would need to change the parameter ENEMY to ALLY.

9.8.2 Movement to Safer Spot

This identifies the location near the agent that has the least amount of enemy physical influence. This is good for finding a location for the character to move that is away from the immediate physical range of enemies.

```
WorkingMap.New(MyLocation);
WorkingMap.AddInverse(LocationMap(MyLocation, ENEMY), 1.0f);
WorkingMap.Multiply(InterestTemplate(MySpeed), 1.0f);

return WorkingMap.GetHighestLocation();
```

By using the inverse of the enemy location map, we are saying that the places where the cell values are low (or even 0)—that is, *away* from enemies—are now the highest points. Correspondingly, the highest points on the map are now the lowest due to the inverse. Since we are looking for place with the fewest enemies, we now can use the `GetHighestLocation()` function. Of course, the highest points would be modified somewhat after the application of the interest map, again as visualized in Figure 9.8.

Note that this code can also be used for moving away from allies (e.g., to keep spacing) simply by changing the parameter ENEMY to ALLY.

Additionally, by changing the code to use the threat map of enemies, we could find a location that had the least amount of enemy threat (but was also close to our location by application of the interest template). The new code would be as follows:

```
WorkingMap.New(MyLocation);
WorkingMap.AddInverse(ThreatMap(MyLocation, ENEMY), 1.0f);
WorkingMap.Multiply(InterestTemplate(MySpeed), 1.0f);

return WorkingMap.GetHighestLocation();
```

9.8.3 Nearest Battlefront Location

To determine a location that is in the area between our allies and our enemies, we multiply the enemy threat map by the ally threat map. The resulting map has high points along a line where the two maps overlap the most (Figure 9.10). By further multiplying this map by the interest template, we can find a location nearest to the agent that is "on the front lines."

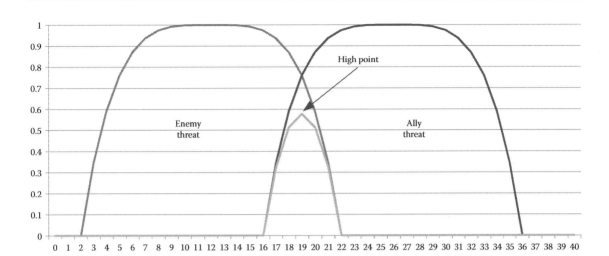

Figure 9.10

Multiplying enemy threat (or location) by ally threat (or location) yields high points along the front lines.

```
WorkingMap.New(MyLocation);
WorkingMap.Add(ThreatMap(MyLocation, ENEMY), 1.0f);
WorkingMap.Multiply(ThreatMap(MyLocation, ALLY), 1.0f);
WorkingMap.Multiply(InterestTemplate(MySpeed), 1.0f);

return WorkingMap.GetHighestLocation();
```

As we noted in the prior section, by subtracting our ally's proximity, we can find a point that is "on the front" but also away from our fellows. This leads to a behavior where allied agents will spread out along a battlefront by selecting a location that is not only in between the bulk of allies and enemies but also physically apart from their comrades. In order for this to work, we need to normalize the result of the map earlier and then subtract a portion of the ally proximity map. The version of the ally proximity map that we need must not include our own proximity. Therefore, a function is created that returns the ally proximity *without our own information*. This would simply be as follows:

```
AllySpacingMap.New(MyLocation);
AllySpacingMap.Add(LocationMap(MyLocation, ALLY), 1.0f);
AllySpacingMap.Add(LocationTemplate(MyLocation, MySpeed), -1.0f);

Return AllySpacingMap&();
```

We can then apply this spacing map into our original formula. The adjusted code would read as follows:

```
WorkingMap.New(MyLocation);
WorkingMap.Add(ThreatMap(MyLocation, ENEMY), 1.0f);
WorkingMap.Multiply(ThreatMap(MyLocation, ALLY), 1.0f);
WorkingMap.Normalize();
WorkingMap.Add(AllySpacingMap(), -0.5f);
WorkingMap.Multiply(InterestTemplate(MySpeed), 1.0f);

return WorkingMap.GetHighestLocation();
```

Note that we are multiplying the ally spacing map by a scaling factor of 0.5 before we subtract it in order to make it less of an impact on the positioning than the battlefront itself.

9.9 Conclusion

As we have demonstrated, influence maps can be a powerful tool for agents to understand the dynamic world around them. By providing a modular system that allows programmers to combine individual map components in a variety of ways, a wide variety of expressivity can be easily created and tuned with relative ease.

References

[Tozour 01] Tozour, P. 2001. Influence mapping. In *Game Programming Gems 2*, ed. M. DeLoura, pp. 287–297. Charles River Media, Hingham, MA.

[Woodcock 02] Woodcock, S. 2002. Recognizing strategic dispositions: Engaging the enemy. In *AI Game Programming Wisdom*, ed. S. Rabin, pp. 221–232. Charles River Media, Hingham, MA.

10

Spatial Reasoning for Strategic Decision Making

Kevin Dill

10.1 Introduction

In the real world, no military decision can be made without taking into account the characteristics of the space in which the decision is taking place. Individual soldiers will use cover and concealment, so as to maneuver on the enemy without being shot. Squad leaders will split their team, with one element pinning the enemy in place while the second maneuvers to attack from a flank. Platoon leaders emplacing a defensive perimeter will use their largest weapons to cover the most likely avenues of approach, and use resources such as minefields and barbed wire to constrain the enemy's maneuverability—forcing them to attack where expected. Beyond small unit tactics, spatial considerations are taken into account in decision after decision—from the placement of diapers in a toy store (at the back, so that parents have to take their children past the toys) to the placement of a city (in a good location for trade, with ready access to water).

While there are exceptions, game AI often does a poor job of thinking about space in these ways. A common justification is that the developer doesn't want to make the game too hard for the player—but there are any number of ways to balance the game, including simply making the enemies weaker or forcing them to make intentional mistakes that the player can exploit. Further, imagine the benefits of making the AI more spatially competent. As Koster so eloquently explained in *A Theory of Fun for Game Design* [Koster 04], one of the things that makes a game fun is *mastery*. Imagine an enemy that could use good spatial tactics and strategies against you in a difficult but not overwhelming way. If the player can learn from the strategies of their enemy, then they are being *shown* how to take advantage of the environment themselves, and we can gradually build upon that experience, imparting mastery step by step much like the game *Portal* gradually imparts mastery in the use of a teleportation gun.

In this chapter, we present a successful spatial reasoning architecture that was originally developed for the real-time strategy (RTS) game, *Kohan II: Kings of War* ("Kohan II") [Kohan II]. This architecture primarily addressed strategic needs of the AI, that is, the large-scale movements and decisions of groups of units across a map.

Spatial reasoning is, by its very nature, highly game- and decision-specific. The information that needs to be tracked and the techniques that will work best depend greatly on the specific nature of the experience that you're trying to create for your players. Further complicating the issue is the fact that the capabilities of your game engine will often drive you toward specific representations of space and away from others. As the approaches in this chapter were largely drawn from *Kohan II*, a tile-based strategy game, our solutions have that flavor about them. Nevertheless, many of the ideas discussed here are directly applicable in a wide range of domains, and others might spur your own ideas for spatial considerations. Our ultimate hope is to spark your imagination and get you thinking about (1) how space is important to your players' experience and (2) how you can represent and reason about that. From there, it's a small step to finding the right solutions for your own game.

It is worth noting that the *Kohan II* AI was discussed in *AI Game Programming Wisdom 3* [Dill 06]. While it's not necessary to read that chapter in order to understand this one, it will help to clarify the larger picture and in particular how some of the techniques discussed here might be used in the context of a utility-based AI.

10.2 Spatial Partitioning

Before any spatial reasoning can be done we need a *spatial representation*, which is created by breaking the game map up into meaningful *regions*. Regions will form the basis of most of the spatial reasoning techniques we will describe, including techniques for driving exploration, picking attack locations, path planning, and spatial feature detection.

The ideal subdivision is of course going to be game-specific, as you create regions that represent the spatial characteristics important to the decisions you want to make. With that said, here are some general characteristics of good regions as they are defined in Kohan II—just keep in mind that (with the possible exception of homogeneity, depending on your intended use) these are intended as fuzzy guidelines, not hard requirements:

- *Homogeneity*: It's often a good idea to have regions composed of a single "type" of space. For example, in a strategy game, your regions might divide space by terrain type, with each region being composed entirely of land, water, or mountain tiles, perhaps further subdivided to call out features like hilltops and roads that are of particular importance. Similarly, in a shooter with indoor maps, you might divide space into room and corridor regions, perhaps with smaller regions to represent areas of cover and concealment, potential snipe points, and so forth. The important thing is that each region should contain exactly one type of space—so a cover region should contain *only* cover, a hilltop region should contain *only* the hilltop, and so forth. This way, the AI knows that anywhere it goes in that region the expected characteristic will pertain.

- *Not too big*: If the regions are too large, then the reasoning becomes muddy and inaccurate—there isn't enough detail represented to make meaningful decisions. At the ridiculous extreme, we could treat the whole map as a single region—but this wouldn't be helpful to the AI at all.

- *Not too small*: If the regions are too small, then we can get buried in details. This can have profound performance implications, as many terrain reasoning techniques are search based and thus potentially expensive. More to the point, wherever possible (and this can be a difficult balancing act), we would like all of the features that go into making a decision about a region to be contained within that region or at least in a few adjacent regions. For example, if considering attacking a settlement in an RTS game, we'd like that settlement to be contained in a single region. If considering an army, we'd like the entire army to be contained in a single region. This is often not possible—armies typically move around and cross region borders freely, for example—so we will often need to consider characteristics of nearby regions when making decisions. Techniques exist for this, the most obvious being influence maps (which are discussed in detail in Section 10.4), but the fewer regions the army traverses, the better our decisions about it are likely to be.

- *Roughly equilateral/square/hexagonal/round*: Long, skinny regions tend not to be ideal—they can easily be too small in one dimension, and too large in the other. Of course, this is an ideal that depends very much on the situation. Long, skinny regions make perfect sense when representing long skinny things, such as a corridor in a building or the area along the side of a country road where the combination of a ditch and a stone wall may provide improved cover.

- *More-or-less convex*: Convexity is not an absolute requirement, even if you're going to use your regions for high-level path planning—in fact, it is often overrated. Nevertheless, if your spatial partition algorithm creates regions that are badly concave (e.g., a region shaped like a giant letter L or like Pacman with his mouth half open), you may want to consider taking a pass over all the regions and splitting these ones in half, particularly if they're large. As a rough rule of thumb, if the center of a region is not inside the region then the region is too concave.

10.2.1 Region Generation

There is no one right way to generate regions. When possible, it's a good idea to lean on the tools provided by your game engine. Techniques that you might consider include the following:

- *Designer defined*: For many games with predefined maps, designers can hand annotate the maps. This gives the most control over the player's experience and can produce very good results, but isn't possible on large open-world games or games with random maps.

- *Navmesh based*: If your game has a navmesh, then it's possible to simply use that, although this may not result in very good regions—many navmesh generation algorithms create regions that are long and skinny or that are widely varying in size. One partial solution is to automatically combine and/or subdivide the navmesh cells to produce better quality regions, perhaps sacrificing a bit of convexity to produce regions that are closer to round and of appropriate size. Of note, if you decide to head in this direction, consider using a technique such as conforming Delaunay triangulation for your navmesh generation—it will provide triangles that are closer to being equilateral (and thus not long and skinny) than many other approaches [Tozour 02, de Berg 08].
- *Tile based*: If you have a tile-based map (or can temporarily lay tiles over your map), you can use a flood-fill algorithm to create your regions. This is the approach that we used in *Kohan II*, so we will discuss it in detail.

For *Kohan II*, we used a greedy flood-fill-based approach to create rectangles from our grid tiles and then, in certain cases, combined adjacent rectangles to create our regions. It wasn't a perfect approach. It was time consuming (on a 2005 era machine, with a large map, it could take well over 20 seconds, so we ran it at load time only) and would sometimes create regions that were long and skinny or oddly shaped. Nevertheless, it was simple to implement and debug and makes a good basis for the rest of this chapter.

The logic for rectangle creation was as follows:

1. Start a new region that consists of a single tile. This tile should be one that has not yet been placed into a rectangle, and that is the farthest to the bottom and left of the map.
2. Using that tile as the bottom-left corner, find the largest homogenous rectangle that we can. We do this by alternately expanding the rectangle one row to the right and one row up, as long as this expansion results in a rectangle that is homogeneous.
3. If the resulting rectangle is "too big," divide it horizontally and/or vertically, creating two or more rectangles of a more reasonable size—for instance, if our maximum width is 16 tiles, then a 20×45 rectangle would be divided into six 10×15 pieces.

This algorithm results in rectangles of terrain that are homogeneous, generally roughly square (although this is not guaranteed), convex, and not too big. However, it can create a lot of very small regions along the borders of different types of terrain (e.g., along the edges of rivers or mountain ranges). These regions are not only too small, they also often aren't very interesting (not a lot of importance happens right on the edge of impassable terrain). Consequently, we would prefer to somehow get rid of them.

The first step to addressing this is to take a second pass over all of the rectangles looking for the undesirable ones. For example, we might search for rectangles that are less than two tiles wide in one direction or the other and that contain less than ten total tiles—although the details of how to tune that are of course game-specific. Whenever we find one of these rectangles, we try to attach it to an adjacent rectangle of the same terrain type. We only do this if the resulting region doesn't exceed some maximum height and width and if its center remains inside of its borders. The result is that we

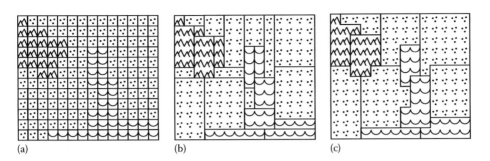

(a)   (b)   (c)

Figure 10.1

A hypothetical tile-based map with land, water, and mountain terrain (a) and the same map divided into rectangles (b) and regions (c).

get a smaller number of more useful, slightly larger, occasionally nonconvex regions. Figure 10.1 shows this entire process step by step.

In *Kohan II*, we retained all three representations. The tiles were useful for low-level path planning and collision avoidance, although we did allow movement within tiles. The rectangles gave a compact representation for the regions (a region consisted of a list of rectangles, and a rectangle simply stored the bottom-left and top-right tiles). Finally, the regions were used for a wide variety of spatial reasoning and decision-making tasks.

10.2.2 Static vs. Dynamic Regions

For many games, it is adequate to use static regions—that is, regions that don't change during gameplay. Static regions are generally baked into the map during development or, if you have random maps, created when the map is generated. Some games, however, have destructible or user-changeable terrain and, as a result, need to be able to update their regions as the map changes.

Dynamic region calculation is a difficult and thorny problem—think hard before deciding to include it in your game! With that said, it's not insoluble. For tile-based maps, a fast localized flood-fill-based solution can work—this is the approach that was taken by *Company of Heroes* [Jurney 07], which was probably the first game to solve this problem. If you're using a triangulation-based navmesh to provide your regions, it is possible to retriangulate the affected area reasonably quickly (e.g., Havok AI does this). Note that neither of these approaches is simple to implement or optimize, and no matter how much you optimize, neither is likely to run in a single frame. Thus, you're going to have to timeslice the calculations and also to figure out how the AI should handle the case where the regions have been invalidated but haven't yet finished recomputing. Regardless, dynamic recalculation of the regions is well beyond the scope of this article (but *Computational Geometry: Algorithms and Applications* might provide at least a starting point [de Berg 08]).

10.3 Working with Regions

So, now we have our regions… what do we do with them? Well, lots of things, but let's start with some examples that take advantage of the granularity and homogeneity of our regions—that is, of the fact that they're not too big, not too small, and made up entirely of a single type of space.

10.3.1 Picking Places to Scout or Explore

As discussed earlier, regions allow us to break the map into larger, less granular, spaces, which can greatly reduce the complexity of decision making. One area where this pays off is in selecting areas to explore or to scout for enemy forces. If we made this decision on a tile-by-tile basis, it would be entirely intractable—there are simply too many tiles to choose from. Instead, we can score the value of exploring a region using information such as the following:

- How much of it is already explored?
- How close is it to our current position?
- Does our current strategy prefer to explore close to the center of our territory (looking for resources) or far away (looking for enemy bases), and how does this region match that preference?

Scouting is similar to exploration, except that the decision is based on how recently that region has been scouted, its proximity to our territory, its proximity to known enemy territory or units, its strategic importance, and so forth.

Of course, once you've picked a region to explore or scout, you need a low-level AI that handles the actual motion over the tiles, perhaps spiraling outward until a new location is picked—but this is generally much more tractable than the high-level decision selecting a general area to explore.

10.3.2 Picking Places to Attack

Regions can also allow us to lump nearby structures or resources together and make decisions based on their aggregate value. For example, deciding where and when to attack is an important part of any strategy game. Lots of factors might go into this decision—the strength of our available units, the enemy strength in the area, the strategic value of the region, etc. Many of these factors are discussed elsewhere in this chapter, but the underlying basis for this evaluation is always going to be the economic and/or military value of the target being attacked.

What we want to avoid is launching multiple separate attacks against targets that are very close together, with each attack individually bringing enough units to defeat the enemy forces in the area. This results in sending far too many units to attack, thus depriving us of the opportunity to use those units in other ways. In order to do this, instead of attacking individual targets, we launch our attacks against *regions*. The value of attacking a region can be considered to be something like the sum of the values of all of the targets in that region, plus 25% of the value of targets in adjacent regions—or zero if there is an adjacent region that has a higher total value.

The result is that if we do launch multiple attacks, then those attacks will be spread out, hitting relatively distant targets. This forces the player to fight a battle on two fronts, which is generally a challenging (and enjoyable) experience.

10.3.3 Picking Unit Positions

In addition to their granularity, the homogeneity of the regions can help drive spatial decision making at the unit level. For example, imagine that our archer units have a bonus to their ranged attack value when they're above their enemies, that all units move slower when travelling uphill, and that spearman units have the ability to hide in tall grass and then spring out and ambush the enemy with a large bonus to their attack.

When picking a place to position a unit, we first need to identify the valid regions. Generally speaking, these are the regions that allow the unit to satisfy its high-level goal. For example, if the unit is participating in an attack, then the region must be close enough to attack the enemy, or if it's standing guard, then the region must be close enough to cover the target it's defending (and ideally located on a likely avenue of approach—more on that in Section 10.5.3). Next, we calculate a score for each of the valid regions based on a number of factors, including the proximity to the unit's current location, the cost of moving there, and the viability of moving there (e.g., it's not a good idea to move your archers through a mass of enemy swordsmen just to get to a good tactical position).

In addition to those factors, however, we can consider the value of the region itself. For example, archers might really like hilltop regions—not only do they get a bonus to their attack but they also have more time to fire at enemies coming up the hill to attack them. Spearmen might have a moderate preference for grassland regions, but only when guarding, since they won't have time to hide during an attack, and only when the region is on a likely avenue of approach, since they can only ambush enemies that go past them.

10.3.4 Path Planning

If our regions are created out of some smaller abstraction, such as tiles, then we can use the regions for hierarchical path planning, which will greatly speed up our path queries. To do this, we first find the shortest path through the regions (which is comparatively fast because the regions are moderately large so there are relatively few of them). Once we have the region path, we find the first region on the path whose region center is not visible from the current position of the unit we're planning a path for. On a tile-based map, we can do this with a series of tile walks, which are also quite fast (linear time on the length of the tile walk). A tile walk is similar to a raycast, except that instead of testing against the collision geometry, it simply determines which tiles are along the line. Finally, we calculate the low-level path (using the tiles) from the unit to that region center. This low-level path should also be very quick to find, because it's more or less straight (it typically has a single turn), which means that A* with a straight-line heuristic will find it in near-linear time (i.e., really, really fast—this is the best case scenario for A*).

One nice thing about this approach is that our regions (i.e., the nodes in our high-level abstraction) are homogeneous, which means that we can weight the high-level path based on the terrain type. For example, we can make a unit that prefers to travel through grassland, or to avoid hilltops, or both, by making regions of those terrain types more or less expensive to travel through. While hierarchical path-planning solutions have been around for some time, they don't typically use a homogenous abstraction, so they lose the ability to weight the path in this way—and thus the ability to choose their paths on the basis of anything other than shortest distance.

In the remainder of this chapter, we'll refer to the connectivity graph through the regions as the *region graph* and to a path through this graph as a *region path* or a *high-level path*.

10.3.5 Distance Estimates

One thing that we frequently want is an estimate of the distance between two distant objects. For example, if we are considering whether to attack an enemy settlement with a particular unit, then we will want to know the distance between that settlement and the unit. If we are considering exploring a particular region, then we will want to know the distance to that region not only from the exploring unit but also from each of our settlements. We could use the full path planner to find these distances, but doing so is likely to be prohibitively expensive, especially if we're going to be doing a lot of these checks (and we will almost certainly be doing a lot of these checks if we want to have good spatial reasoning). The obvious simplification is to use straight-line distance, but if your map is at all complex then straight-line distance often badly underestimates the actual distance.

The solution is to find the region path, which is fairly quick, and then calculate the distance from region center to region center along that path. The result isn't a perfect estimate—it will overestimate the distance to some extent. The good news, however, is that the extent to which it overestimates the distance is bounded by the size of the regions, so unless your regions are enormous, this estimate can be expected to be fairly good.

10.3.6 Region Path Caching

Given the frequency with which we'll be using distance estimates, even finding a region path may not be fast enough. In this case, if you can spare a few megabytes of memory, it's possible to cache the region paths as you discover them. In order to do this, you need to have your regions numbered from $0 \dots n - 1$, where n is the number of regions in your game. You can then create an $n \times n$ lookup array. In this array, you store the first step to get from every region to every other region. So, for example, if the path from region 17 to region 23 is $17 \to 12 \to 23$, then position [17][23] in the array would contain 12 (because the first step to get from 17 to 23 takes us to region 12). Similarly, position [12][23] would contain 23, position [23][17] would contain 12, and position [12][17] would contain 17.

If the region count is low enough, this "next step" lookup array could be precomputed fully at map generation time using an algorithm such as Floyd–Warshall [Floyd 62], which runs in $O(n^3)$ in the number of regions. If this cost is prohibitive, however, the contents of the array could also be computed in a just-in-time fashion. A single high-level path doesn't take long to calculate, so you can always run the path planner the first time you need a path between two particular regions and then store them in the path cache as you go. This works out well, because there are generally fewer units to work with (and thus, less work for the AI to do) early in the game, which gives us more time for path planning. In addition, even though the AI will ask for a lot of distance estimates all at once, many of them will start and end in the same general area. If the path planner uses the path cache to look up shortest partial paths, then groups of queries from similar locations will be very fast because most of the paths are just slight modifications of previous searches.

Clearly, one concern is that this array can get quite big if you have a lot of regions. If you have 2000 regions, and you store the region indices in 2-byte integers (since 1 byte isn't big enough), then the size of the array is 2000·2000·2 = ~8 MB. That's not a completely unreasonable amount of memory on a modern system—although it's not viable on something like the Nintendo 3DS or a cell phone—but it's enough to catch the attention of the rendering team (who will no doubt want the space for more polygons). It's possible to optimize this a bit by compressing the region indices into less than 16 bits (e.g., we can handle 2000 regions with 11 bit indices), but this makes the code quite a bit more complicated for only an incremental savings.

Another trick is to only store the shortest path from the lower-numbered region to the higher-numbered region. Since the shortest path from region 17 to region 23 is the same as the shortest path from region 23 to region 17 (assuming that we don't have any unidirectional connections, like jump downs or one-way teleports), we can just store the first step from the lower-numbered region to the higher-numbered region. Working out the sequence of queries to rebuild the path is a bit tricky, but doable. The essence of it is that you work from both ends toward the middle, filling in pieces until you have the full path. So, in our example earlier, if we wanted to find the path from 23 to 17, first, we'd look up the first step from 17 to 23 (because we don't store the first step from 23 to 17) and find that it is 12. This tells us that we need to go from $23 \rightarrow [\text{unknown}] \rightarrow 12 \rightarrow 17$. Next, because 12 is less than 23, we look up the path from 12 to 23 and find that we can go directly there. Thus, our final path, as expected, is $23 \rightarrow 12 \rightarrow 17$. If implemented properly, there should always be a single [unknown] location as we fill in the path—the trick is to look up the next step from the lower-indexed to the higher-indexed region adjacent to that location.

10.3.7 Recognizing Cul-de-Sacs and Chokepoints

Cul-de-sacs are areas that have only a single point of access (like dead-end streets). *Chokepoints* are narrow places in the terrain that connect two or more larger areas. Previous work has discussed a variety of ways to detect and make use of these features, but these approaches are often complex and computationally expensive [Forbus 02, Obelleiro 08] or require that the region graph be extremely sparse [Dill 04]. Unfortunately, most games have maps that are fairly open and easily traversable, which means that the region map is typically not sparse at all.

If your map has been divided into regions, then cul-de-sacs are dead simple to recognize. A cul-de-sac is simply a region that is passable (i.e., units can move through it), which has only one adjacent passable region. Looking back at the map in Figure 10.1c, there are three cul-de-sacs (though on a less constrained map, they would not be nearly so common): the southeast, southwest, and northwest land regions.

Detecting chokepoints is a bit more complicated. One approach is to look for a region R that separates the adjacent regions into two (or more) groups, which we will call *areas*, that are only connected through R. For example, in Figure 10.2a, region 2 is a chokepoint because you can only get from region 1 to region 3 by passing through it. In Figure 10.2b, it is not (at least, not according to this definition), because there is an alternate route around to the west. We can detect regions like this by doing a breadth-first search from each region adjacent to R and excluding R itself from the search. If the search from any adjacent region fails to find any other adjacent regions, then those two adjacent regions must be in different areas and R is a chokepoint.

There are two major problems with this solution. First, it is expensive to compute (unbounded breadth-first search from every region adjacent to every other region… yick!). Second, it is too strict. For example, in Figure 10.2b, region 2 is not considered a chokepoint, but in reality this region and the region directly to its west between them do a nice job of dividing the map into two areas. More generally, a region can be useful as a chokepoint even if there's an alternate route between the adjacent areas, as long as the alternate route is convenient or costly to take.

Fortunately, the solution to both of these problems is the same. We can simply limit the depth of our breadth-first search. This keeps the cost of the search down and also reflects

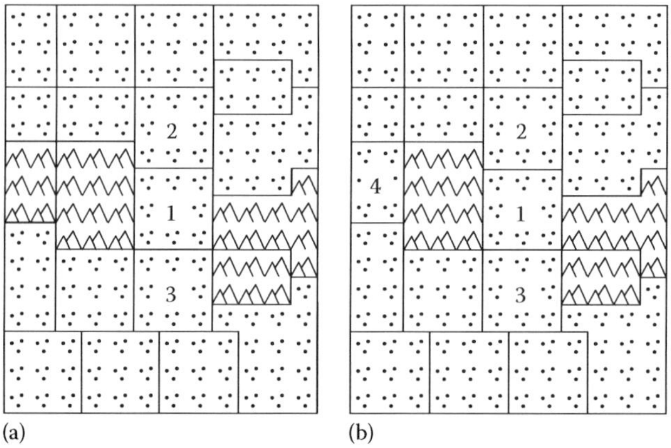

Figure 10.2

(a) Region 1 is a chokepoint because you can't get from region 2 to region 3 without going through it. (b) There are no chokepoints because there is an alternate route around the mountains to the west (through region 4).

the fact that a region can be a chokepoint merely by creating a local division between two areas—it doesn't have to create a global division between them. Finding the right depth for the search is another of those fuzzy, game-specific problems, but in general, a value somewhere between 5 and 10 is probably good for the sorts of maps we've been discussing.

Of note, both cul-de-sacs and chokepoints are generally only interesting if they are reasonably narrow. This is one of the reasons why we want to ensure that our regions aren't too large. As long as the regions have an appropriate maximum width, that width can serve as our definition of "reasonably narrow."

Once you have identified the chokepoints, there are all sorts of ways that you can put them to use. They are often excellent ambush points, for example. One trick is to keep track of how much enemy traffic goes through each chokepoint (or is likely to go through each chokepoint—more on this in Section 10.5.2) and place ambushes on the high-traffic spots. Furthermore, if you can identify a set of chokepoints that separate your territory from the territory of an enemy (i.e., they're along likely avenues of approach—again, more on this is discussed in Section 10.5.3), then they become excellent places to put defensive units and/or fixed defenses (such as forts or walls). This allows you to mass your defenses in fewer locations, giving you a better chance of defeating an incoming attack. At the very least, placing a few forces to stand guard there can warn you that an attack is on the way (in the Army, we called this an LP/OP, or listening post/observation post). Finally, if the chokepoints constrain movement then you might be able to mass your forces at the exit of a chokepoint and defeat the enemy as they come out of it. This tactical advantage may enable a small force to defeat a much stronger enemy—the Battle of Thermopylae, in which 300 Spartans famously held off a massive Persian army (for a time, at least), is perhaps the best known example of this.

On some maps, chokepoints can also be used to plan an attack. If the map is fairly constrained, you may be able to find the chokepoints closest to your target and stage your attacking forces into a multipronged attack, simultaneously striking from two or more different chokepoints. Alternately, you can launch a diversionary attack at one chokepoint and then send a much larger force against the other. As in real life, these sorts of maneuvers can be difficult to time and can go horribly wrong if they're detected in time—but when you're an AI opponent, allowing the player to defeat an overly clever maneuver might be the whole point!

Cul-de-sacs are generally less interesting than chokepoints precisely because they are out-of-the-way spaces that are not normally visited very often. On the other hand, they can be good places to hide economic buildings or other things that we don't want the player to see. We also might be able to optimize some aspects of our AI by excluding the cul-de-sacs from consideration.

One last note on chokepoints and cul-de-sacs: if a chokepoint only has two adjacent passable regions, and one of those regions is a cul-de-sac, then the chokepoint can also be considered part of the cul-de-sac. In other words, if the only place a chokepoint leads to is a dead end, then the chokepoint is really part of the dead end as well. Recognizing this can help to avoid placing units in a region that you think is a chokepoint when in fact nothing interesting is likely to happen there.

10.4 Influence Maps

Influence maps (as they are used in video games) have been around at least since the 1990s [Tozour 01]. They are typically used in the context of tile-based maps [Hansson 10] or on tile-like abstractions such as those proposed by Alex Champandard [Champandard 11]. With a few minor adaptations, however, they can be applied to regions with outstanding results.

10.4.1 Influence Map Basics

The key idea behind an influence map is that each unit has an *influence*, which is *propagated* out from the unit's position. The propagated influence of a unit decreases with distance in accordance with some formula, the simplest of which is simply to decrease the influence by some fixed amount for every tile that you traverse. The overall influence in each tile is the sum of the propagated influences of all of the units on the map.

As an example, consider Figure 10.3. In Figure 10.3a, we see a single lefty unit (whose icon and influence appear on the left side of the tile) with an influence of 5. This influence could represent any property that we wish to track over space, but for the purposes of our example let's assume that it is the combat strength of the unit. Influence propagates outward from the unit, so that adjacent tiles have an influence of 4, and the next tiles beyond those have an influence of 3, and so forth. Thus, on any tile, we can see the influence of this unit— which is to say, how relevant the unit is to combat decisions made with respect to that tile. In the tile where the unit is located, it exerts its full combat strength, but in more distant tiles, which it would have to travel for some time to reach, its influence is decreased.

In Figure 10.3b, we see how the influence of multiple units can be combined to give the overall influence of a player. Thus, instead of a single unit, we have three lefties, each with an influence of 5. The influence in any tile is simply the sum of the influences of the three units and represents the amount of combat strength we can expect that player to be able to bring to bear on a fight that occurs in that tile. There's no particular magic to calculating this—you can simply set all the influence values on the map to 0 and then go

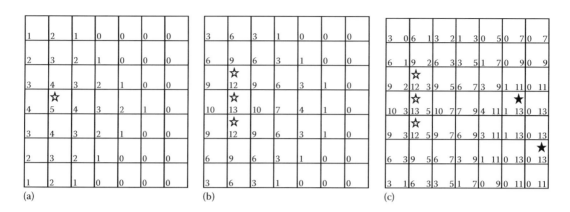

Figure 10.3

An example of an influence map with a single unit (a), three units belonging to the same player (b), and units belonging to two different players (c).

through each unit and add its influence to the map. Addition is commutative, so it doesn't matter what order you add the units in—the end result will be the same. Also of note, in this example we show each unit in its own tile, but the technique works exactly the same if you have multiple units in a tile—simply propagate their influence one at a time and the math will work.

Figure 10.3c is where things start to get interesting. Two righty units have come into the area. These units are a bit more powerful—perhaps they are cavalry units, rather than infantry—and so they each have an influence of 8. Righty influence propagates in the same way as lefty influence, and now we can see how much influence each side has and recognize areas that are contested (i.e., the areas where both sides have high influence, such as the tiles to the immediate right of the three lefty units), areas that are largely unoccupied (i.e., the areas where neither side has much influence, such as the upper and lower left-hand corners), and areas that are cleanly under the control of one side or the other (i.e., the areas where one side has high influence and the other low, such as the entire right side of the map).

Some authors suggest that when calculating the relative influence between two sides, you simply subtract enemy influence from friendly influence and look at the result—so, for example, the lefty influence in the tile with the middle lefty unit would be 8 (because $13 - 5 = 8$), and the righty influence would be -8. This approach loses critical information, however. There is a big difference between a hotly contested tile and one that is far from the action, for example, and yet if you use subtraction to combine the scores, then in both cases you'll end up with an influence of 0.

Another point to consider is that if we keep the influences separately, we can recombine them in any way that we want as alliances change or as we consider different aspects of the situation. For instance, when considering my own attack power in a tile I might include 25% of the influence of my allies, since there is a reasonable chance (but not a certainty) that they will jump into the fight to support me, especially if it's a close thing. This single trick was the only thing that we did to encourage teamwork between AI players that were allies in *Kohan II*, and it resulted in really nice coordinated attacks and/or one-two punches (where one enemy would hit you, and then just as you defeated them another enemy would swoop in to finish you off).

10.4.2 Propagation Calculations

One detail that was glossed over in the aforementioned example is the rate at which influence decays while it propagates. In the example, we simply reduced the influence by 1 for each tile it propagated through—so, for example, the righty units (which were more powerful) exerted their influence over a larger area. This approach uses the formula in the following equation:

$$I_D = I_0 - (\text{distance} \cdot k) \tag{10.1}$$

where
I_D is the influence at some distance
I_0 is the initial influence that the unit will exert in the tile where it's located
Distance is the distance between those two tiles
k is a tuning constant (which can be adjust to make the AI behave appropriately)

It's worth noting that for tile-based influence, we sometimes use Manhattan distance rather than straight-line distance (i.e., we calculate the distance as the sum of the change in x and the change in y, rather than using the Pythagorean theorem to calculate it). This makes sense if our units only move along the axes, but it can also just be easier to compute. This is the approach that was used in Figure 10.3.

We should also note that influences that are less than 0 should be discarded, but for the sake of brevity we have removed the *max()* statement from this and all of the following formulae.

Although the simple distance-based approach given earlier is appropriate for some applications (such as border calculations, which we discuss in Section 10.4.5), we can do better when reasoning about combat strength. Conceptually, the influence in each tile represents the ability of a player's units to get to a fight in a given tile fast enough to have an impact on the outcome of that fight. The farther away the units are, the less impact they'll have, because a significant amount of fighting will already have occurred by the time that they arrive. Thus, the real limiting factor in how far the influence propagates is not simply distance but rather the travel time to arrive at a distant tile. We can model this with a formula like the one in the following equation:

$$I_D = I_0 \cdot \frac{max\_time - travel\_time}{max\_time} \tag{10.2}$$

where
max_time is the maximum travel time at which a unit is considered to exert influence (e.g., 60 seconds)
travel_time is the actual amount of time it will take to travel to the distant tile

The aforementioned formulae are *linear* and *continuous*, which is to say that if you graph them then you will get a single straight line. There are times when we want nonlinear formulae (the line isn't straight), noncontinuous formulae (there is more than one line), or both. For example, an artillery unit that can fire over several tiles might use a discontinuous formula. For tiles within its range of fire, it will exert full influence. Beyond that distance, its influence will depend on the time to pack and unpack the artillery piece, but the travel time will just be the time to get in range. In order to accomplish this, we will need two formulae. Tiles within firing range simply use $I_D = I_0$, while more distant tiles use a formula such as the one given in the following equation:

$$I_D = I_0 \cdot \frac{max\_time - \left(time\_to\_pack + time\_to\_get\_in\_range + time\_to\_unpack\right)}{max\_time}$$

(10.3)

Thus, the influence is constant and high out to some distance and then it drops to a significantly smaller value (because beyond that distance, the unit needs to pack and unpack as well as travelling before it can enter the fight).

Similarly, a commander unit might have a nonlinear influence that looks like an inverted parabola—that is, the commander remains strong in the vicinity of its troops (where it is highly effective) but then drops off more and more sharply with distance. We could model this with a formula such is the one in the following equation:

$$I_D = I_0 - \left(\text{distance}\right)^k$$

(10.4)

Finally, the designers may want to be able to determine the influence themselves. If they are mathematically inclined, they may be able to help design these sorts of formulae—but if not, allowing them to give you a simple lookup table with the desired influence at any distance may be a good approach. Tables that are created in a spreadsheet and saved as .csv files can be easy for them to create and are also easy to parse in the code.

Ultimately, much of the intelligence in your influence maps comes from the way you choose to propagate the influence. For more detail on constructing AI logic out of mathematical formulae, much of which is directly applicable here, we highly recommend *Behavioral Mathematics for Game AI* [Mark 09].

10.4.3 Force Estimates over Regions

So far, we've talked about mapping influence over tiles, but it's straightforward to map the influence over regions instead. To do this, we first need to ensure that our propagation formula is based on distance (or travel time). All of the aforementioned formulae meet this requirement. Then, when propagating influence, we work our way through the region graph, just as we did through the tiles. In each region, we calculate the distance to the original region along the region graph (which we can track as we go—we don't have to recompute it each time) and use that value to calculate the local influence for that unit.

The only tricky bit in all of this is that we need to ensure that, as we walk the graph, we find the shortest path to each region. In order to do this, as we're walking the graph, when we're deciding which node to expand next, we always expand the node that has

Listing 10.1. The influence propagation algorithm. The regions variable is an array of region pointers, unit is a pointer to the unit whose influence we're propagating, and startRegion is a pointer to the region where unit is located.

```
for (int i = 0; i < numRegions; ++i)
{
    regions[i]->traversed = false;
}

heap<float, int> openList;
openList.push_back(0, startRegion->id);

while (!openList.empty())
{
    pair<float, int> nextRegionEntry = openList.pop();
    int nextRegionID = nextRegionEntry.second;
    Region* nextRegion = regions[nextRegionID];
    nextRegion->traversed = true;

    float distSoFar = nextRegionEntry.first;
    float influence = CalcInfluence(unit, distSoFar);
    if (influence <= 0)
        continue;

    nextRegion->influence += influence;

    Region* child = nextRegion->GetFirstChild();
    for (; child; child = child->GetNextSibling())
    {
        if (!child->IsPassable(unit) || child->traversed)
            continue;

        float dist = distSoFar + GetDist(nextRegion, child);
        openList.push_back(dist, child->id);
    }
}
```

the shortest total path from the starting region. Listing 10.1 shows pseudocode for this algorithm, and Figure 10.4 shows a new map with the influence for the lefty (white) and righty (black) players.

When calculating influence over regions, rather than over tiles, you lose some of the fine-grained precision. On the other hand, the resulting values are much easier to work with. If I have a settlement, three defensive units, and a fort all in close proximity, it's much easier to reason about how they interact if they're all in one region, or at least are in adjacent regions.

Another advantage of this approach is that even though we lose some precision, the resulting values can actually be more accurate. For example, note that the region with the three lefty units has their full influence—that is, the lefty influence in that region is 15. Compare this to Figure 10.3b, where the highest lefty influence was only 13. An influence of 15 is more accurate, since those units are close enough that they are able to—and are very likely to—support one another. Of course, there are border cases as well—for example, the two righty units in adjacent regions still end up with a maximum influence

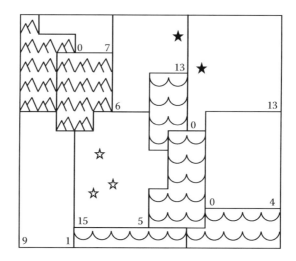

Figure 10.4

Influence propagation over the regions.

of 13, rather than 16. If these cases bother you, it's easy enough to check for them and adjust the influence values accordingly.

10.4.4 Illusion of Intelligence

One possible criticism of influence maps is that they are "cheating," in that they give the AI information that it could not otherwise have. In other words, even though the AI may not know the exact locations of the player's units, it knows generally where they are because it knows about their influence.

One solution is simply not to count influence for units that the AI can't see (or that it hasn't seen recently), but this approach has its own pitfalls. For example, this approach might make it easy to dupe the AI into attacking or defending in places where it shouldn't, which can then be exploited by the player. This will make the AI look stupid and will make the game less fun.

You could argue that the AI should scout better, but building a good scouting algorithm is a hard problem in its own right! Humans intuit how much force they should expect to face based on partial information—if they see two or three enemy units, they can make a guess as to how many they might not have seen and also as to what types of units the enemy is likely to have. Influence maps can provide a nice balance between a truly noncheating AI and an AI that doesn't blatantly cheat but does have a way to compensate for a human's innate intuition and stronger spatial reasoning skills. We don't allow the AI full knowledge, but we allow it enough knowledge to make the sorts of judgments that a human makes naturally.

More to the point, however, it's worth asking ourselves what our true goal is. Is it to build an AI that doesn't cheat or is it to provide a compelling experience for the player? One of the great advantages of basing your attack and defense decisions on influence maps is that it helps to *ensure* that the player's experience will be compelling. It is no fun to battle an enemy who doesn't fight back. It's a huge disappointment to build up your resources, amass an enormous army, and march on the enemy's stronghold—and discover that there are no defenders there, allowing you to win easily. It doesn't matter whether this occurs because the AI is truly stupid or because it made a poor choice and sent its units to the wrong place—it *looks* stupid and will rapidly erode the player's interest in your game.

Because the influence system gives the AI some warning that an attack is approaching— the enemy influence rises—we can avoid this hazard. When the enemy launches their massive attack, the AI will know that it's coming and will be able to ensure that there's something there to meet it. How the AI manages this is of course up to us (the solution used in *Kohan II* can be found in *AI Game Programming Wisdom 3* [Dill 06]), but now we have the information that we need to make a response possible.

Influence maps help to make our attacks appear more intelligent as well. Because the AI will tend to attack where the enemy is weakest, we get an enemy that is "smart" about where it strikes. This forces the player to maintain a broad defense, which adds to the challenge and sense of excitement. Furthermore, if we don't commit all of our forces to an attack immediately, but do require the ones who have actually engaged the enemy to remain where they are, then we get emergent skirmishes and diversionary attacks. The AI will initially attack with just a part of its total force. If the player rushes units from else-where to defend against the attack then the next attack may either be held back (because the player now has overwhelming force) or may go in at the new weak spot (which was exposed when the defensive units were pulled away). This result was actually a bit of a surprise for us on the *Kohan II* team—we didn't anticipate it—but it is borne out by the many reviews that said things like "the CPU uses smart battlefield tactics like trying to get the flank and attacking your weak spots" [Abner 04] or that it is "capable of drawing the player away or diverting his attention from a secondary attack." [Butts 04] The AI didn't explicitly reason about these things, they happened emergently as a result of our use of influence maps.

The best of all is that this cheating is hard for players to detect, because it's not blatant, it's not explicit, and it's not perfect knowledge. The AI sometimes does the perfect thing—but sometimes it doesn't. In Kohan II, we allowed players to go back and watch any game from beginning to end, from any viewpoint (i.e., they could turn fog of war off or even watch from the perspective of another player). We never heard complaints of the AI cheating, and indeed, some reviewers described the game as having a "noncheating AI." [Ocampo 04]

It might seem that this will make the AI too hard to beat but honestly, that's a good problem to have. There are a host of ways to tone down a difficult AI, but very few simple ways to increase the challenge when the AI isn't smart enough. What's more, players seem to genuinely enjoy the challenge of beating an AI that maneuvers well. Very nearly with-out exception, the reviews of *Kohan II* not only mentioned the AI but cited its ability to maneuver intelligently as one of the major strengths of the game.

10.4.5 Border Calculations

So far, we've talked about influence as a way to reason about combat power, but the same techniques can have much broader application. Space being limited, we will give one other example.

It is often beneficial to have a clear sense of what space is inside your borders, what space is clearly under somebody else's control, and what space is contested. This infor-mation can have broad-reaching implications. It can affect where you attack, where you position defensive forces, where you choose to expand, how many supporting forces you send to escort noncombat units such as builders or trade caravans, and so forth. On tightly constrained maps it's possible to extract this information directly from the region map [Dill 04], but as we discussed earlier, most strategy games have broader, more loosely constrained maps that don't yield well to this approach.

When a graph-based approach to border calculation is not practical, a less precise but more generalizable approach is to use influence. To do this, simply apply a certain amount of *border influence* to each major structure (e.g., buildings, bases, cities, settlements—whatever is important in your game). When propagating this influence, we want it to spread farther if the initial influence is higher. Thus, we can propagate it using the simple formula given in Equation 10.1.

Figure 10.5 shows an example in which the lefty and righty players each have one settlement. The lefty settlement is fairly small, and so it only has an influence of 15. The righty settlement is a bit larger and has an influence of 25. By examining the influence in each region, we can determine regions that are clearly controlled by the lefties (D and E), regions that are clearly controlled by the righties (C and F), and regions that are contested (A and B). From this, the lefties might identify region B as a good place to position defensive forces (it is contested, is reasonably close to their settlement, and is a chokepoint). Region A is less attractive for defensive forces, since it is a cul-de-sac with nothing in it, but it might be a good position for an ambush force. If the righties were to attack our settlement, forces hidden there could attack from behind and envelop them, blocking their line of retreat. Similarly, the lefties might identify regions D and E as good places to build economic structures, like mines or new settlements, which will need to be defended. Finally, they might pick region C as a good place to build an offensive fort, which will support an attack against the enemy, because it is the one where the lefties have the highest influence.

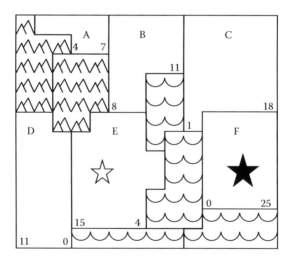

Figure 10.5

An example of how border influence could propagate over regions.

10.5 Spatial Characteristics

Much of the art of making your AI intelligent, whether in terms of spatial reasoning or in any other domain, comes from finding the right way to recognize and capture some distinction that you can then reason about. In this final section we will briefly discuss a number of easy-to-track distinctions that we can use to reason about space.

10.5.1 Scent of Death

One common trick, used in many games, is to keep track of how many things have died in each tile or in each region. We can use this in numerous ways, but two obvious ones are to prefer paths that avoid those regions and to only go into those regions in greater strength. So, for example, if we're considering building a gold mine in a region where we've previously lost a number of units, we might want to send extra defenders along to protect our builder unit (and our new gold mine).

A similar approach can be used to dynamically adjust the strength of enemy units who unexpectedly win battles. If, for example, we lose a battle that we expected to win, then we might increase the influence of the units that defeated us (or even increase the influence of all enemy units) in order to recognize the fact that this player is more wily and tactically competent than we expected. This will help to avoid sending losing attacks against the same target over and over without at least ensuring that each attack is stronger than the last.

10.5.2 High-Traffic Areas

It's often useful to know where other players are *likely* to travel. You can use this information to sneak around them, to ambush them, to place toll posts along their path, and so forth.

One way to gather this information is to simply keep track of the number of units of any given type (military units, caravans, etc.) that have moved through each region. This is guaranteed to be accurate (assuming that you cheat and log units that the AI didn't actually see) but only gives information about what has already happened—it doesn't necessarily predict the future.

Another approach is to plan region paths between all major sites, such as settlements, and keep track of the number of these paths that go through each region. This approach doesn't account for things like the likelihood of travelling between any two sites and can be exploited by players who deliberately choose obscure paths, but it can do a better job of predicting traffic that has not yet occurred.

10.5.3 Avenues of Approach

It is often important to be able to consider not only where the enemy is likely to attack but also *how they are likely to get there*—that is, the likely *avenues of approach*. For example, in real life, when a light infantry platoon is placed in a defensive perimeter, the commander will ensure that somebody is covering every direction, but they will place the heaviest weapons (e.g., the machine guns or grenade launchers) to cover the likely avenues of approach, while placing the lighter weapons (e.g., rifles) to cover the flanks and rear. This isn't foolproof, but it does make it more likely that the enemy will face your heaviest fire when they attack—or else that they'll be forced to work around your sides and attack through more difficult terrain. Likely avenues of approach are also good places to position

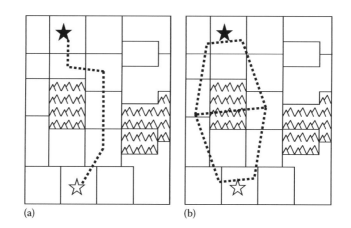

Figure 10.6

The avenues of approach between enemy settlements calculated using the region path (a) or two trapezoids (b).

LP/OPs, screening forces (i.e., defensive forces that will engage the enemy *before* they get to their target), and/or ambush forces (which can be used either to surprise enemies on their way in or to entrap them once they've engaged).

Of course, figuring out where the avenues of approach are is as much art as science, even in the real world. While computers aren't likely to do this as well as humans, there are some simple heuristics that you can use. The most obvious, shown in Figure 10.6a, is simply to calculate the shortest region path to nearby enemy sites or known enemy positions. The problem with this approach is that it doesn't catch alternate routes that might be used if enemy units don't start exactly where expected or deliberately take a longer path, such as the path to the west side of the mountains.

One alternative is to search some number of regions out from the shortest path. For example, if we search two regions out from the path in Figure 10.6a, then we would find the western pass through the mountains—but we would also identify a lot of inappropriate regions as avenues of approach (e.g., the cul-de-sac in the southeast corner of the map). We can add further complexity in order to try to identify and eliminate these regions, but that sort of special-case logic is prone to be brittle and difficult to maintain.

Another alternative, shown in Figure 10.6b, is to superimpose two adjacent trapezoids onto the map such that they stretch between the region you're defending and the nearby enemy position. These trapezoids should be narrower at the origin and destination and wider where they connect. Any region underneath these trapezoids can be considered an avenue of approach. This solution works well in this particular example, but one can easily imagine maps on which the only path goes well to the side of a straight line or even wraps around behind your defensive position, and so the actual avenue of approach is quite different from what the trapezoids suggest.

The best solution might be to combine the two techniques, for example, by only using the trapezoids if they cover every region on the shortest path or by warping the trapezoids to expand to the side of the shortest path, but this is certainly an area in which more work is merited.

10. Spatial Reasoning for Strategic Decision Making

It's also worth noting that while these examples have, for simplicity, only shown a single enemy location from which avenues of approach can originate, in reality, there are often multiple sources for enemy forces. In that case you may need to consider the approaches from all of them.

10.5.4 Flanking Attacks

In the infantry one learns numerous techniques for attacking an enemy position. Without question, when it is possible to achieve, the preferred approach is to first have one element of your force fix the enemy in place with suppressive fire (i.e., fire at the enemy position, keeping their heads down and preventing them from moving), while another element maneuvers around to their flank and then cuts across from the side to finish them off.

This tactic is rarely seen in video games and indeed runs a significant risk of making the enemy "too good" (especially since they typically outnumber the player as well). With that said, it certainly could add a significant element of both realism and stress to the game. It is actually not difficult to achieve. Divide the AI force into two groups. One group lays down suppressive fire, pinning the player in place. The other group calculates an area similar to the double trapezoid in Figure 10.6b. They then plan a path to the enemy that excludes the area inside of the trapezoids, which will bring them around the side of the enemy and across their flank.

10.5.5 Attackable Obstacles

Many fantasy strategy games have maps that are littered with lairs, lost temples, magic portals, mana springs, and other areas that your units can attack and exploit. At the same time, these games usually also feature enemy players who you need to overcome.

When assigning units to attack a distant target such as an enemy settlement, we don't want our units to get bogged down fighting smaller targets. At the same time, if a unit is going to have to path well out of the way of a spider lair, for example, then it might not be the most appropriate unit to use on that attack—or at the very least, we should probably deal with the spider lair first, so that our line of retreat will be clear.

In *Kohan II*, we solved this problem by not allowing a unit to be assigned to an attack if the region path between it and the target was not clear of enemies. This led to a new problem, however, which was that the player could prevent the AI from attacking a settlement simply by placing smaller, low-value forts in front of it.

We solved this second problem by adding a portion of the priority for attacking the distant target onto the intervening target any time that we found an intervening target that blocked one of our units from joining in an attack. As an example of this solution, consider Figure 10.7. The lefties have a priority of 100 to attack the righty settlement located in region F with their infantry units in region E, but there is a lost temple located in region C that will block their advance. As a result, we don't allow the AI to use those units in an attack on the settlement, but we do transfer 25% of the priority to attack the settlement to a goal to attack the lost temple. There was already a priority of 10 to attack the lost temple, so that priority is now increased to 35.

The end result is that if there is a good place to attack a high-priority target, such as an enemy settlement, then the AI will find it and perform the attack. If the high-priority

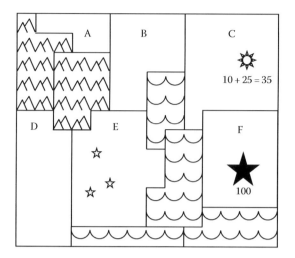

Figure 10.7

The lefties want to attack the enemy settlement in region F, but can't because of the lost temple in region C.

targets are all screened, then the AI will transfer the attack priority for hitting those targets to the screening obstacles and they will be attacked instead.

10.5.6 Counterattacks and Consolidation

In the infantry, one is trained that whenever you take an enemy position, the first thing you do is get into defensive positions and prepare for a counterattack. Only after some time has passed without counterattack do you move on to other tasks.

In strategy games, this same concept can serve us well. We can expect players to counterattack when we take territory away from them, if only because they may have defensive units that are late to arrive, and we can also enhance the player's experience by counterattacking when they take territory away from us. In the words of one reviewer, "[In] most RTS single player games… your armies run into predetermined clumps of foes and they duke it out. Once subdued, you can rest assured that the region is secured and pacified. Not in Kohan II. Fight over a town and take it; you'll find yourself beating a hasty retreat as a counter attack will soon follow unless you can consolidate your advance and secure your line of supply" [WorthPlaying 04].

Accomplishing this is relatively simple. Any time the enemy captures one of our settlements, we increase the priority for attacking the region that the settlement was in for the next several minutes. If we have enough remaining units to launch an attack (which we determine using the enemy influence in the region), then a counterattack will result. If we don't have the strength for a counterattack, as is often the case, then we'll preserve our forces for other goals—but if the enemy influence should drop too quickly (i.e., if the player pulls his units out of the region right after capturing it) then the counterattack goal will still be there for consideration.

We can brace against player counterattacks and follow-up attacks in a similar way. Any time that we win a fight against the enemy (whether offensive or defensive), we boost the priority for defending in the corresponding region. The influence map will tell us how much strength we need to bring to that defense, but boosting the priority lets the AI know that defending that specific area is particularly important because of the increased likelihood of further attack.

10.6 Conclusion and Future Thoughts

Spatial reasoning is a vast topic and this chapter has done little more than scratch the surface. We have concentrated most heavily on strategy game AI and particularly on techniques drawn from the RTS *Kohan II*, although ideas for other types of games are sprinkled throughout. For example, small unit tactics (such as those found in most first-person shooters) rely heavily on concepts such as cover and concealment, fire and maneuver, aggressive action, suppressive fire, lanes of fire, high ground, restricted terrain, kill zones, and so forth—and we have at best handwaved at those. Although true military tactics may be overkill for most games, they are a good place to begin—and they are full of spatial reasoning problems. The U.S. Army's FM 3-21.8, *The Infantry Rifle Platoon and Squad* [US Army 07], is publically available and is an excellent starting point for learning about how real-world forces operate.

Of course, many games are neither strategy games nor first-person shooters. Spatial reasoning solutions are as varied as the (often game-specific) problems that require them and the types of player experience that the game designers want to create. As with any aspect of game AI, it is best to start by thinking over the problem space. What would a human do? How would the human decide, and how can those decisions be simulated in code? What would those decisions look like to the enemy? What portion of that would make the game more compelling for our players and what would make it less? What would be fun?

In this chapter, we discussed some of the tools that can be used to help answer those questions, including techniques for creating a spatial partition, characteristics of a good spatial partition, a number of example uses of that spatial partition, influence maps and example uses of those, and a smattering of additional spatial characteristics that can be used to drive AI decisions. Although some of these concepts are directly applicable to broad classes of games, most require modification and customization to be truly useful. Our hope here is not to have provided a complete solution that can be dropped into any new game, but rather to have given a few ideas, starting points, hints, and most of all to have inspired you, the reader, to take space into account in more meaningful and compelling ways in your next game.

References

[Abner 04] Abner, W. 2004. Reviews: Kohan II: Kings of War. GameSpy.com. http://pc.gamespy.com/pc/kohan-ii-kings-of-war/549000p2.html (accessed May 18, 2014).
[Butts 04] Butts, S. 2004. Kohan II: Kings of War. IGN.com. http://www.ign.com/articles/2004/09/21/kohan-ii-kings-of-war?page=2 (accessed May 18, 2014).
[Champandard 11] Champandard, A.J. 2011. The mechanics of influence mapping: Representation, algorithm and parameters. http://aigamedev.com/open/tutorial/influence-map-mechanics/ (accessed May 18, 2014).

[de Berg 08] de Berg, M., O. Cheong, M. van Kreveld, and M. Overmars. 2008. *Computational Geometry: Algorithms and Applications*, 3rd edn. New York: Springer-Verlag.

[Dill 04] Dill, K. 2004. Performing qualitative terrain analysis in master of orion 3. In *AI Game Programming Wisdom 2*, ed. S. Rabin, pp. 391–398. Hingham, MA: Charles River Media.

[Dill 06] Dill, K. 2006. Prioritizing actions in a goal-based RTS AI. In *AI Game Programming Wisdom 3*, ed. S. Rabin, pp. 321–330. Boston, MA: Charles River Media.

[Floyd 62] Floyd, R.W. 1962. Algorithm 97. *Communications of the ACM* 5–6, 345.

[Forbus 02] Forbus, K.D., J.V. Mahoney, and K. Dill. 2002. How quality spatial reasoning can improve strategy game AIs. *IEEE Intelligent Systems* 17(4), 25–30. http://citeseerx.ist.psu.edu/viewdoc/download?doi=10.1.1.27.1100&rep=rep1&type=pdf (accessed May 18, 2014).

[Hansson 10] Hansson, N. 2010. Influence maps I. http://gameschoolgems.blogspot.com/2009/12/influence-maps-i.html (accessed May 18, 2014).

[Jurney 07] Jurney, C. and S. Hubick. 2007. Dealing with Destruction: AI from the trenches of COMPANY OF HEROES. In *Game Developer's Conference,* San Francisco, CA. http://www.gdcvault.com/play/765/Dealing-with-Destruction-AI-From (accessed May 18, 2014).

[Kohan II] Kohan II: Kings of war. [PC]. TimeGate Studios, 2004.

[Koster 04] Koster, R. 2004. *A Theory of Fun for Game Design*. Phoenix, AZ: Paraglyph Press.

[Mark 09] Mark, D. 2009. *Behavioral Mathematics for Game AI*. Boston, MA: Cengage Learning.

[Obelleiro 08] Obelleiro, J., R. Sampedro, and D. H. Cerpa. 2008. RTS terrain analysis: An image-processing approach. In *AI Game Programming Wisdom 4*, ed. S. Rabin, pp. 361–372. Boston, MA: Course Technology.

[Ocampo 04] Ocampo, J. 2004. Kohan II: Kings of war updated hands-on impressions. GameSpot.com. http://www.gamespot.com/articles/kohan-ii-kings-of-war-updated-hands-on-impressions/1100-6104697/ (accessed May 18, 2014).

[Tozour 01] Tozour, P. 2001. Influence mapping. In *Game Programming Gems 2*, ed. M. DeLoura. Hingham, MA: Charles River Media.

[Tozour 02] Tozour, P. 2002. Building a near-optimal navigation mesh. In *AI Game Programming Wisdom*, ed. S. Rabin, pp. 171–185. Hingham, MA: Charles River Media.

[US Army 07] US Army. 2007. *FM 3-21.8: The Infantry Rifle Platoon and Squad*. Washington, DC: Department of the Army. http://armypubs.army.mil/doctrine/DR_pubs/dr_a/pdf/fm3_21×8.pdf (accessed September 7, 2014).

[WorthPlaying 04] WorthPlaying.com. 2004. Kohan II: Kings of War. http://worthplaying.com/article/2004/11/26/reviews/20850/ (accessed May 18, 2014).

11

Extending the Spatial Coverage of a Voxel-Based Navigation Mesh

Kevin A. Kirst

11.1 Introduction

An AI navigation mesh, or *navmesh* for short, is a structure that can be used by an AI agent for pathfinding through a world. A voxel-based navmesh is one that is generated through the use of voxels. A *voxel*, representing a cube-shaped volume of space in a 3D grid, can be combined with other voxels to represent any volume of space. With voxels, a navmesh can be generated, which conforms greatly to the physical volume of a world, resulting in a navmesh that closely resembles the space in the world where an AI agent can physically fit. A voxel-based navmesh exists only where an AI agent can travel without colliding with or protruding into any physical body in the world.

A voxel-based navmesh is typically generated using parameters (notably height and radius) that describe the AI agent's dimensions while standing. This results in a navmesh that exists only where the AI agent can stand. Any space that is too low or too narrow for the AI agent to fit in while standing is excluded from the navmesh.

What follows is an explanation of how a voxel-based navmesh can be generated that includes the nonstanding spaces in the world: areas where the AI agent could fit if it were to crouch, lie prone, sidestep, swim, or otherwise contort its physical body appropriately.

Through appropriate markup, a more complete navmesh can be computed with a higher degree of spatial awareness. At a high level, an AI agent will continue to simply request a path from the pathfinder and travel along that path. Should that path take the AI agent through a small hole in the wall, the AI agent can use information embedded within the navmesh to dynamically contort its body to fit through the hole. Annotating navmeshes is nothing new; however, when combined with a voxel-based navmesh generator, the resulting procedurally built navmesh with extended spatial coverage can be used to give greater depth to an AI agent's ability to navigate through the world.

11.2 Overview of Voxel-Based Navmesh Generation

Before exploring this idea further, it's important to have a good understanding of the fundamentals behind a voxel-based navmesh. The goal here is to understand the steps involved in the generation process from a high-level perspective. This is important for understanding later how the process can be expanded to include other types of spaces in the navmesh. There are many articles on navmeshes and navmesh generation techniques (voxel based and otherwise). Greg Snook has done a wonderful job explaining the benefits and details of an AI navmesh [Snook 00]. David Hamm takes it one step further by discussing the benefits of utilizing an automatic navmesh generator while detailing the algorithm involved [Hamm 08]. There also exists a very well-respected voxel-based navmesh implementation known as *Recast*, written by Mikko Mononen, which is fully open sourced [Mononen 14]. This is a great resource containing example algorithms and a general code structure of a voxel-based navmesh generator.

11.2.1 Voxel-Based Navmesh Goals

Every voxel-based navmesh implementation out there is trying to solve the same problems and satisfy the same set of goals:

1. Maximize the coverage of the AI navmesh in the level.
2. Minimize the amount of human interaction required when placing the AI navmesh in the level.
3. Reduce the time spent when updating the AI navmesh during level iterations.

To maximize the AI navmesh's coverage, the navmesh needs to be extended across the entire level. The coverage will also need to be constrained by the physical world: ledges that are too high to jump over, slopes that are too steep to walk up, and walls that block the way forward should be omitted from the final navmesh.

To minimize the setup cost for building this AI navmesh in the level, the process needs to be automated as much as possible. The task should be no more difficult than painting the area where the AI agent can go in one broad stroke and having some automation fill in the blanks. To maximize the AI navmesh's coverage, this automation must be able to break apart the physical world and figure out what areas the AI agent can and cannot fit in the physical space (collision detection between the AI agent and physical objects) and ensure the navmesh extends only to the areas where the AI agent does physically fit.

To reduce the time spent in maintaining this AI navmesh, this automation process ought to continuously run and refresh the AI navmesh whenever the physical space in the level changes. Keeping true with the idea of automation, this process should happen seamlessly in the background without any additional interaction needed by the level designer. For example, if the designer drops a large object down in the middle of the room, puts up a new wall, or changes the degree of the slope in the terrain, then the AI navmesh needs to reflect these changes immediately after the action is carried out.

11.2.2 Enter Voxelization

Voxels are generated for the purpose of understanding algorithmically the space being constrained by the level's physical world. Figure 11.1 shows a simple in-engine scene. Figure 11.2 shows the same scene after voxelization.

Using these voxels, it is possible to calculate a set of planar polygons (hereafter referred to as only polygons), which cover the surfaces of the physical world and include in their areas as much of the navigable space as possible. These polygons are nontriangulated and consist of only a set of vertices that form the edges of the shape.

Figure 11.1

The world partitioned into grid for parallel voxelization.

Figure 11.2

Voxels generated in a single grid, slightly overlapping the boundaries.

To generate the polygons, it must be determined which voxels form the edge of a polygon and how many polygons will be needed to cover the area. The area within these polygons will make up the AI navmesh in the level—anything outside these shapes are deemed nonnavigable by the AI agent. To find which voxels lay on the edge of a polygon (which subsequently will tell us how many polygons exist in the area), each voxel must be asked this single question: If an AI agent were to occupy the same space as this voxel, would that AI agent be able to legally move away from that space in any possible direction?

One obvious check for answering that question would be physical clipping. If the voxel is right up beside a wall and the AI agent stood centered on top of that voxel, then chances are the AI agent's arm or leg may be clipping into the wall. This is probably not ideal, and so it will be necessary to ensure that this voxel is left outside of all of the polygon shapes. We have another scenario: suppose the voxel is located just above the terrain on a slope with a steep gradient. Should the AI agent stand centered on top of this new voxel, then there is a strong certainty that the AI agent's feet may clip through the surface once it begins to play the run forward animation cycle. Since this is not ideal, it will again be necessary to ensure that this voxel is left outside of all of the polygon shapes.

To answer this question for each one of the voxels, a table of agent-driven parameters will be used. These parameters, when paired, describe two things:

1. The physical space that a single AI agent takes up (i.e., no other physical items should be within this space to ensure that the AI agent will not collide or clip through a nearby physical object while the AI agent plays any possible animations)
2. The maximum tolerance of the restrictions placed on the AI agent by motion-controlling animation

Listing 11.1 shows an example of what an agent-driven parameter table might look like.

The `radius` and `height` parameters are examples of description #1. With just these two parameters, it is ensured that the AI navmesh only covers areas where the AI agent can physically fit given its physics cylinder. The remaining parameters are examples of description #2. They do not describe anything about the physical world, but instead simply impose limitations on what would otherwise be legal navigable area. `maxStepHeight` can help in differentiating between a staircase and a large pile of rocks. `maxSlopeRad` can ensure the AI navmesh stays away from mountain slopes and sticks to just the rolling hills. Lastly, `minWaterDepth` and `maxWaterDepth` can be used to extend the AI navmesh a bit beyond the coastline.

With these parameters in hand, each of the voxels need to be flagged in one of three ways: **nonwalkable** (violates the parameters), **walkable** (passes the parameters), and **border** (passes the parameters but one of the neighboring voxels violates the parameters). Figure 11.3 shows the previous scene's voxels after they have been flagged. The nonwalkable and walkable voxels can safely be thrown away once all the voxels have been flagged. The remaining border voxels will be used to draw the outlines of the polygons—the voxels that neighbor one another are part of the same polygon. After going through all of

```
struct SAgentParameters
{
    //Radius (in meters) of the AI agent's physics cylinder
    float radius;

    //Height (in meters) of the AI agent's physics cylinder
    float height;

    //Maximum height (in meters) of a step that the AI agent
    //can climb without breaking feet anchoring.
    float maxStepHeight;

    //Maximum angle (in radians) of a slope that the AI
    //agent can walk across without breaking animation.
    float maxSlopeRad;

    //Minimum height (in meters) from a sea floor where
    //the AI agent can stand and still keep its head above
    //water.
    float minWaterDepth;

    //Maximum height (in meters) from a sea floor where
    //the AI agent can stand and still keep its head above
    //water.
    float maxWaterDepth;
};
```

Figure 11.3

Flagged voxels. Lighter are walkable. Darker are border and nonwalkable.

these border voxels, one or any number of polygons may be determined, but it is important to remember which voxels belong to which polygon. Islands can form, as shown in Figure 11.4. These polygons may or may not be convex (some in fact might even have holes inside of them). This is perfectly okay, but should be remembered when moving on to the next step in the generation process.

Figure 11.4

Two polygons generated from the border voxels.

11.2.4 Triangulating the Polygons

To facilitate pathfinding through the navmesh, nodes need to be placed within the polygon shape to act as points along the calculated path. Any concave polygons, or polygons with holes, must also be handled correctly. No calculated paths should ever cut through a hole in a polygon or otherwise exit that polygon's borders and enter area not included in any of the other polygons. In order to use these polygons in the navmesh, they must be rendered convex. This can be done through a standard triangulation algorithm. Jonathan Richard Shewchuk describes a great triangulating algorithm that can handle both the convex, concave, and hole-filled polygons that may have been generated in the previous step [Shewchuk 02].

If the polygons shown in Figure 11.4 are triangulated without any additional modifications, the resulting triangle mesh would include an excessive number of small triangles in the parts around the polygon edges, due to the blocky border leftover from the voxelization process. See Figure 11.5 for an illustration of this point. This is not ideal, as it will result in placing a lot of nodes within a relatively small area, which is wasteful to both memory and computation time during pathfinding. What would be preferred is a polygon with a sloping side instead of a staircase side.

It is ideal if the polygon's border is simplified before it is triangulated, turning these staircases into slopes. Note that since the outside space is now entirely made up of nonnavigable areas for the AI agent, the polygon border should be simplified by shaving away interior space without including any nonnavigable exterior space. We are sacrificing coverage of the navigable area in exchange for an increase in performance. Figure 11.6 shows the same polygon border after it has been simplified.

The triangle list calculated through the triangulation algorithm will become the basis of the AI navmesh—the centers of each triangle representing a node and each neighboring triangle receiving a path connection between the two nodes. Figure 11.7 shows our previous scene's grid after triangulating the two polygons. Figure 11.8 shows the completed navigation mesh.

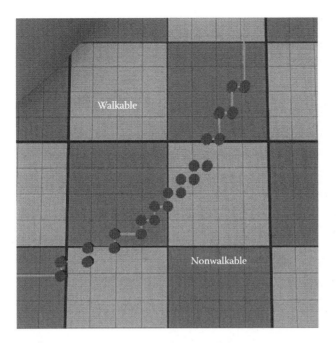

Figure 11.5

Polygon with a staircase side before simplification.

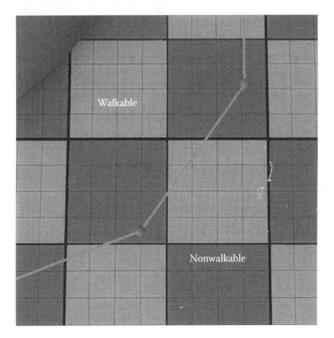

Figure 11.6

Polygon with a sloping side after simplification.

Figure 11.7

Simplified polygons after being triangulated.

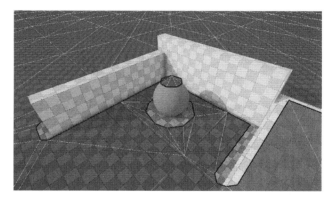

Figure 11.8

Completed triangulated AI navigation mesh.

11.2.5 Recap

Here's a quick recap of the voxel-based AI navmesh generation process.

1. Segment the world into individual cells using a grid. Overlap each grid on top of its neighbors slightly.
2. Using parallelization, perform the following on each cell:
   a. Voxelize the empty space in the cell (space not occupied by a physical body).
   b. Using the agent-driven parameters, flag all voxels as nonwalkable, walkable, or border.
   c. Throw away all nonwalkable and walkable voxels.
   d. Using the remaining border-flagged voxels, generate planar polygon shapes using the voxels as the edges.
   e. Simplify the polygon border shapes to prepare for triangulation, removing unnecessary vertices without increasing the area of the polygon.
   f. Triangulate the polygon and add the resulting localized triangle list to the master triangle list.

3. Once all cells have been processed, generate pathfinder nodes for all triangles in the master triangle list.
4. Create connections between the nodes that border each other—if they share the same triangle parent or if their parent triangles neighbor one another in the master triangle list.

This process gives us a workable AI navmesh that conforms to the physical world accurately, given a single static set of parameters based on an AI agent's physical state and motion behavior. As long as the AI agent does not deviate from its parameters, it will safely be able to travel anywhere along this navmesh without getting stuck or blocked by some physical body—as long as the physical bodies don't move around either! But if those physical bodies do move or change in some way, you could always regenerate the localized triangle list for the cells that contain that physical body and stitch the updated triangles back into the navmesh.

11.3 Extending the Navmesh's Spatial Coverage

Suppose an AI agent were to deviate from its physical parameters for a moment. Most action games support having an AI agent that can crouch down low, reducing its physical height. Suppose now the AI agent were to begin moving around while in this crouched state. As long as the new physical space that the AI agent occupies is less than the space used to generate the navmesh, there won't be any issues. Small objects can always fit in large spaces; therefore, the AI agent will still be able to safely travel everywhere along the navmesh. From that AI agent's perspective, the world has seemingly become much larger. Now, the space under a table looks easily passable. The AI agent could now fit through the air-conditioning duct opening. Even the holes blown out of the walls look passable from this state. But the navmesh was generated in a way that only considers where the AI agent could fit while standing. These new hiding places and shortcuts were passed over during the generation process. The voxels that filled these spaces were flagged as nonwalkable and were discarded.

11.3.1 Reintroducing the Discarded Space

It would be great if all of this discarded nonwalkable-flagged space could be reintroduced into the navmesh. But before that is done, it is important to flag this space with appropriate annotations. Without any additional metadata associated with the space, there is no way for the AI agent to determine if the space can be navigated while standing upright. Therefore, two rules must be satisfied:

1. The crouch-only triangles must be clearly separated from the stand-only triangles. Stand-only triangles should only exist in spaces where the AI agent can legally stand. Crouch-only triangles should only exist in spaces where the AI agent can legally crouch.
2. The crouch-only triangles must be flagged in some way, so that it is possible to later delineate what area is stand only and what area is crouch only on the navmesh.

The first rule is easily satisfied. The navmesh will be generated using the voxel-based generation process described earlier as usual; however, instead of discarding the nonwalkable

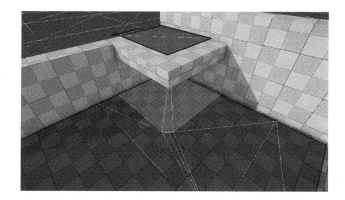

Figure 11.9

Crouch-only triangles (light) bordering stand-only triangles (dark).

voxels, these voxels will simply be set aside and sorted into a separate container for later revisiting. Once the generation process has finished constructing the localized triangle list for a cell, step #2 can be repeated in its entirety using the nonwalkable voxels that were set aside as a result of the previous pass' step #2a. That is, instead of voxelizing the cell space again, the nonwalkable voxels will be used as the starting pool of voxels, with all of their flags discarded. These voxels are then processed once again like before, but with a different set of agent-driven parameters—parameters that describe the AI agent's physical state and motion behavior from a crouching perspective. This will result in a new localized triangle list that spans across the remaining space in the cell where the AI agent can physically fit so long as it is crouched. And since the space in the cell where the AI agent could physically fit while standing is not being considered again (as those voxels were not included in the crouch-only pool of voxels), the edges of the newly calculated crouch-only triangles will exactly border the edges of the previously calculated stand-only triangles. Figure 11.9 illustrates this point.

Table 11.1 shows a side-by-side comparison of what the agent-driven parameters could look like for standing and crouching.

Notice how the `height` has decreased while the `radius` has stayed the same. While the AI agent is crouched down, the height of its collision cylinder has naturally lowered to match the difference in displacement from the floor to its head. The `maxWaterDepth` has also decreased proportionally. While crouched, the AI agent's motion behavior has been altered as well. The AI agent can no longer climb steep slopes like it used to and it cannot

Table 11.1 Standing and Crouching Agent-Driven Parameters

Parameter	Standing	Crouching
radius	0.4 m	0.4 m
height	2.0 m	1.2 m
maxStepHeight	0.5 m	0.25 m
maxSlopeRad	0.5 rad	0.35 rad
minWaterDepth	0.0 m	0.0 m
maxWaterDepth	1.5 m	0.7 m

raise its legs high enough to pass over certain steps. As a result, the `maxStepHeight` and `maxSlopeRad` values were decreased to better match its movement restrictions while crouched.

When these crouch parameters are used to flag the remaining voxel pool (remember the voxels in the pool were the ones that were flagged as nonwalkable by a standing AI agent), the voxels will then reflect if they are nonwalkable, walkable, or border for a crouching AI agent. For example, the voxels that were placed just above the floor but below the table were nonwalkable by a 2 m tall AI agent but are now clearly walkable by a 1.2 m tall AI agent. Voxels that are being found are now walkable, some of which are forming borders due to the absence of neighboring voxels that did not carry over from the previous pass. These newly flagged border voxels can generate new polygons, which once simplified and triangulated will fill a new localized triangle list full of crouch-only triangles.

If this localized triangle list were to be combined with the localized triangle list from the previous pass and merged into the master triangle list "as is," only the first rule will have been satisfied. The triangles from both passes will be clearly separated with no overlapping occurring. But the crouch-only triangles will have no distinguishing annotations associated with them that separate them from the stand-only triangles. An AI agent will still think it can traverse over these triangles while standing. These crouch-only triangles must be annotated in some way before being combined with the stand-only triangles, so that it is possible to distinguish between the two triangle types at path-planning time.

To satisfy the second rule, metadata are incorporated into the triangle data type. These metadata inform an AI agent of how it must alter its physical state or motion behavior in order to successfully travel over the triangle.

11.3.2 Using the Metadata

The last key of the puzzle involves getting the AI agent to make use of the metadata. When an AI agent requests a path of the pathfinder, triangle nodes in the navmesh become the vertices of the path. In the end, the AI agent is simply walking from one triangle node to another until the AI agent reaches the node from the last triangle (the one that contains the destination point within its area). The AI agent can always figure out which triangle it's currently standing over and which it's moving toward next, just by looking at the nodes in the path that it is following.

By including the metadata associated with the triangle in the path vertex, it then becomes possible for the AI agent to refer to the metadata while following its path. As an example, Listing 11.2 shows a simple structure describing a path vertex. The vertex is constructed from a triangle node. The metadata from that triangle node is included in the path vertex.

With the inclusion of the metadata in the path vertices, it is now just a matter of using the data at the right time. While the AI agent is following its path, it can look at the next path vertex and determine if it should be crouching or not. If the next path vertex has a true value for `bCrouch`, then the AI agent needs to set its stance to be crouching. If there is a false value for `bCrouch`, then the AI agent needs to set its stance to be standing. See Figure 11.10 as an example. A path can now be generated through standing-only space and crouch-only space interchangeably. The AI agent will set its stance correctly based on which area it is about to enter next.

Notice how the previous triangle node is passed in to the `SPathVertex` constructor if available. Figure 11.10 illustrates why this is needed. Six triangles are shown, forming

Listing 11.2. Path vertex structure which records if it came from a crouch-only triangle.

```
struct SPathVertex
{
    //Position of the path vertex
    Vec3 vPosition;

    //True if AI agent should crouch while navigating
    //to this vertex
    bool bCrouch;

    explicit SPathVertex(const STriangleNode &node,
        const STriangleNode *prevNode = 0)
    {
        vPosition = node.vPosition;
        bCrouch = node.bCrouchOnly;

        if (prevNode)
        {
            //Stay crouching if the previous triangle
            //was crouch-only
            bCrouch |= prevNode->bCrouchOnly;
        }
    }
};
```

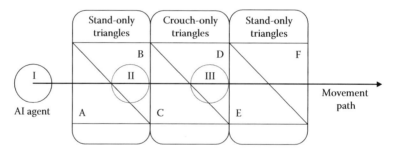

Figure 11.10

An AI agent's movement path on top of the navmesh. Six triangles are shown from the navmesh (A through F), with the middle two (C and D) being flagged as crouch only. Three points of interests are shown as circles labeled with the numerals I through III.

the navmesh. A movement path is passing through all six triangles (the nodes originating from the midpoints of the triangle segments), with the AI agent being located at the start of the path (point I). Note that triangle B is stand only, while triangle C is crouch only. When the AI agent has reached the path vertex from triangle B and begins to move toward the path vertex from triangle C (point II), the AI agent will begin to crouch. This is the correct behavior, as it gives the AI agent time to crouch before leaving the stand-only space of triangle B and entering the crouch-only space of triangle C. Now look at triangles D and E. Triangle D is crouch only, while triangle E is stand only. When the AI agent has reached the path vertex from triangle D and begins to move toward the path vertex from triangle E (point III), the AI agent will have begun to stand. This is because triangle E has a false value for `bCrouch`, and since the path vertex made using triangle E is the next path vertex, the AI agent ought to set its stance to be standing. But the AI agent is still within the crouch-only space of triangle D. The AI agent needs to exit this space before it can stand up. The safest way to know if the AI agent has cleared the crouch-only space of triangle D is to wait until the AI agent has reached triangle E and has moved on to the next path vertex from triangle F. To keep the AI agent crouching while navigating toward triangle E, we set its `bCrouch` value to be true, not because triangle E's metadata say so but because the previous node (triangle D) is crouch only.

11.4 Identifying Other Spaces

Crouch navigation is just one example of how the recycling process can be applied to a voxel-based navmesh generator. The following is an assortment of other possibilities that can be explored. Each one of these possibilities involves just adding another recycling pass of the leftover nonwalkable voxels using a different tweak to the agent-driven parameters and another entry in the triangle metadata.

11.4.1 Prone Navigation

Just like with crouch navigation, prone navigation works off the `height` parameter—just with a much lower value. For prone navigation, the agent-driven parameters might contain the values in Table 11.2.

The `radius` parameter has doubled that of the standing height. This is because, while in the prone position, the AI agent will be lying flat down on its stomach, and so from its pivot point located near its pelvis joint, the maximum radius of a circle that fully encloses the AI agent is half its standing height, or 1 m. The `height` parameter and the various motion behavior parameters are lowered and adjusted to fit the new height of the AI agent.

11.4.2 Swim Navigation

Swim navigation works off of the `minWaterDepth` and `maxWaterDepth` parameters. By using a `minWaterDepth` equal to the standing `maxWaterDepth` and a much larger value for the new `maxWaterDepth`, a navigation mesh can be generated along the sea floor of a very deep lake or even an ocean. The agent-driven parameters might contain the values in Table 11.3.

The `radius` and `height` parameters match those used in the proning parameters, as the AI agent will be swimming, which involves lying flat on its stomach.

Table 11.2 Proning Agent-Driven Parameters

Parameter	Standing	Proning
radius	0.4 m	1.0 m
height	2.0 m	0.5 m
maxStepHeight	0.5 m	0.1 m
maxSlopeRad	0.5 rad	0.15 rad
minWaterDepth	0.0 m	0.0 m
maxWaterDepth	1.5 m	0.35 m

Table 11.3 Swimming Agent-Driven Parameters

Parameter	Standing	Swimming
radius	0.4 m	1.0 m
height	2.0 m	0.5 m
maxStepHeight	0.5 m	48.5 m
maxSlopeRad	0.5 rad	2π rad
minWaterDepth	0.0 m	1.5 m
maxWaterDepth	1.5 m	50.0 m

The minWaterDepth matches the maxWaterDepth used in the standing parameters. This ensures only surfaces below sea level that are lower than the standing height of the agent up to its neck are considered. The maxWaterDepth parameter uses a value of 50 m, but this value can be however low or high as is necessary for the world. It will just cap how far out into the water the AI agent can swim, given how deep the water is at that point. The maxSlopeRad parameter is set to 360°. Since the AI agent will be swimming along the surface of the water, the slope of the ground or objects underneath the water surface is irrelevant, and using a value of 360° ensures any legal calculated slope will always pass.

The maxStepHeight parameter is a bit more interesting here and was calculated as

$$maxStepHeight = maxWaterDepth - minWaterDepth \qquad (11.1)$$

Imagine a large cube resting on the sea floor 50 m below the water surface. If the height of that cube is less than 48.5 m, the AI agent can float on the water surface and not touch the top of the cube. If the height of the cube is greater than or equal to 48.5 m, then the AI agent could stand on the surface of the cube and be nearly or fully out of the water, meaning the height difference from the water surface to the top of the cube is too small for the AI agent to swim through.

Keep in mind that the AI navmesh is being generated along the sea floor and not the water surface. When constructing the path vertices along this section of the navmesh, the height of the vertex should be adjusted to match the height of the water surface, so that the AI agent does not attempt to follow a path underwater.

11.4.3 Sidestep Navigation

Sidestepping navigation involves moving one's body without extending one's legs forward. If one is moving to their left, then to sidestep, they would extend their left leg out to the left of their body and then retract their right leg so that it comes to rest beside their left leg again. This style of motion allows one to move through very tight spaces, as long as they can suck their gut in enough! For an AI agent, sidestepping translates into a navigation method that works with a much smaller radius. The agent-driven parameters might look something like Table 11.4.

These parameters are identical to the standing parameters, with the exception of radius, which has been halved to a mere 20 cm. If these parameters are used to generate sidestep-only triangles after a stand-only pass, the navmesh would be extended in tighter-fitting areas where the AI agent could still stand. An example of such an area

Table 11.4 Sidestepping Agent-Driven Parameters

Parameter	Standing	Sidestepping
radius	0.4 m	0.2 m
height	2.0 m	2.0 m
maxStepHeight	0.5 m	0.5 m
maxSlopeRad	0.5 rad	0.5 rad
minWaterDepth	0.0 m	0.0 m
maxWaterDepth	1.5 m	1.5 m

might be a narrow ledge along the parameter of a building or a room packed with boxes making a maze of walkways.

To navigate this space requires a more stylized approach for an AI agent. A unique set of locomotion animations that drive the AI agent's character to move forward by sidestepping is required. The collision cylinder around the AI agent might also need to be temporarily adjusted, so that the radius of the cylinder matches the maximum 20 cm space.

11.4.4 Multiple Generation Parameter Passes and Hierarchy

Due to the recursive nature of the multiple generation passes when using different parameters, the order in which the parameters are parsed is critical in determining the resulting navmesh. As each pass only considers those voxels that have previously been flagged as nonwalkable, the next set of parameters can only add (and consequently mark up) space that has not yet been included in the navmesh.

For example, consider generating the navmesh with standing, crouching, and proning parameters. If the hierarchy is standing, then proning, then crouching, the resulting navmesh will mostly consist of only standing- and proning-marked space. Since it is possible to prone anywhere where one can crouch (with the slight exception of the slightly wider radius for prone vs. crouch), all of the nonwalkable voxels from the stand-only pass will be consumed during the prone-only pass. The crouch-only pass will have very few nonwalkable voxels left for it to consider. Should the hierarchy be modified to consider crouching before proning, a better mixture of crouch-only and prone-only space will be distributed throughout the navmesh. Sometimes one method may be preferred over the other, and so there is no right or wrong answer for the order of hierarchy. This leaves the door open for many interesting combinations and resulting navmeshes to experiment with!

11.5 Playing with the Heuristic

Here is one additional footnote for consideration: it might be the case that having an AI agent that avoids crouching, proning, swimming, or whatever nonstanding navigation is preferable, if it is possible. Consider a table in the middle of the room. If the AI agent were to walk from one end of the room to the other, is it better for that AI agent to walk up to that table in the center, crouch down, crawl through the space underneath, emerge at the other end, and continue on? Or should that AI agent simply walk around the table?

Level of effort comes into play here. It requires far less energy to take the few extra steps and navigate around the table than it does to contort one's body to fit through the space underneath the table. Unless the point beneath the table top is the destination, there most likely isn't a logical reason for the AI agent to spend that extra energy to pass under it. This level of effort can be described through your pathfinding heuristic. By artificially scaling the pathfinding cost to move into a crouch-only triangle, an AI agent can usually be convinced that the pathway around the table is a far cheaper alternative than the direct path under the table.

11.6 Conclusion

Voxel-based navmeshes, when generated using the recycling strategy here described, can greatly enhance an AI agent's spatial awareness through its navigation. The examples that were covered (crouching, proning, swimming, and sidestepping) are just the tip of the iceberg of possibilities. Any tweak that is made to the agent-driven parameters to cover previously discarded areas can be merged into the navmesh, and with the addition of another aggregate in the triangle metadata, an AI agent can discern the information needed to contort their bodies to fit these newly covered spaces.

We have some parting food for thought: your triangle metadata can be used for much more than what has been stated thus far. Consider including other spatial information in your triangle metadata. For example, the triangles of your navmesh that lay under a forested area could include metadata flagging the area as forested. This information could then be read by an AI agent as it paths through the forest and used to modify its behavior, perhaps guiding it to take more advantage of the abundance of cover provided by trees as good hiding spots to seek or investigate. The navmesh will almost certainly be under an AI agent's feet at all times, so use it to your advantage! Store whatever information you can in the navmesh to help your AI agents understand the space they're in, and opportunity will surely come knocking.

References

[Hamm 08] Hamm, D. 2008. Navigation mesh generation: An empirical approach. In *AI Game Programming Wisdom 4*, S. Rabin, Ed. Charles River Media, Boston, MA.

[Mononen 14] Mononen, M. 2014. Recast navigation solution. https://github.com/memononen/recastnavigation (accessed September 10, 2014).

[Shewchuk 02] Shewchuk, J.R. May 2002. Delaunay refinement algorithms for triangular mesh generation. *Computational Geometry: Theory and Applications*, 22(1–3):21–74.

[Snook 00] Snook, G. 2000. Simplified 3D movement and pathfinding using navigation meshes. In *Game Programming Gems*, M. DeLoura, Ed. Charles River Media, Boston, MA.

12

Being Where It Counts
Telling Paragon *Bots Where to Go*

Mieszko Zieliński

12.1 Introduction

From an AI point of view, multiplayer online battle arena (MOBA) games have two distinct layers: the tactical layer, which is responsible for the individual behavior of the AI-controlled players (aka "bots"), and the strategic layer, which is responsible for the broader, team-level, strategic decision-making. The goal of the tactical layer is to handle moment-to-moment combat in a fashion that will not break the players' suspension of disbelief. Although this is visually appealing, it has a relatively small impact on the game's outcome (assuming a certain level of skill among the players). The strategic layer, on the other hand, has a much more important goal of providing the bots with their strategic, long-term goals. It is responsible for knowing where the enemies are, deducing what the opponent's next strategic step might be, and determining which defensive structures are in danger, which enemy structures to attack, who should attack them, and so on. This is the part of the AI that can win or lose the game and that can keep players engaged over the course of the entire match.

Paragon is the latest MOBA from Epic Games. This chapter will describe the approach taken while developing the first version of the strategic layer for *Paragon's* bots. It is a simple solution that can be applied to a wide range of games, but despite its simplicity, it has achieved powerful results.

12.2 Problem Description

From a strategic point of view, being in the right place at the right time is the key to success in a MOBA. Assuming that all players are more or less on the same skill level, the only way to win an encounter is to have an advantage in numbers or the element of surprise. You need to be able to concentrate your forces to attack or defend in the right places, at the right times, without leaving an opening that the enemy can exploit. Both are extremely difficult to achieve if every bot thinks for itself. This is not an AI-specific problem—in Player versus Player (PvP) games, the teams using voice communication have an enormous advantage over the teams that do not.

Any kind of cooperation is better than no cooperation. The simplest form of cooperation is "going together." If two teammates head down the same map route, they will help each other even if only by accident, splitting the danger in two, doubling the firepower. From this point of view, it should be enough, at least initially, to just make sure bots are where they are needed. If there are three enemy heroes attacking a bot team's tower and only one bot is defending it, for example, then the obvious course of action is to get some teammates over to boost the defense. Merely having bots show up in such a scenario is enough to create an illusion of cooperation—anything achieved on top of that is a bonus.

Before the systems described in this chapter were implemented, the *Paragon* bots already had their individual behaviors in place. They had a basic understanding of how their abilities should be used. They could use healing potions when low on health points. They had reasonable target selection policies. They also knew to run for their lives when in mortal danger. Although the bots' behavior was perceived as correct, the absence of cooperation between the bots lacked the strategy necessary to compete against humans.

In summary, the problem can be formulated in simple terms as *making sure bots go where they are needed*. Once they arrive, the tactical layer can take over and do the rest.

12.3 The Graph

The very first thing needed when deciding where to go is a knowledge of the places that one can go. Experienced human players have it easy: they look at the mini-map and get information about all important places at a glance. They see where their teammates are, where the minions are going, which towers are still alive, and so on. Tracking minions, the lesser AI-controller soldiers, is especially important since players need minions to be able to attack enemy towers. The AI needs the same information, but those data need to be somehow gathered or generated, which is done using specialized AI subsystems.

Every MOBA game map has a similar structure: There are two team bases at far ends of the map, and there are defensive structures (called *towers* in *Paragon*), which are arranged into chains, forming *lanes*. There is usually more than one lane, and in between the lanes, there is a *jungle* that hides additional interesting places. In *Paragon*, those include *experience (XP) wells* and *jungle creeps' camps*. XP wells are places where teams can place *harvesters* to extract and store XP. The stored XP needs to be retrieved on a regular basis by a player hero because harvesters have limited capacity. Jungle creeps' camps are places where heroes can kill neutral inhabitants of the jungle for experience and buffs (temporary stat improvements).

The strategic AI needs to know about all such places—both the towers and the contents of the jungle—because every one of them has some strategic significance and can become an objective for the AI. Using information regarding the important places on the map, we can build a graph for the AI to use as the game-world's abstraction. Since nodes represent potential objectives, we call it the *Objective Graph*.

Let us take a step back from *Paragon* for a second. Our approach for generating a graph from relevant locations on the map does not depend on *Paragon's* specifics and can be easily applied to nearly any game that deals with spatial reasoning. The algorithm will be described in the following subsections.

12.3.1 Nodes

Every important location (such as a tower or XP well in *Paragon*) should have a corresponding graph node. Nodes are packed nicely in an array. Every node has an index, a pointer to the related structure on the map, a location (which is polled from said structure), and some additional cached properties. Examples of these properties include the structure type, which team currently owns it, and in which lane (if any) the node lies.

In addition to structures, places of strategic importance like vantage points, spawn locations, good places for an ambush, and so on, are all good candidates for graph nodes. In short, any location that bots might be interested in for strategic reasons should be represented as a node in the graph.

12.3.2 Edges

The edges in the graph represent the game-world connections between the locations symbolized by nodes. A connection is created between two game-world locations if there is an AI navigable path between them. Building edge information can be done in two steps. The first step is to generate all possible connections so that every node has information about every other reachable node. A game-world pathfinding query from every node to every other node is performed; if the path is found, the path's length is stored on the edge. This information is referred to as the edge's *cost*. Connections need to be tested both ways because path-length information is going to be used in a meaningful way later, and for nontrivial maps, A-to-B and B-to-A paths will sometimes have different lengths.

In most games, there are no isolated locations. Given enough time, a player can reach every location on a map from any other location—otherwise, why include that location in the game at all? With that in mind, the resulting graph is a *complete digraph*, which means it has an edge between every pair of nodes in the graph. This graph may sound expensive to create, but for our maps, it took less than three seconds. In any case, the computation is done offline when the game is created, so the cost does not impact the player's experience.

The second step of the edge-building process is to prune unnecessary connections. By unnecessary, we mean edges that, when replaced with a combination of other edges, still sum up to a similar cost (within some configurable tolerance). Listing 12.1 describes the algorithm with pseudocode.

The EdgeCostOffset variable defines the tolerance that we allow in the combined cost of the edges that are replacing a single edge and is designer-configurable, which gives the map maker a degree of control over the edge generation process. The offset value should be ideally configurable for each map, as the values that work well on one map may

```
Graph::PruneEdges(InNodes, InOutEdges)
{
  SortEdgesByCostDescending(InOutEdges)
  for Edge in InOutEdges:
    for Node in (InNodes - {Edge.Start, Edge.End}):
      if Edge.Cost >= InOutEdges[Edge.StartNode][Node].Cost
        + InOutEdges[Node][Edge.EndNode].Cost
        + EdgeCostOffset:
          Edge.IsPruned = true
          break
}
```

not be as good on another. Having a way to force connections (i.e., shield them from pruning), as well as a way to manually prune edges, can come in handy as well.

Note that in the algorithm presented, pruned edges are not being removed, just marked as pruned. This is an important point. As described in Section 12.4, in some cases, it is advantageous to use the pruned edges, whereas in others, it is not.

12.3.3 Closest Graph Node Lookup Grid

There is one more piece of information that we incorporate as part of the graph building process—a *closest graph node lookup grid*. This is a coarse grid covering the whole map that stores calculated information regarding the closest nodes. Since this information is calculated offline, in the editor or as part of some build process, it is not limited to simple-and-fast distance checks. Instead, full-featured path-length testing can be used to maximize the quality of the data stored. For every grid cell, an arbitrary location is picked (center is arbitrary enough), and paths are found to every node in the graph. Then a note is taken of the node closest in terms of path length. Optionally, the specific path-length value can be stored as well; there are a plenty of ways to prove that this kind of information is useful.

Note that the grid's resolution is arbitrary, but it has consequences—the smaller the cells, the higher the resolution of data, but it will take more time to build that information (a lesser problem), and it will take up more memory (a potential deal breaker).

12.4 Enemy Presence

One type of data that would be beneficial to associate with graph nodes, which is available only at runtime, is *enemy presence* or *influence* (Dill 2015). On the strategic level, where the graph lives, it does not really matter which hero is where exactly, or how many minions are left alive from which wave (minions move in waves). The relevant information is what the "combat potential" is or how "in danger" a given area is.

A simple runtime update step can be performed on the graph periodically. There should already be a way to query other game systems for information regarding the location and state of all heroes and all minion waves. This information can be used to build influence information with the algorithm shown in Listing 12.2.

Listing 12.2. Influence calculations.

```
Graph::UpdateInfluence(InAllHeroes, InAllMinionWaves)
{
  ResetInfluenceInformation()

  for Hero in InAllHeroes:
    Node = LookupClosestGraphNode(Hero.Location)
    Influence = CalculateHeroInfluence(Hero, 0)
    Node.ApplyInfluence(Influence)
    for Edge in Node.Edges:
      Influence = CalculateHeroInfluence(Hero, Edge.Cost)
      Edge.End.ApplyInfluence(Hero.Team, Influence)

  for Wave in InMinionWaves:
    Node = LookupClosestGraphNode(Wave.CenterLocation)
    Influence = CalculateWaveInfluence(Wave, 0)
    Node.ApplyInfluence(Influence)
    for Edge in Node.Edges:
      if Edge.EndNode.LaneID != Wave.LaneID:
        continue
      Influence = CalculateWaveInfluence(Wave, Edge.Cost)
      Edge.End.ApplyInfluence(Wave.Team, Influence)
}
```

Note that `LookupClosestGraphNode` takes advantage of the closest graph node lookup grid described in the previous section.

In essence, what the code in Listing 12.2 is doing is calculating the influence score for every relevant source and distributing it across the graph. This is one of the places where information from pruned graph edges is being used. `Cost` information is relevant regardless of whether an edge is pruned or not, and here it is being used as a reliable indication of game map distance.

Minions' influence is limited to lane nodes because minions are restricted to a specific lane. Minion influence should not seep through the jungle to another lane, since that would result in misinformation—minions are not allowed to change lanes.

12.5 Putting the Graph to Use

By now, it should be clear that the graph described in previous sections is the top level of a *hierarchical navigation graph*. It has nodes corresponding to actual locations in the game world. It has connections corresponding to paths in the game world. This means any path calculated in the graph can be translated into a regular navigation path in the game world.

Using the information regarding dangers on the map, strategically smart paths can be found. Pathfinding can be configured to find paths serving multiple purposes, like paths that avoid an enemy, paths that go through enemy-dense areas, paths that stick to lanes as much as possible, and so on. With this ability, there are a large number of possibilities for an AI programmer to explore.

Regular A* search (Buckland 2004) can be used to find paths along unpruned edges of the graph. Using unpruned edges promotes bots moving between interesting locations. The resulting paths are sequences of nodes that the AI should visit to reach its goals. If we do not want the AI to visit "interesting locations," then we can skip this or better yet apply a heuristic to the search which forces it to avoid "bad" nodes (such as those with high enemy influence). This ensures that we pick a smart path, and the graph node is small enough that the use of a heuristic will not make our searches overly expensive.

The bot's path-following code uses a graph path to generate consecutive navigation paths. When a bot following a graph path reaches a graph node on the path, it then searches a regular path to the next node on the path, repeating the process until the last node is reached. This saves us some path-finding performance cost, since finding a series of short paths is cheaper than finding one long path. Building the full path ahead of time would be a waste: the bot usually will not even utilize the whole hierarchical path. Often, it will get distracted by petty things like enemies or death.

12.6 The Objectives

Every node in the graph has some strategic importance. They might be places to attack, or to defend, or places where a bot can go to gather XP or wait in an ambush, for example. Thus, every node of the graph can have some kind of objective associated with it.

A *Bot Objective* in *Paragon* is a type of behavior modifier. When a bot is assigned to an objective, the objective tells it where to go and what to do when it gets there. An objective is usually associated with a structure on the game map and, by extension, with a node in the objective graph. An objective knows how to deal with the structure: for example, defend it, attack it, or stand on it to get XP. It also knows which agents would be best suited to deal with the structure and how many agents are required. An objective can also influence how agents are scored.

Not all objectives are equally important. An objective's priority is based on a number of factors. These include the objective's type (for example, defending is more important than attacking) and its location (e.g., defending the base is more important than defending a tower somewhere down the lane). It is also related to the structure's health and enemy presence in the area. The enemy presence is read directly from the Objective Graph, using the influence information described in Section 12.4.

There are also objective-specific factors influencing the objective's priority. The "experience well" objective is an interesting example in this regard. The longer an XP harvester is waiting at full capacity, the more XP potential gets wasted and the more important it is to retrieve XP from it. On the other hand, the higher the level of heroes on the team, the less important it is to acquire that XP.

12.6.1 Where do Objectives Come From

Every type of objective has its own generator, and all generators create instances of objectives before the match starts. These objectives then register themselves with their respective graph nodes, as well as with any game system they need notifications from. For example, a defend objective would register to be notified when its tower gets destroyed, and an XP harvesting objective would register to be notified when the XP harvester on a particular well is full. In all cases, these objectives register with the *AI Commander*.

12.7 The AI Commander

The AI Commander is responsible for assigning objectives to bots based on all the information described above. Objective assignment is done as a response to events in the game world. Each team is processed separately, and human-only teams get skipped altogether. The pool of available objectives is also separate for each team, which is pretty intuitive—bots should not know whether the other team is planning to attack a given tower that would be cheating! However, some of the objectives do care about aspects of the other team's actions or state. For example, the "experience well" objective has two modes—it is "regular" when the well is unoccupied, or owned by the objective's team, and it switches to "offensive" when the enemy team takes possession of the well by placing its own harvester on it. This kind of knowledge gathering is encapsulated inside each specific objective's logic.

The objective assignment process can be split into multiple steps. As a first step, each team's objectives have a chance to update their own state. Every objective can be in either a "Dormant" or "Available" state. It is up to each objective's internal logic to determine which state it is in. If an objective is dormant, then it is skipped by the AI Commander during the objective assignment process. As part of the update, objective priorities are calculated as well. As previously mentioned, the objective's priority is based on multiple factors, and every objective can also specify how much a given factor influences its score. For example, "experience well" objectives are not concerned with enemy influence, while tower defense objectives treat it very seriously. Once every objective is updated and scored, all the available objectives are sorted by priority.

In step two, each available objective filters and scores all of the teammates, and stores the results for use in step three. Filtering gives objectives a chance to exclude unfit agents on a case-by-case basis. For example, a special ability is required to place a harvester on an experience well, so that objective excludes heroes who do not have that ability. Agent scoring is described in greater detail in Section 12.7.1. It would actually be more efficient to do the scoring and filtering as part of step three, but splitting the process this way makes it easier to explain.

The third step of the objectives assignment process is responsible for assigning agents to objectives. We do this by iterating over the following loop until all agents have been assigned:

1. Find the highest priority objective.
2. Allow that objective to pick a minimum set of resources (e.g., a single Brawler, or a Support and Caster pair).
3. Reduce the priority of that objective according to the amount of resources it took. The amount of priority reduction per agent assigned is in relation to all active objectives' max priority. It means that with every agent assigned, an objective will lose MaxPriority/TeamSize priority.

One potential tweak some adopters might want to consider is to use different limits to how many resources an objective is allowed to take. Allowing only the minimum amount will result in carrying out as many objectives as possible, but for some games, it would make more sense to focus all the power on just one or two objectives.

It is important to note that the result of this process depends heavily on how the objectives' priority is calculated and on how the individual objectives calculate their agent scores. Tweaking those two elements is necessary for good results.

12.7.1 Agent Scoring

There are two ways the agents' scoring can be performed by an objective. One is fully custom scoring, where the objective is the only scoring authority and calculates the scores itself. The other way, the default method, allows an objective to specify a hero role preference (Support, Tank, Caster, etc., as a single hero can have multiple roles). The preference is expressed as a set of multipliers for every role, and the score is based on the best role that the agent has. For example, if a hero is a Tank and a Brawler, and the objective has 0.1 preference for Tanks but 0.3 for Brawlers, then that given hero's score will be 0.3.

Regardless of the method, the agents' scores are calculated per objective. This makes it easier to tweak the results of the whole objective assignment process since potential mistakes in agent scoring will be localized within individual objectives and will have limited effect on which objectives are being carried out.

Distance (or travel time, if you have agents that move at different speeds) is another component of agent score. It usually makes most sense to assign a medium-scoring agent that is close to an objective rather than picking the highest scoring one that is on the other side of the map. Calculating a reliable distance-based portion of the score is really fast, since that information is already available within the Objective Graph; it already knows the path cost for every node pair in the graph! The path distance is retrieved from the graph and multiplied by a factor supplied by the objective.

Using one fun trick, a distance to the objective can be calculated even for dead heroes. To do this, we have to use travel time (that is, how long will it take the unit to travel to the objective) rather than distance. We then treat dead heroes as standing in their team's base but needing an additional X seconds (X being the time left to respawn) to arrive at the destination. This way, if one additional agent is needed to defend the base, then from two similarly adequate bots, the one that respawns in 10 seconds will be picked over the one that would need 20 seconds to get there.

12.7.2 Humans

The AI Commander treats human players in mixed human-bot teams just like other agents. The objective assignment code makes no exception for human agents. An assumption is made that the AI Commander will pick a reasonable objective for every agent, including players. If so, a player can be expected to carry out the assigned objective without being directly controlled by the game AI. Moreover, the on-screen team communication system can be used to request players to do something specific, like "defend left" or "group up!" (just like human players can do in regular PvP games). In any case, both the game and AI Commander are flexible in this regard, so even if an agent does not fulfill its role, the game will not break, and adjustments will be made during the next objective assigning iteration.

An interesting possible extension should be pointed out here. Since human players can use team communication, we could include messages from them as hints and temporarily increase the priority of the objectives associated with received messages. We cannot have human players control which objectives the AI Commander picks directly, since that would have a potential of ruining the experience by sending the AI to all the wrong places, but we can use it to influence the decisions in a weaker way.

12.7.3 Opportunistic Objectives

When a bot carries out an objective, it usually involves following an objective graph path. The path-finding algorithm can be configured to prefer graph nodes containing unassigned objectives. Then as a bot progresses through the graph path on every node, a check can be done to see if there is an unassigned objective that said bot can carry out. The objective gets a chance to specify if it is interested in being assigned this way. For some objective types, it simply does not make sense to be picked up "on the way." Good opportunistic objectives should be easy and quick to carry out, for example, gathering XP from wells or destroying a jungle creeps' camp.

12.8 Future Work

The ideas described in this chapter have a lot more potential uses. The Objective Graph is a convenient abstraction of the map, and more data can be associated with every node. Below are some examples.

12.8.1 Probabilistic "Presence" Propagation

As of this writing, the *Paragon* AI Commander has perfect knowledge of all heroes' locations. Human players only know about enemy heroes that they have seen themselves or that have been sighted by the team. Although this is not completely fair, it helps compensate for other shortcomings (such as not being able to synchronize ability usage with their teammates).

It would be possible to build a probabilistic net of locations of all heroes based on the objective graph. If an enemy hero is visible to any of the team's heroes or minions, the graph node closest to the enemy's location gets annotated with information that the given hero is at that node with probability of 1. If a hero is not visible, then that hero's last known location is used; based on the time of last sighting, propagate information to all neighbors of the last known location node. The probability of a hero being at any other graph node is proportional to the distance (read directly from the graph nodes) and the time passed; it may also be influenced by the knowledge of currently hot locations on the map and where a hero could be interested in being. An information diffusion step could also be added to the process. This whole idea is a variation of Occupancy Maps (Isla 2006).

12.8.2 Map Evaluation

One of the few reliable use cases of neural networks (NNs) in game AI is data classification. It is possible to imagine a NN that would take the "world state" as input and generate a sort of "quality" or "desirability" value as output. Having a map abstraction such as a graph already at hand makes converting the world state into a vector of values into a relatively straightforward process. Data from games played online by human players can be used to construct a training set. Grabbing graph snapshots at regular intervals and associating them with the final result of the match would be a good start. Once trained, the net could be used to help the AI Commander to evaluate current game's state and guide high-level strategy, such as by hinting whether the current world state requires a more defensive or a more offensive stance.

12.9 Conclusion

As proven by our internal user experience tests, the introduction of a strategy layer to the *Paragon* bot AI greatly improved players' experiences. The game did not instantly become harder, because no behavioral changes have been made to the bots' individual behaviors, but users did notice the game being more interesting. Bots started showing signs of a deeper strategic understanding of the game: filling in for fallen comrades, switching lanes, attacking enemy harvesters, and even *ganking* (which is MOBA-speak for *ambushing*), although the latter behavior was entirely emergent. The system telling the bots where to go was simple but competent. Players will generate their own explanations for what is going on in the game as long as the AI is doing its job well enough!

A graph representation, due to its discrete nature, is an easy way to represent complex data like a level filled with gameplay. Pathfinding over long distances is a breeze. Estimating enemy danger at a node location is a simple lookup operation (provided regular influence updates are performed). Last but not least, the Objective Graph gives spatial context to the otherwise abstract concept of objectives. This is just a start; there is so much more that could be done with a graph abstraction of the game map. There is no (good) excuse not to give it a try and build one of your own!

References

Buckland, M. 2004. *Programming Game AI by Example*. Jones & Bartlett Learning.

Dill, K. 2015. Spatial reasoning for strategic decision making. In *Game AI Pro 2: Collected Wisdom of AI Professionals*, ed. S. Rabin. Boca Raton, FL: A. K. Peters/CRC Press.

Isla, D. 2006. Probabilistic target tracking and search using occupancy maps. In *AI Game Programming Wisdom 3*, ed. S. Rabin. Hingham, MA: Charles River Media, pp. 379–388.

13

Combat Outcome Prediction for Real-Time Strategy Games

Marius Stanescu, Nicolas A. Barriga, and Michael Buro

13.1 Introduction

Smart decision-making at the tactical level is important for AI agents to perform well in real-time strategy (RTS) games, in which winning battles is crucial. Although human players can decide when and how to attack based on their experience, it is challenging for AI agents to estimate combat outcomes accurately. Prediction by running simulations is a popular method, but it uses significant computational resources and needs explicit opponent modeling in order to adjust to different opponents.

This chapter describes an outcome evaluation model based on Lanchester's attrition laws, which were introduced in Lanchester's seminal book *Aircraft in Warfare: The Dawn of the Fourth Arm* in 1916 (Lanchester 1916). The original model has several limitations that we have addressed in order to extend it to RTS games (Stanescu et al. 2015). Our new model takes into account that armies can be comprised of different unit types, and that troops can enter battles with any fraction of their maximum health. The model parameters can easily be estimated from past recorded battles using logistic regression. Predicting combat outcomes with this method is accurate, and orders of magnitude are faster than running combat simulations. Furthermore, the learning process does not require expert knowledge about the game or extra coding effort in case of future unit changes (e.g., game patches).

13.2 The Engagement Decision

Suppose you command 20 knights and 40 swordsmen and just scouted an enemy army of 60 bowmen and 40 spearmen. Is this a fight you can win, or should you avoid the battle and request reinforcements? This is called the *engagement decision* (Wetzel 2008).

13.2.1 Scripted Behavior

Scripted behavior is a common choice for making such decisions, due to the ease of implementation and very fast execution. Scripts can be tailored to any game or situation. For example, *always attack* is a common policy for RPG or FPS games—for example, guards charging as soon as they spot the player. More complex strategy games require more complicated scripts: attack closest, prioritize wounded, attack if enemy does not have cavalry, attack if we have more troops than the enemy, or retreat otherwise. AI agents should be able to deal with all possible scenarios encountered, some of which might not be foreseen by the AI designer. Moreover, covering a very wide range of scenarios requires a significant amount of development effort.

There is a distinction we need to make. Scripts are mostly used to make decisions, while in this chapter we focus on estimating the outcome of a battle. In RTS games, this prediction is arguably the most important factor for making decisions, and here we focus on providing accurate information to the AI agent. We are not concerned with making a decision based on this prediction. Is losing 80% of the initial army too costly a victory? Should we retreat and potentially let the enemy capture our castle? We leave these decisions to a higher level AI and focus on providing accurate and useful combat outcome predictions. Examples about how these estimations can improve decision-making can be found in Bakkes and Spronck (2008) and Barriga et al. (2017).

13.2.2 Simulations

One choice that bypasses the need for extensive game knowledge and coding effort is to simulate the battle multiple times, without actually attacking in the game, and to record the outcomes. If from 100 mock battles we win 73, we can estimate that the chance of winning the engagement is close to 73%. For this method to work, we need the combat engine to allow the AI system to simulate battles. Moreover, it can be difficult to emulate enemy player behaviors, and simulating exhaustively all possibilities is often too costly.

Technically, simulations do not directly predict the winner but provide information about potential states of the world after a set of actions. Performing a playout for a limited number of simulation frames is faster, but because there will often not be a clear winner, we need a way of evaluating our chances of winning the battle from the resulting game state. Evaluation (or scoring) functions are commonly employed by look-ahead algorithms, which forward the current state using different choices and then need to numerically compare the results. Even if we do not use a search algorithm, or partial simulations, an evaluation function can be called on the current state and help us make a decision based on the predicted combat outcome. However, accurately predicting the result of a battle is often a difficult task.

The possibility of equal (or nearly equal armies) fighting with the winner seeing the battle through with a surprisingly large remaining force is one of the interesting aspects of strategic, war simulation-based games. Let us consider two identical forces of 1000 men each; the Red force is divided into two units of 500 men, which serially engage the single (1000 men) Blue force. Most linear scoring functions, or a casual gamer, would identify this engagement as a slight win for the undivided Blue army, severely underestimating the "concentration of power" axiom of war. A more experienced armchair general would never make such a foolish attack, and according to the Quadratic Lanchester model (introduced below), the Blue force completely destroys the Red army with only moderate loss (i.e., 30%) to itself.

13.3 Lanchester's Attrition Models

The original Lanchester equations represent simplified combat models: each side has identical soldiers and a fixed strength (i.e., there are no reinforcements), which governs the proportion of enemy soldiers killed. Range, terrain, movement, and all other factors that might influence the fight are either abstracted within the parameters or ignored entirely. Fights continue until the complete destruction of one force, and as such the following equations are only valid until one of the army sizes is reduced to 0. The general form of the attrition differential equations is:

$$\frac{dA}{dt} = -\beta A^{2-n} B \quad \text{and} \quad \frac{dB}{dt} = -\alpha B^{2-n} A \tag{13.1}$$

where:
  t denotes time
  A, B are force strengths (number of units) of the two armies assumed to be functions
      of time

By removing time as a variable, the pair of differential equations can be combined into $\alpha(A^n - A_0^n) = \beta(B^n - B_0^n)$.

Parameters α and β are attrition rate coefficients representing how fast a soldier in one army can kill a soldier in the other. The equation is easier to understand if one thinks of β as the relative strength of soldiers in army B; it influences how fast army A is reduced. The exponent n is called the *attrition order* and represents the advantage of a higher rate of target acquisition. It applies to the size of the forces involved in combat but not to the fighting effectiveness of the forces which is modeled by attrition coefficients α and β. The higher the attrition order, the faster any advantage an army might have in combat effectiveness is overcome by numeric superiority.

For example, choosing $n = 1$ leads to $\alpha(A - A_0) = \beta(B - B_0)$, which is known as Lanchester's *Linear Law*. This equation models situations in which one soldier can only fight a single soldier at a time. If one side has more soldiers, some of them will not always be fighting as they wait for an opportunity to attack. In this setting, the casualties suffered by both sides are proportional to the number of fighters and the attrition rates. If $\alpha = \beta$, then the above example of splitting a force into two and fighting the enemy sequentially will have the same outcome as without splitting: a draw. This was originally called Lanchester's Law of Ancient Warfare, because it is a good model for battles fought with melee weapons (such as spears or swords, which were the common choices of Greek or Roman soldiers).

Choosing $n = 2$ results in the *Square Law*, which is also known as Lanchester's Law of Modern Warfare. It is intended to apply to ranged combat, as it quantifies the value of the relative advantage of having a larger army. However, the Squared Law has nothing to do with range—what is really important is the rate of acquiring new targets. Having ranged weapons generally lets soldiers engage targets as fast as they can shoot, but with a sword or a pike, one would have to first locate a target and then move to engage it. In our experiments for RTS games that have a mix of melee and ranged units, we found attrition order values somewhere in between working best. For our particular game—*StarCraft Broodwar*—it was close to 1.56.

The state solution for the general law can be rewritten as $\alpha A^n - \beta B^n = \alpha A_0^n - \beta B_0^n = k$. Constant k depends only on the initial army sizes A_0 and B_0. Hence, if $k > 0$ or equivalently $\alpha A_0^n > \beta B_0^n$, then player A wins. If we denote the final army sizes with A_f and B_f and assume player B lost, then $B_f = 0$ and $\alpha A_0^n - \beta B_0^n = \alpha A_f^n - 0$, and we can predict the remaining victorious army size A_f. We just need to choose appropriate values α and β that reflect the strength of the two armies, a task we will focus on in the next section.

13.4 Lanchester Model Parameters

In RTS games, it is often the case that both armies are composed of various units, with different capabilities. To model these heterogeneous army compositions, we need to replace the army effectiveness with an average value

$$\alpha_{\text{avg}} = \frac{\sum_{j=1}^{A} \alpha_j}{A} \tag{13.2}$$

where:
   α_j is the effectiveness of a single unit
   A is the total number of units

We can see that predicting battle outcomes will require strength estimates for each unit involved. In the next subsections, we describe how these parameters can be either manually created or learned.

13.4.1 Choosing Strength Values

The quickest and easiest way of approximating strength is to pick a single attribute that you feel is representative. For instance, we can pick $\alpha_i = \text{level}_i$ if we think that a level k dragon is k times as strong as a level 1 footman. Or maybe a dragon is much stronger, and if we choose $\alpha_i = 5^{\text{level}_i}$ instead, then it would be equivalent to 5^k footmen.

More generally, we can combine any number of attributes. For example, the cost of producing or training a unit is very likely to reflect unit strength. In addition, if we would like to take into account that injured units are less effective, we could add the current and maximum health points to our formula:

$$\alpha_i = \frac{\mathrm{Cost}\,(i)\,\mathrm{HP}\,(i)}{\mathrm{MaxHP}\,(i)} \qquad\qquad (13.3)$$

This estimate may work well, but using more attributes such as attack or defense values, damage, armor, or movement speed could improve prediction quality, still. We can create a function that takes all these attributes as parameters and outputs a single value. However, this requires a significant understanding of the game, and, moreover, it will take a designer a fair amount of time to write down and tune such an equation.

Rather than using a formula based on attack, health, and so on, it is easier to pick some artificial values: for instance, the dragon may be worth 100 points and a footman may worth just one point. We have complete control over the relative combat values, and we can easily express if we feel that a knight is five times stronger than a footman. The disadvantage is that we might guess wrong, and thus we still have to playtest and tune these values. Moreover, with any change in the game, we need to manually revise all the values.

13.4.2 Learning Strength Values

So far, we have discussed choosing unit strength values for our combat predictor via two methods. First, we could produce and use a simple formula based on one or more relevant attributes such as unit level, cost, health, and so on. Second, we could directly pick a value for each unit type based mainly on our intuition and understanding of the game. Both methods rely heavily on the designer's experience and on extensive playtesting for tuning. To reduce this effort, we can try to automatically learn these values by analyzing human game replays or, alternatively, letting a few AI systems play against each other.

Although playtesting might ensure that AI agents play well versus the game designers, it does not guarantee that the agents will also play well against other unpredictable players. However, we can adapt the AI to any specific player by learning a unique set of unit strength values taking into account only games played by this player. For example, the game client can generate a new set of AI parameters before every new game, based on a number of recent battles. Automatically learning the strength values will require less designer effort and provide better experiences for the players.

The learning process can potentially be complex, depending on the machine learning tools to be used. However even a simple approach, such as logistic regression, can work very well, and it has the advantage of being easy to implement. We will outline the basic steps for this process here.

First, we need a dataset consisting of as many battles as possible. Some learning techniques can provide good results after as few as 10 battles (Stanescu et al. 2013), but for logistic regression, we recommend using at least a few hundred. If a player has only fought a few battles, we can augment his dataset with a random set of battles from other players. These will be slowly replaced by "real" data as our player fights more battles. This way the parameter estimates will be more stable, and the more the player plays, the better we can estimate the outcome of his or her battles.

An example dataset is shown in Table 13.1. Each row corresponds to one battle, and we will now describe what each column represents. If we are playing a game with only two types of soldiers, armed with spears or bows, we need to learn two parameters for each player: w_{spear} and w_{bow}. To maintain sensitivity to unit injuries, we use $\alpha_j = w_{spear}HP(j)$ or $\alpha_j = w_{bow}HP(j)$, depending on unit type. The total value of army A can then be expressed as:

$$L(A) = \alpha_{avg}A^n = A^{n-1}\sum_{j=1}^{A}\alpha_j = A^{n-1}\sum_{j=1}^{A}w_j HP(j)$$

$$= A^{n-1}(w_{spear}HP_s + w_{bow}HP_b)$$

(13.4)

HP_s is the sum of the health points of all of player A's spearmen. After learning all w parameters, the combat outcome can be estimated by subtracting $L(A) - L(B)$. For simplicity, in Table 13.1, we assume each soldier's health is a number between 0 and 1.

13.4.3 Learning with Logistic Regression

As a brief reminder, logistic regression uses a linear combination of variables. The result is squashed through the logistic function F, restricting the output to $(0,1)$, which can be interpreted as the probability of the first player winning.

$$y = a_0 + a_1 X_1 + a_2 X_2 + \cdots \qquad F(y) = \frac{1}{1+e^{-y}}$$

(13.5)

For example, if $y = 0$, then $F = 0.5$ which is a draw. If $y > 0$, then the first player has the advantage. For ease of implementation, we can process the previous table in such a way that each column is associated with one parameter to learn, and the last column contains the battle outcomes (Table 13.2). Let us assume that both players are equally adept at controlling spearmen, but bowmen require more skill to use efficiently and their strength value could differ when controlled by the two players:

$$y = L(A) - L(B)$$

$$= w_{spear}\left(A^{n-1}HP_{sA} - B^{n-1}HP_{sB}\right) + w_{bowA}\left(A^{n-1}HP_{bA}\right) - w_{bowB}\left(B^{n-1}HP_{bB}\right)$$

(13.6)

This table can be easily used to fit a logistic regression model in your coding language of choice. For instance, using Python's *pandas* library, this can be done in as few as five lines of code.

Table 13.1 Example Dataset Needed for Learning Strength Values

Battle	HP_s for A	HP_b for A	A	HP_s for B	HP_s for B	B	Winner
1	3.80	0.95	5	4.20	0.00	6	**A**
2	10.00	1.00	11	7.00	3.00	10	**B**
...	...	...	...	...	...	...	...

Table 13.2 Processed Dataset (All But Last Column Correspond to Parameters to be Learned)

$A^{n-1}HP_{sA} - B^{n-1}HP_{sB}$	$A^{n-1}HP_{bA}$	$-(B^{n-1}HP_{bB})$	Winner
...	...	...	...

13.5 Experiments

We have used the proposed Lanchester model but with a slightly more complex learning algorithm in UAlbertaBot, a *StarCraft* open-source bot for which detailed documentation is available online (UAlbertaBot 2016). The bot runs combat simulations to decide if it should attack the opponent with the currently available units if a win is predicted or retreat otherwise. We replaced the simulation call in this decision procedure with a Lanchester model-based prediction.

Three tournaments were run. First, our bot ran one simulation with each side using an *attack closest* policy. Second, it used the Lanchester model described here with static strength values for each unit based on its damage per frame and current health: $\alpha_i = \text{DMG}(i)\text{HP}(i)$. For the last tournament, a set of strength values was learned for each of 6 match-ups from the first 500 battles of the second tournament. In each tournament, 200 matches were played against 6 top bots from the 2014 AIIDE *StarCraft* AI tournament. The results—winning percentages for different versions of our bot—are shown in Table 13.3. On average, the learned parameters perform better than both static values and simulations, but be warned that learning without any additional hand checks might lead to unexpected behavior such as the match against Bot2 where the win rate actually drops by 3%.

Our bot's strategy is very simple: it only trains basic melee units and tries to rush the opponent and keep the pressure up. This is why we did not expect very large improvements from using Lanchester models, as the only decision they affect is whether to attack or to retreat. More often than not this translates into waiting for an extra unit, attacking with one unit less, and better retreat triggers. Although this makes all the difference in some games, using this accurate prediction model to choose the army composition, for example, could lead to much bigger improvements.

13.6 Conclusions

In this chapter, we have described an approach to automatically generate an effective combat outcome predictor that can be used in war simulation strategy games. Its parameters can be static, fixed by the designer, or learned from past battles. The choice of training data provided to the algorithm ensures adaptability to specific opponents or maps. For example,

Table 13.3 Our Bot's Winning % Using Different Methods for Combat Outcome Prediction

	Bot1	Bot2	Bot3	Bot4	Bot5	Bot6	Average
Simulations	60.0	79.0	84.0	65.5	19.5	57.0	60.8
Static	64.5	**81.0**	80.5	69.0	22.0	66.5	63.9
Learned	**69.5**	78.0	**86.0**	**93.0**	**23.5**	**68.0**	**69.7**

learning only from siege battles will provide a good estimator for attacking or defending castles, but it will be less precise for fighting in large unobstructed areas where cavalry might prove more useful than, say, artillery. Using a portfolio of estimators is an option worth considering.

Adaptive game AI can use our model to evaluate newly generated behaviors or to rank high-level game plans according to their chances of military success. As the model parameters can be learned from past scenarios, the evaluation will be more objective and stable to unforeseen circumstances when compared to functions created manually by a game designer. Moreover, learning can be controlled through the selection of training data, and it is very easy to generate map- or player-dependent parameters. For example, one set of parameters can be used for all naval battles, and another set can be used for siege battles against the elves. However for good results, we advise acquiring as many battles as possible, preferably tens or hundreds.

Other use cases for accurate combat prediction models worth considering include game balancing and testing. For example, if a certain unit type is scarcely being used, it can help us decide if we should boost one of its attributes or reduce its cost as an extra incentive for players to use it.

References

Bakkes, S. and Spronck, P., 2008. Automatically generating score functions for strategy games. In *Game AI Programming Wisdom 4*, ed. S. Rabin. Hingham, MA: Charles River Media, pp. 647–658.

Barriga, N., Stanescu, M., and Buro, M., 2017. Combining scripted behavior with game tree search for stronger, more robust game AI. In *Game AI Pro 3: Collected Wisdom of Game AI Professionals*, ed. S. Rabin. Boca Raton, FL: CRC Press.

Lanchester, F.W., 1916. *Aircraft in Warfare: The Dawn of the Fourth Arm*. London: Constable limited.

Stanescu, M., Hernandez, S.P., Erickson, G., Greiner, R., and Buro, M., 2013. October. Predicting army combat outcomes in StarCraft. In *Ninth Annual AAAI Conference on Artificial Intelligence and Interactive Digital Entertainment* (*AIIDE*), October 14–18, 2013. Boston, MA.

Stanescu, M., Barriga, N., and Buro, M., 2015, September. Using Lanchester attrition laws for combat prediction in StarCraft. In *Eleventh AIIDE Conference*, November 14–18, 2015. Santa Cruz, CA.

UAlbertaBot github repository, maintained by David Churchill., 2016. https://github.com/davechurchill/ualbertabot.

Wetzel, B., 2008. The engagement decision. In *Game AI Programming Wisdom 4*, ed. S. Rabin. Boston, MA: Charles River Media, pp. 443–454.

14

Guide to Effective Auto-Generated Spatial Queries

Eric Johnson

14.1 Introduction

Intelligent position selection for agents—that is, analyzing the environment to find the best location for a given behavior—has evolved rapidly as spatial query systems such as CryENGINE's Tactical Point System and Unreal Engine 4's Environment Query System have matured. Once limited to evaluating static, preplaced markers for behaviors such as finding cover or sniping posts, dynamic generation gives us the ability to represent a much wider and more sophisticated range of concepts. The ability to generate points at runtime allows us to sample the environment at arbitrary granularity, adapting to changes in dynamic or destructible environments. In addition, when used to generate a short-term direction rather than a final destination, we can represent complex movement behaviors such as roundabout approaches, evenly encircling a target with teammates, or even artificial life algorithms such as Craig Reynold's boids (Reynolds 1987), all while navigating arbitrary terrain.

Originally developed as a generalized, data-driven solution for selecting pregenerated points in the environment, Crysis 2's Tactical Point System (TPS) is now freely available to the public as part of CryENGINE, while Bulletstorm's Environmental Tactical Querying system is now integrated into Unreal Engine 4 as the Environment Query System (EQS), making these techniques accessible to a massive audience (Jack 2013, Zielinsky 2013). As game environments grow increasingly complex, other studios are also adopting this approach with implementations like the Point Query System in *FINAL FANTASY XV* and the SQL-based SpatialDB in MASA LIFE (Shirakami et al. 2015, Mars 2014).

Designing effective queries is the key to maximizing the quality of agent position selection while dramatically reducing the amount of work required to implement and tune these behaviors. Done well, you can consolidate the majority of a game's position selection logic into a library of queries run on a spatial query system, rather than managing a collection of disparate and independent algorithms. However, the functionality of these systems has become increasingly sophisticated as they gain wider adoption, presenting developers with more possibilities than ever before. This introduces new challenges to use the array of tools and techniques at our disposal effectively.

In this chapter, we present a selection of tricks and techniques that you can integrate into your agent's queries to ultimately deliver higher quality, more believable behavior. Each component of a spatial query is covered, from sample generation to failure resistance, to improve the effectiveness of spatial queries in your project.

14.2 Overview

In modern implementations, a single spatial query generally consists of the following components:

- *Sample points*: Locations in the world which we want to evaluate in order to determine their suitability for a particular movement task.
- *Generator*: Creates the initial set of sample points in the environment. For example, one type of generator might create a 100 m 2D grid of points along the floor of the level, whereas another might create a ring of points at a radius of 10 m.
- *Generator origin*: The location around which we want to run the generator—for example, the center of the grid or ring of points that are created. Most often, the generator origin is either the agent itself or some target that it is interacting with.
- *Test*: Measures the *value* of a sample point, or defines an *acceptance condition* for it. For example, the sample's distance from the agent can be a measure of value, while its visibility to the agent's target can serve as an acceptance condition.
- *Test subject*: A location, object, or list of locations/objects that serve as the subject of comparison for a test. For example, a distance test might compare each sample point's location against the querying agent, its destination, the set of nearby enemies, recently discovered traps, etc.

To get an idea how these components work together, consider a scenario in which we need to implement a typical approach-and-surround behavior for a group of melee enemies (Figure 14.1). Our goal is to get them into attack range quickly while at the same time fanning out in a circle around the player. To accomplish this, we might begin by using a *ring generator*, using the player as the *generator origin* to create a set of *sample points* in range of our target. Next, by using a series of *tests* measuring the distance from each sample point to the player, the agent, and the agent's teammates (as *test subjects*), we can combine their

Figure 14.1

Four enemies using spatial queries to approach and surround the player.

value to find positions that get the agent closer to the player from its current location while avoiding areas occupied by teammates. A visibility test from each point to the player, used as an *acceptance condition*, can additionally discard destinations where the agent would be unable to see the player. Finally, the location with the highest total score across all tests is returned as the query result.

The remainder of this chapter assumes a basic familiarity with publicly available query system implementations such as TPS and EQS.

14.3 Generating Sample Points

The first step in selecting a useful destination for an agent is to generate a set of potentially viable locations to evaluate. When using pregenerated points this is trivial; we typically collect all marker objects in a given range and move on to the ranking phase. For dynamically-generated points, things are more complex as the generation method itself can heavily impact the quality of the final result.

14.3.1 Generation on the Navigation Mesh

The simplest method of dynamically generating a set of sample points is to create a localized 2D grid on the surface of the agent's environment. Although it is possible to use collision raycasts against level geometry to map out the level floor, this is not only computationally expensive, but the generated points may not be reachable by the agent (e.g., if they lie on a steep slope or narrow corridor). By sampling along the surface of the navigation mesh instead of the actual level geometry, we can both reduce generation cost and ensure that the sample position is reachable by the agent.

However, the overhead of finding the navmesh surface for a large number of sample points can still be significant. To be practical at runtime, we can further minimize generation cost by localizing our projection test to a limited set of navmesh polygons that match as closely as possible the area to be sampled by the generator. The caveat is that there are multiple valid techniques we can use to define this subset, and the one we choose can significantly affect the outcome of the query. For example, two common approaches are either to gather the set of navmesh polygons within a bounding box centered on the query origin, or to gather the navmesh polygons within a given path distance of the query origin, and then to generate points only on those polygons. The bounding box approach is straightforward to implement, but can generate positions that, measured by path distance, are distant or even unreachable (Figure 14.2a). For behaviors such as finding ranged attack locations, this can be a good fit. Using path distance on the other hand ensures that the origin is reachable from all positions, but ignores locations that are spatially indirect, even if they are physically close (Figure 14.2b). Thus the bounding box approach may work better for behaviors that only require line-of-sight (such as ranged attacks), whereas the path distance method is preferable for behaviors dependent on spatial distance, such as following or surrounding.

Other options exist as well. For instance, we can merge both techniques, relaxing the path distance requirement to find reachable points within a given radius even when the path to that location is long and indirect. For example, given a radius r, we can gather all navmesh polygons within some multiple of that radius (say, $2r$). Then, during generation, we can eliminate sample points with a linear distance greater than r, giving us better coverage over an area while still ensuring a path to the generator origin.

After we have selected the most appropriate method for gathering navmesh polygons, we have a few different methods for generating samples that will impact the effectiveness of our final query:

1. *One-to-one mapping*: Some common navigation libraries, such as Recast/Detour, provide functionality to find the nearest point on the navmesh, given a point and bounding box. We can thus run a search over the gathered polygons at each (x, y) position on the grid, with some reasonably large z value, to verify that a point lies on the section of the navmesh gathered in the previous step. Although efficient, a weakness of this technique is that if your environment has vertically overlapping areas, such as a multi-floored building or bridges, only one level will be discovered (Figure 14.2c).

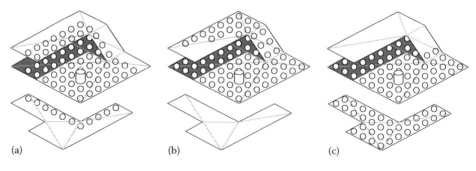

(a)   (b)   (c)

Figure 14.2

(a) Navigation mesh-based sample generation restricted by bounding box distance. (b) Sample generation restricted by path distance. (c) Sample generation restricted to a one-to-one mapping from the original grid coordinates to the nearest location on the navmesh.

2. *One-to-many mapping*: A second technique is to use a vertical navigation ray-cast over the gathered polygons at each (x, y) position, generating multiple hits along the z axis whenever we pass through a gathered navmesh polygon. Here, we trade efficiency for accuracy, handling multi-level terrain at the cost of some performance.

14.3.2 Generation Structure

Grids are not the only way to arrange our generated sample points. A custom generator can produce items along walls, arranged in rings, hexes, along waypoint graphs, inside Voronoi cells, or countless other configurations depending on the situation. This decision is important; a poor layout can introduce bias into your query, causing agents to cluster around or avoid certain locations. For tests that are intended to create a smooth scoring gradient, such as distance from a target, it is immediately noticeable when this distribution becomes uneven as agents will begin to approach targets only from specific directions, or settle into locations at specific intervals from the target.

For example, consider a query that wishes to find a location that is as close to an agent's target as possible, while leaving a 3 m buffer zone around the target. With a grid-based approach, we can first generate a set of sample points around the target, discard those closer than 3 m away, and rank the rest based on their distance from the target. Unfortunately, this exposes a problem, as illustrated in Figure 14.3. Depending on the desired radius, the closest points to the target invariably lie either on the diagonal or cardinal directions. As a result, agents not only cluster around four points, they may also approach the target at an unnatural angle to do so—that is, instead of moving directly toward the target to a point that is 3 m away, they will veer to one side or the other to get to one of the "optimal" points found by the search. In addition, selecting a grid layout for a circular query is intensely inefficient; a large portion of the sample points will either be too close (and thus

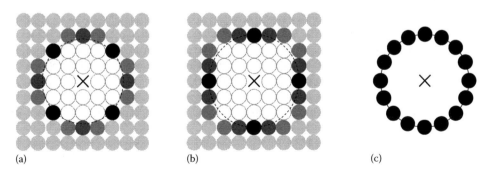

(a) (b) (c)

Figure 14.3

(a, b) Examples of diagonal and cardinal distance bias introduced by range tests over grid-generated points. (c) Elimination of distance bias by using a ring generator. Darker circles indicate higher priority positions. Empty circles indicate points that were generated but discarded, whereas light circles indicate positions that were ranked but have no possibility of being used.

immediately discarded by the distance test) or too far (and thus will never be selected, because a closer valid point exists).

In this instance, we can replace the grid generator with a ring generator, eliminating distance bias by guaranteeing that all points closest to the target are the same distance from the target. In addition, we gain an efficiency boost, as we need only generate a fraction of the sample points to perform the same test.

In our projects, this category of query was by far the most common. By changing approach/surround queries to use ring generators, agents selected more natural destinations, and the improved efficiency allowed us to enhance these queries with more complex sets of tests.

14.4 Testing Techniques and Test Subjects

Tests are the building blocks that allow complex reasoning about the environment, and are thus the most crucial components of a query system. Although projects invariably require some domain-specific tests, knowing how to combine and reuse simple, generic tests to produce complex results is the key to rapid development. For example, by only mixing and matching the two most versatile tests in a query system's toolkit, distance and dot product, we can support a surprisingly wide range of tasks beyond the common but simple "move within X meters of target Y" or "find the closest cover point between myself and the target" behaviors. Section 14.8 provides several practical examples of queries built with these two tests.

14.4.1 Single versus Multiple Test Subjects

Some query systems, such as EQS, allow a test to be run against multiple reference locations. By preparing specific concepts such as "all nearby allies," "all nearby hostiles," or "all agent destinations," we can add tests to our queries to improve the final result.

For example, a minimum distance test (Section 14.4.3) weighted against both ally locations and ally destinations can prevent agents from attempting to move not only into currently occupied locations, but also into locations that *will be occupied in the near future*. For agents that do not require advanced coordinated tactical movement, this single powerful addition can eliminate most location contention without the need to implement specific countermeasures such as point reservation systems.

14.4.2 Distance Test Scoring

When performing a test against multiple test subjects, we have a choice to make: What score do we keep? For example, is it better to record the shortest distance or the average? As shown in Figure 14.4, each can be used to express a different concept. Minimum distance helps us create local attraction or avoidance around the test subjects; this allows us to keep our distance from any area of the map occupied by a test subject. Conversely, average distance gives us the centroid of the subjects, useful for enforcing team cohesion by prioritizing samples within a specific distance from the centroid.

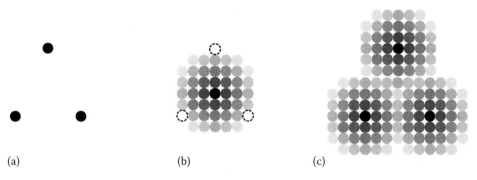

(a)   (b)   (c)

Figure 14.4

(a) Multiple targets used as the context of a distance test. (b) Score using average distance from targets. (c) Score using minimum distance from targets.

14.4.3 Dot Product Test Techniques

Within our project, this test is the most frequently used after the distance test, and these two as a pair have been used to express more movement concepts than all other tests combined. The dot product test measures the angle between two directions, allowing us to, for example, prioritize sample points in front of or behind an agent. By choosing our test subjects carefully, we can handle virtually any direction-related weighting by stacking dot product tests. Some examples:

- Testing the vector from the agent to a sample point against the agent's orientation allows us to prioritize locations in front of (or behind) the agent.
- Similarly, testing points against the agent's right vector instead of its orientation (forward vector) lets us prioritize locations to its right or left.
- We can use one of the tests above to prioritize a heading in front of, behind, to the left or to the right of the agent. However, using both together will prioritize the area where they overlap, allowing us to represent a diagonal heading instead.
- Testing against the world forward and right vectors, instead of the agent's, can give us prioritization along cardinal or ordinal directions.
- Using a target as the test subject, rather than the agent, gives us the ability to position ourselves in a specific direction relative to that target—for instance, to stand in front of an NPC vendor, to attack an armored enemy from behind, or to walk alongside the player in formation.
- For even more flexibility, we can accept an optional orientation offset in the dot product test itself: By applying a user-defined angle to the set of forward vectors above, we can prioritize points in any direction, not just the cardinal and ordinals.
- By defining both directions as vectors between two subjects, rather than the orientation of the subjects themselves, we can go even further:
- Comparing the vector from the agent to a sample point against the vector from the sample point to an agent's target prioritizes locations between the agent and the target. This provides us with locations that get us closer to the target from our current position, ranked by the directness of that approach.

- By using a sine scoring function (Section 14.5.1) over the same vectors, we prioritize locations where the dot product value approaches zero, generating destinations ranked by *indirectness*. While still approaching the target, these locations allow us to do so in a curved, flanking manner.
- Flipping the direction of the first vector (i.e., using the vector from a sample point to the agent instead of the agent to a sample point) reverses the prioritization, providing retreat suggestions ranked by directness away from the target (Figure 14.5).

We can even apply these concepts beyond actors in the scene. For example, ranking sample points based on the dot product of the vector from the camera to a sample point against the camera's orientation provides us with locations near the center of the screen (though potentially obstructed). Used with a minimum threshold and low weight, this can provide encouragement for buddy AI characters or other agents we want the player to see as much as possible.

14.4.4 Subject Floor Position

In action games where the player can fly, jump, or climb walls, an agent's target can easily become separated from the navmesh. When used as a generator origin, this results in the entire query failing, as there is no navmesh at the origin location to generate sample points around. On our project, we used two techniques to resolve this issue:

1. We provided a "Target Floor" test subject to supplement Target (the default). This modified version projected the agent's position down to the navmesh floor, if present.
2. We provided a "Closest Navmesh Point to Target" test subject, which scanned the immediate area when the target was off mesh.

Both of these techniques allowed agents to find a suitable location to approach the player when jumping or performing off-mesh traversal. For ground-based enemies, this solution was robust enough to become the default test subject used for engaging the player.

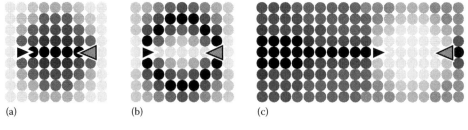

(a) (b) (c)

Figure 14.5

(a) Approach locations prioritized by directness. (b) Approach locations prioritized by indirectness. (c) Retreat locations prioritized by directness.

14. Guide to Effective Auto-Generated Spatial Queries

14.5 Test Scoring Functions

Once all sample points have been scored, they must be normalized and ranked. Most commonly, we use this value as-is, inverting the priority when needed with a negative test weight. However, as the final post-processing stage in a test's evaluation, we can pass the normalized score of each sample point to a scoring function to transform its value. Doing so allows us to increase or decrease the influence of certain samples, adding precision to our test's intent, or transforming the concept it measures entirely.

- *Linear scoring* (Figure 14.6a) is the backbone of most tests, returning the value of normalized test scores exactly as they were passed in.
- *Square scoring* (Figure 14.6b) strongly deemphasizes all but the highest ranked samples in the test. Useful when we want emphasis to drop off rapidly.
- *Square root scoring* (Figure 14.6c) does the opposite; overemphasizing all but the lowest-ranked samples in the test.
- *Sine scoring* (Figure 14.6d) differs from other methods, in that it emphasizes mid-range values, and de-emphasizes both the highest- and lowest-ranked sample points.
- Where scoring functions describe the *rate* at which emphasis should change, a test's weight determines the *direction* of change. When a test's weight is negative, an increase in score is replaced with a corresponding decrease, inverting the scoring curve (Figure 14.6b and e, c and f).

Queries typically require several tests to express a useful concept. In these cases, the highest ranked location will almost always represent a compromise between multiple competing goals. The role of scoring equations is to allow each test to define how tolerant it is of suboptimal locations, and how quickly that tolerance changes. In conjunction with the test weight, this lets us define how that compromise should be met.

For example, if we want an agent that steps away from others as its personal space is encroached, how should we express its level of discomfort? We might approximate it using

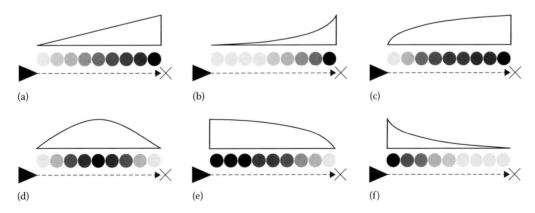

(a)　　　　　　　　(b)　　　　　　　　(c)

(d)　　　　　　　　(e)　　　　　　　　(f)

Figure 14.6

Normalized result of a distance test from sample points to an agent's target, after applying linear (a), square (b), square root (c), sine (d) scoring functions. Response curves become inverted when a negative scoring weight is used, as shown in (b) and (e), and (c) and (f), respectively. Darker shades indicate better locations.

two tests: A distance test against our current location, expressing our desire to move as little as possible, and a second distance test, negatively weighted against other actors in the scene, expressing our desire to move as far away from them as possible. The balance of these two tests determines when the agent will react. For example, if we use square scoring with a negative weight on the second test (Figure 14.6e), in general other actors will have little effect on the agent's evaluation of its current location, but when approached extremely closely its desire to stay in its current location will be outweighed by its desire to avoid others and it will try to find a slightly less crowded position. Alternatively, if we instead use square root scoring with a negative weight (Figure 14.6f) then even the influence of distant actors will quickly become overwhelming, creating a nervous agent with a strong desire to keep far away from anyone in the area.

The advantage to expressing satisfaction with scoring functions is that it allows us to produce a dynamic, natural response that is not easily expressed by the hard edges of an acceptance condition. If, instead of measuring satisfaction, we simply invalidated all locations within 2 m of another actor, our agent's response becomes predictable and artificial. However, by defining a level of comfort for all sample points in the test, our response can change along with the environment. For example, when entering a quiet subway car the agent in our scoring equation example will naturally maintain a polite distance from other passengers, but will gradually permit that distance to shrink as it becomes packed at rush hour, continuously adjusting its reaction as the environment becomes more or less crowded.

14.5.1 Sine Scoring Techniques

Although square, square root, and other monotonic scoring functions can be used to tune test results by compressing or expanding the range of suitable positions, sine scoring gives us an opportunity to use existing tests in altogether new ways. For example, applied to a distance test with a minimum and maximum range, we can define a specific ideal radius to approach a target—the average of the two ranges—while still accepting positions closer or further from the target, but with reduced priority.

When applied to the dot product, we have even more options:

- When used against the agent's orientation, we can express preference for positions to both the left and right, or both forward and behind with a negative weight.
- If we use the absolute value of the dot product with an agent's orientation, this produces the same result. However, when both are combined, we can now represent preference for either the cardinal or intermediate directions.
- As described in Section 14.4.3, applied to the dot product *(Agent→Sample Point)·(Sample Point→Target)*, we can create a circle between the agent and the target, representing a roundabout approach.

There are many other instances where the most interesting samples are those that lie in the mid-range of a test's scoring function; sine scoring is the key to discovering them!

14.6 Continuous versus Sequential Updates

Most queries are designed to be executed once, at the start of a behavior, to provide the agent with a suitable destination for its current goal (Figure 14.7a). To adapt to changing world conditions, such as a cover point becoming exposed, it is common to periodically run a validation test on the agent's destination while en route, but for efficiency we typically do not execute another full query until after we have arrived. In some cases, however, it is worth the expense to update continuously, periodically reexecuting the original query without waiting to arrive, and thus generating new recommendations as world conditions change (Figure 14.7b). Not only does this allow us to react more dynamically, it opens the door to new types of query-based behaviors that previously could only be expressed in code. Common concepts like surrounding, orbiting, zig-zag approaches and random walks can all be expressed as a single, repeatedly executed query without any programming required.

14.6.1 Continuous Query-Based Behaviors

By periodically rerunning the same query, providing frequent updates to the agent's destination, we can create the illusion of sophisticated navigation or decision-making. For example, as shown in Figure 14.8, by generating a ring of points on the navigation mesh around the agent's target, then simply prioritizing samples a few meters away as well as those in front of our current position, an agent will begin to circle-strafe around the target, avoiding obstacles as it moves and even reversing direction when it becomes stuck.

Traditional positioning can be enhanced by this technique as well. For example, when approaching a target as part of a group, not only can we maintain ideal distance from the target as it moves, but by negatively weighting the area around the agent's teammates the group can dynamically reposition themselves in relation to each other, creating a natural and responsive surround behavior (Figure 14.9).

14.6.2 Continuous Querying versus Destination Validation

While promising, there are caveats to this method. Compared to destination validation, continuous querying is responsive and can produce high-quality results, but is also

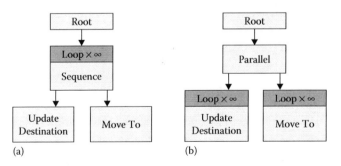

Figure 14.7

Behavior tree implementation of a sequential query-based behavior (a) versus a continuous query-based behavior (b).

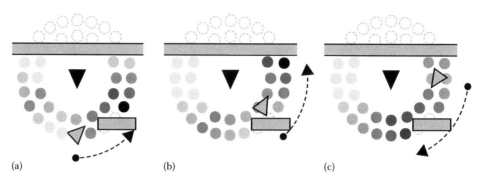

(a)   (b)   (c)

Figure 14.8

Orbiting a target with a continuously updated query (a). As positions in front of the agent become increasingly unsuitable, positions behind the agent gradually gain utility (b), ultimately causing the agent to automatically reverse direction when it can no longer proceed (c).

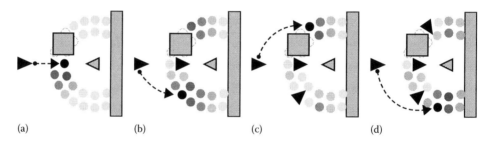

(a)   (b)   (c)   (d)

Figure 14.9

A group of agents approach and surround a target in sequence. In this example, agents prefer locations that are near the target, as well as along the vector between the agent and the target (a), but negatively weight locations near other agents to prevent clustering (b, c, and d). This produces an organic surround behavior that maintains formation continuously as the target moves, and adapts naturally as the number of agents increases or decreases.

computationally expensive. If too many agents in the scene are issuing too many queries, you can easily burn through your AI's CPU budget. It is also more challenging to avoid degenerate behavior: agents becoming stuck in local minima, oscillating between destinations unnaturally, or moving in a stop-and-go fashion by selecting destinations too close to their current position. Nevertheless, the benefits can be substantial and are well worth consideration.

14.7 Reducing Query Failure

Using the techniques thus far, we have been able to reason about the ideal layout for generated points, apply tests on single or multiple subjects, and adjust their scoring based on our needs. In theory, this should be enough to produce high-quality results from a spatial

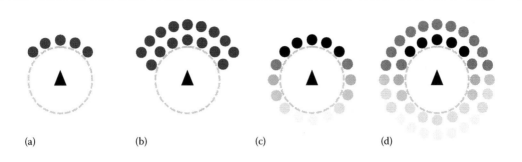

(a)   (b)   (c)   (d)

Figure 14.10

Reducing query failure of a strict, brittle query (a) by increasing robustness (b), permissiveness (c), or both (d). Whenever possible, strategies (c) and (d) will return the same result as the original query.

query system for most position selection tasks. However, in practice we rarely are so lucky. For example, the player may be in a narrow corridor, causing all samples in our flanking query to fail, or they may be facing a wall, making a dramatic surround from the front impossible. A query is useless if it never works and, unfortunately, it is common to design one that fails too easily in unexpected circumstances like these. Fortunately, by making some simple adjustments, a brittle query can be adapted to provide graceful degradation of position quality in unfavorable conditions. In this section, we show how a query can be modified to give the AI the ability to execute a behavior in a wider range of conditions while still returning the ideal result when possible, making them resilient to the complexities of a modern game environment (Figure 14.10).

14.7.1 Increasing Permissiveness

The first action we can take to make a brittle query more failure-resistant is to make it more *permissive*. That is, we can relax our success conditions so that we have more sample points that can serve as a destination, but use tests to give them a lower final rank so that they are only selected when the ideal conditions are unavailable. In Figure 14.10, we have an example query that attempts to find an attack position in front of the agent's target. If it is acceptable to attack from behind, but not preferred, we can add additional sample points around the target, but weight them with a dot product test so that the samples behind the target receive a low rank. Done this way, agents will still approach the player from the front, unless it is impossible due to the player's location (near the edge of a cliff, facing a wall, etc.).

14.7.2 Increasing Robustness

The next action we can take is to make the query more *robust*. In this case, we relax our concept of the ideal case entirely, providing a larger pool of sample points to draw from under ideal circumstances. For example, our query may specify a position 5 m away and up to 30° from the front of the target, but in reality it may be the case that it will actually work fine at any distance between 5 and 8 m away, and up to 45° in front of the target. Figure 14.10 also shows an example of this solution.

14.7.3 Fallback Queries

Some query systems, such as EQS, provide multiple query *options*, or strategies, that can be defined as part of a single query. These can be thought of as fallback queries, providing alternative location suggestions to consider if the initial query fails. Thus if the initial option has no usable samples, subsequent ones are executed in order until one succeeds. Only when all options fail does the query itself fail. Clever use of fallback queries can also create opportunities for optimizing high-quality behavior: By defining a narrow initial sample set, we can run more expensive tests in the primary option that would normally be cost prohibitive, such as collision raycasts. In the fallback query, with a wider range of sample points, we can remove these tests to find a more mediocre, but still acceptable, location.

14.7.4 Preserving Quality

Taking advantage of these techniques, we can adapt our queries to be both permissive and robust, while still returning the same results as the initial query when possible. In Figure 14.9, the result of the rightmost query can be achieved in two ways:

1. Combine permissive and robust testing strategies: Pair a dot product gradient ranking with a larger valid sample area, then further add a distance test to weight the closest points higher. This layering results in the original set of points receiving the highest rank whenever they are available.
2. Define the leftmost query as the initial query strategy; if this fails, execute a fallback query that combines the permissive and robust testing strategies. This has the benefit of only incurring additional cost when ideal conditions are unavailable, at the expense of a higher overall cost of running both queries in suboptimal conditions.

14.8 Example Behaviors

In this section, we provide a handful of the many behaviors possible using only the most basic tests and the continuous movement behavior tree in Figure 14.7. For each behavior listed below, the only difference in the agent's AI is the query itself.

14.8.1 Directed Random Walk

By selecting a random item from the set of sample points, instead of the one that has the highest rank, we can add variety and unpredictability to a query-based behavior. For example, the classic NPC random walk (moving a short distance in an arbitrary direction, stopping briefly between moves) can be represented as a query by generating a filled circle of points up to a specified radius, ranking them by sine-scored distance to define an ideal move distance, and finally selecting randomly among the top 25% highest ranked points. By adding a dot product test to favor the agent's current direction, we eliminate harsh turns and unnatural oscillations, creating an agent that takes a long winding path through its environment. Finally, a minimum distance test weighted against other agents keeps agents evenly distributed and avoids collisions in crowded environments. By including our current position in the set of generated points, an agent that is boxed in can choose not to move until a reasonable location becomes available (Table 14.1).

Table 14.1 Directed Random Walk: Moves Relatively Forward, Avoiding Others

Weight	Type	Parameters	Scoring
N/A	Ring generator	0–8 m around agent	
1	Distance	Relative to agent	Sine
1	Dot	(Agent→Sample)· (Agent rotation)	Sigmoid
1	Minimum distance	Relative to other agents	Linear, 2–10 m range

14.8.2 Stay on Camera

If we want to position agents where they can be seen by the player, we can use the location and orientation of the camera to prioritize sample points based on their distance from the center of the screen. A camera frustum test can be approximated with a dot product, using a lower clamp to define the angle of a view cone. A negatively weighted distance test relative to the agent ensures the agent moves as little as possible to stay in view. Optionally, adding a raycast test between each point and the camera will eliminate points in front of the camera but hidden behind other objects or scenery, improving behavior quality at the cost of performance (Table 14.2).

14.8.3 Orbit

To walk or run in a circle around a target, we generate a ring of points within the minimum and maximum acceptable radius, then use a set of tests that when combined generate forward movement around the ring. The first, a sine-scored distance test around the agent, defines an ideal movement distance a few meters away from its current position; far enough that we should not arrive before reexecuting the query, but close enough to ensure small, smooth adjustments in heading. Next, a dot product test prioritizes items in the direction that the agent is currently heading, which encourages stable forward movement along the ring (clockwise or counter-clockwise). A second sine-ranked dot product test prioritizes points on the tangent line from the agent to the ring. This serves two purposes: It directs the agent to approach the ring along the tangent line (rather than head on, then turning 90° to begin orbiting), and it strongly prioritizes items directly in front of and behind the agent, allowing the agent to reverse direction when blocked while further stabilizing forward movement. Finally, clamped minimum distance tests around the positions and current destinations of other agents provide local avoidance (Table 14.3).

Table 14.2 Stay on Camera: Agent Attempts to Stay on Screen While Moving as Little as Possible

Weight	Type	Parameters	Scoring
N/A	Grid generator	20 m around agent	
−1	Distance	Relative to agent	Linear
1	Dot	(Camera→Sample)· (Camera rotation)	Linear, 0.85–1.0 range

Table 14.3 Orbit: Moves in a Circle around a Target Avoiding Others

Weight	Type	Parameters	Scoring
N/A	Ring generator	5–9 m around target	
8	Distance	Relative to agent	Sine, 0–6 m range
4	Dot	(Agent→Sample) (Agent→Destination)	Linear
2	Dot	(Agent→Sample)·(Agent→Target)	Sine
1	Minimum distance	Relative to other agents	Sigmoid, 0–5 m range
1	Minimum distance	Relative to other agent destinations	Sigmoid, 0–5 m range

Note: If forward movement is obstructed by the environment or other agents, the agent will turn around and continue orbiting in the opposite direction.

14.8.4 Boids

Spatial queries can even represent artificial life simulations. Craig Reynold's historic boids program, simulating the flocking behavior of birds, produces complex, emergent group behavior from an unexpectedly simple set of rules (Reynolds 1987). By implementing these rules using spatial query tests, we can recreate the original boids simulation as a continuous query behavior. In the original SIGGRAPH paper, individual boid movement was produced by combining the influence of three separate rules:

- Separation, to avoid crowding
- Alignment, to coordinate the flock direction
- Cohesion, to prevent the flock from dispersing

Within a query, separation can be represented as a minimum distance test against other agents, alignment as a dot product test against the average heading of the group, and cohesion as a distance test against the group centroid. By tuning the weights and ranges of these tests, we can adjust the emergent properties of the behavior (Table 14.4).

Table 14.4 Boids: Simulates Boid Flocking Behavior

Weight	Type	Parameters	Scoring
N/A	Ring generator	1–20 m around agent	
1.2	Minimum distance	Relative to other agents	Linear, 0–4 m range
0.5	Dot	(Agent→Sample)· (Average rotation of other agents)	Linear
−1	Distance	Relative to other agents	Linear

Note: Simulates boid flocking behavior using minimum distance, dot product, and average distance tests to represent separation, alignment, and cohesion respectively.

14. Guide to Effective Auto-Generated Spatial Queries

14.9 Conclusion

Once a novel alternative to traditional techniques, over the past five years spatial query systems have evolved into indispensable tools for AI development. Now commonplace and supported by multiple widely used game engines, integrating spatial query systems into your AI is more practical than ever, providing faster iteration time and higher quality position selection in dynamic and complex environments. By understanding the strengths and weaknesses of each component of a query, we can improve query quality and flexibility over a wider range of environmental conditions. Single queries, executed continuously, can even express traditionally code-driven movement behaviors, making query systems an increasingly versatile tool, able to single-handedly support most, if not all, destination selection in a project.

References

Jack, M. 2013. Tactical position selection: An architecture and query language. In *Game AI Pro*, ed. S. Rabin. New York: CRC Press, pp. 337–359.

Mars, C. 2014. Environmentally conscious AI: Improving spatial analysis and reasoning. *GDC 2014*, San Francisco, http://www.gdcvault.com/play/1018038/Spaces-in-the-Sandbox-Tactical.

Reynolds, C. W. 1987. Flocks, herds, and schools: A distributed behavioral model. *Computer Graphics*, 21(4) (SIGGRAPH '87 Conference Proceedings), 25–34.

Shirakami, Y., Miyake, Y., Namiki, K. 2015. The decision making Systems for Character AI in Final Fantasy XV -EPISODE DUSCAE-. *CEDEC 2015*, Yokohama, http://cedec.cesa.or.jp/2015/session/ENG/5953.html.

Zielinski, M. 2013. Asking the environment smart questions. In *Game AI Pro*, ed. S. Rabin. Boca Raton, FL: CRC Press, pp. 423–431.

The Role of Time in Spatio-Temporal Reasoning
Three Examples from Tower Defense

Baylor Wetzel and Kyle Anderson

15.1 Introduction

In Akira Kurosawa's film *Seven Samurai*, a small group of defenders are hired to defend a small village from an invading army of bandits. Vastly outnumbered, their survival depended on mastering their environment. Humans are good at spatio-temporal reasoning. Understanding how objects flow through space over time is how we know whether we can cross the street when there's a car coming. It is also how samurai know where to place ambushes when defending a village.

Spatio-temporal reasoning is an important part of many decisions (in and out of games). It is how armies know where to place gun nests, prisons know where to place cameras, firemen know where to place firebreaks, cities know where to place highways, and malls know where to place stores. Much has been written about the spatial aspect of spatio-temporal reasoning. Identifying choke points, flanks, and avenues of approach is an important part of video game AI, and at this point is fairly well understood. Far less has been written about time. Consequently, this chapter will focus specifically on the temporal aspect of spatio-temporal reasoning.

Temporal strategies are harder to visualize than spatial ones and, we believe, best explained by working through examples. Like Kurosawa's *Seven Samurai*, this chapter will focus on protecting a location from incoming enemies by identifying the best place to deploy our limited defenses. Defending a location is a common scenario in games that include any amount of strategic planning, such as tower defense games, strategy games, and "hold out until help arrives" missions in first-person shooters or action games. We will look at three examples. The first can be solved without directly thinking about time, whereas the second cannot be solved. The third shows how changing one's focus from space to time can produce new solutions.

15.2 Defend the Village

To keep our focus on the temporal part of spatio-temporal reasoning, our examples will use a tower defense game. This gives us difficult problems to solve but abstracts out the details not relevant to the topic.

For those unfamiliar with tower defense games, the genre grew out of real-time strategy games, with many players realizing they enjoyed designing the defenses around their base more than they liked attacking other players. The player is given a location to protect and one or more paths to that location. The player cannot directly attack the enemies (generically referred to as *creeps*) that will come down the path. Instead, they are given a set of objects (generically referred to as *towers*) that attack any enemy in range. Specifics vary by game—in some games the towers are soldiers with fast rifles or slow rocket launchers, in other games the towers are pits of acid, wizards with fire, or monkeys with darts. But what is always the same is that the gameplay revolves around placing towers strategically, in such a way that they prevent the enemies from getting past them.

Our examples come from *GopherTD*, a game we built to study how humans play strategy games. It is based on the popular tower defense game *Vector TD*. These are the details relevant to this chapter:

- There are 28 enemies (creeps) divided into two lines of 14 creeps each.
- Each line of creeps follows a fixed path through the map. Normally the two lines move side-by-side.
- Creeps move at a constant, fixed speed unless slowed by a slowing tower.
- Towers have a fixed rate of fire, do not run out of ammo, and never miss.
- There are several types of towers. To keep things simple, our examples will use only two types:
  - Attack towers attack the closest creep in range, staying on them until the creep dies or moves out of range, after which it moves to whichever creep is closest at that time. A creep must be hit multiple times before it is stopped.
  - Slowing towers attack the closest creep. Attacked creeps move at half speed for two seconds.
- The score is the number of creeps prevented from reaching the exit.

Figure 15.1 shows three examples of *GopherTD* levels.

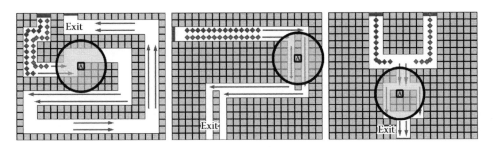

Figure 15.1

Maps from *GopherTD*. Creeps are shown at the entrance. Their goal is to make it to the spot marked Exit, representing the location you are trying to protect. The player's goal is to stop them by placing defenses (towers) along the path. Arrows show the direction the creeps move. A tower can be placed on any gray square. Circles show the range of the attack tower located at the cell marked A.

15.3 Example 1: U-Turns and the Maximum Usable Range Strategy

Our first example, while simple, illustrates some important concepts we should understand before tackling more complex problems.

15.3.1 The Problem

Consider the leftmost map in Figure 15.1. If you had only one attack tower, where should you place it? Figure 15.2 shows five options, each representing a different type of spatial structure—a hallway, corner, U-turn, double-sided wall, and an interior corner. Which is the best position and why?

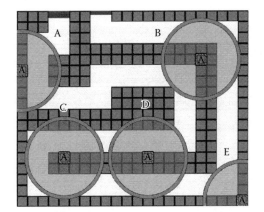

Figure 15.2

An attack tower placed at five different types of positions. (A) A wall. (B) A corner. (C) A U-turn. (D) A wall. The tower overlooks two hallways. (E) An interior corner.

We wanted to design an AI that thought like a human so we began by studying humans. We asked 59 people, a mixture of gamers and nongamers, where they would put the tower (among other things [Wetzel 2014]). The answer was nearly unanimous: C, the U-turn (only one person disagreed, choosing D, the hallway).

What makes the U-turn a better position than the others? People answered in different ways. Some said that it covers three hallways, whereas B and D only covered two and A and E covered one. Some said C covered everything positions such as D did plus more. Others said that C simply looked like it covered more area. Unsurprisingly, given how good humans are at visual estimation, they were correct: position C has a usable range of 30 (i.e., there are 30 path tiles the creeps move across that are inside the tower's range) as opposed to 29 at B, 26 at D, 16 at A, and 8 at E.

15.3.2 Discussion: Space-Time Equivalence

Each of the above explanations means essentially the same thing: maximize the tower's usable range, meaning place the tower where it covers the largest number of tiles that the creeps will walk over. We call this the *Maximum Usable Range* strategy and it is a common and obvious strategy.

Words say a lot about our thinking process. If you look at the reasons given for selecting position C you should notice that the language is almost entirely spatial. If this does not seem surprising, it might be because you believe the problem is a spatial problem. It is not. The goal is nonspatial: maximize the score, with one point earned for each creep destroyed. The action is spatial: place the tower on the map. The effectiveness of the action is temporal: since the tower fires at a fixed rate of speed doing a fixed amount of damage per shot, maximizing the tower's effectiveness means maximizing the amount of time it spends firing. Since the tower only fires when creeps are in range (a spatial property), maximizing the tower's effectiveness means maximizing the amount of time there are creeps in the tower's range.

As with many terrain reasoning problems, the problem is a mixture of spatio-temporal reasoning and nonspatio-temporal goals. Why, then, do people treat it like a spatial problem? One reason is that is easier for people to think about space than time. A large part of the human brain is dedicated to understanding space, something that is not true for time. If a spatio-temporal problem can be converted to a spatial one, it can leverage that hardware.

Two other reasons why people convert spatio-temporal problems to spatial ones are that it works well and that it makes sense. In many cases, space and time are proportional and linearly correlated. In this case, the more area inside a tower's range, the longer it takes the creeps to move through it and therefore the more time creeps are in range and the more time the tower has to fire at them. Increasing a tower's usable range (space) increases the amount of time it spends firing (time).

15.3.3 Discussion: Strategies and Affordances

We wrote AIs to solve each of the maps mentioned in this chapter. The best AIs perform as well as the best human players we studied (which is perhaps unsurprising given that we based them on those players). All of the AIs work in the same way: they are given a set of affordance-keyed strategies and query our Spatial Affordance Query System for places to apply their strategies. We will give examples later but first we need to define how we use the terms "affordance" and "strategy."

An *affordance* is something that affords (allows) an action. More importantly, it suggests an action. The classic example is a door handle (Norman 1988). A plate on a door says (to most people) "push me," whereas a handle says "pull me." In our example, the U-turn was an affordance that said (to most people) "place your tower here." Alternately, for those who measured usable range directly rather than using the U-turn as a proxy for maximum usable range, usable range is an affordance. There are many types of affordances. In the case of U-turns, the affordance is spatial geometry, whereas in the case of usable range, it is a variable to be maximized.

It is important to point out that affordances are contextually defined—whether something is an affordance depends on a number of things including one's goal, capabilities, and other relevant factors. In our example, several things must be true for position C to be a U-turn. First, the creeps must move all the way around it. If the creeps came from two different directions and met in the middle, as they do in the rightmost map in Figure 15.1, the space might still be shaped like a U-turn but it does not afford the expected behavior of creeps moving around the U-turn. Second, C is only a U-turn if the attack tower's range is large enough to cover all three sides. If the tower's range were significantly wider, position D would also be a U-turn, whereas if it were taller, position B would be a U-turn (i.e., it would cover the U-turn that is down and to the left). Third, we only notice the U-turn because the action it affords is relevant to our Maximum Usable Range strategy. If we had different goals, the U-turn might stop affording us actions we care about. The important point for the AI developer is this: You cannot identify an affordance without knowing how you intend to use it. In this example, you not only need to know the map geography, you need to know the path the creeps take and the range of the tower to be placed.

In our experience, a *strategy* tends to be a simple action designed to achieve a single, concrete goal. Strategies exploit or otherwise rely upon an affordance. A player only considers using a U-turn strategy when the map contains U-turn affordances (i.e., areas that can be used as a U-turn by the strategy). Likewise, a player that does not know the U-turn strategy does not notice the afforded U-turns on the map.

Strategies are, in our view, small things. Most problems require the use of multiple strategies, which we refer to alternately as *strategy sets* or a person's *play-* or *problem solving-style*. In this example, where we only have one tower and wish to place it at the spot where it has the most usable range, a single strategy is sufficient. We will see more complicated playstyles in the next examples.

The implementation for the maximum usable range agent is given in Listing 15.1. It is only a few lines: Define the strategy then ask the solver to solve it. Defining a placement strategy involves specifying a *PlacementDecision*, which consists of three parts: *placement object*, *placement relationship*, and *anchor* (Wetzel 2014). For this AI, the strategy is to place the tower (placement object) on a spot that has the maximal (placement relationship) value for the relative property `PhysicalPathCellsInRange` (anchor). Relative properties can vary in magnitude (e.g., usable range), whereas an absolute property does not (e.g., a location either is or is not a corner). The relative property used by this AI is usable range, which it wants to maximize. The anchor could be a spatial feature but more often it is an affordance, as it is here. Other examples of strategies include placing an attack tower's range (placement object) so that it overlaps (placement relationship) another tower's range (anchor) or placing a slowing tower so that the exit to its range

```
Solution AI::getSolution(MapModel map)
{
    SolutionRequest request = new SolutionRequest(map);
    GroupToPlace group = new GroupToPlace();
    request.groups. Add(group);
    group.towers. Add(new AttackTower());
    Strategy strategy =
        new PlaceTowerOnRelativePropertyStrategy(
            MapPropertyOrdinal. PhysicalPathCellsInRange,
            StrategyOperator. Maximum));
    group.placementStrategies. Add(strategy);
    return Solver.getSolution(request);
}
```

(placement object) is in front of (placement relationship) the start to an attack tower's range (anchor) (Wetzel 2014).

The solver code (Listing 15.2) is equally simple: Find the affordances on the map and execute the strategy for each affordance. In this case, the AI asked the solver to place

Listing 15.2. The Solver creates a solution (list of tower placements) by instantiating the strategy for each group of towers. In practice, this means identifying affordances on the map and matching towers to those using each tower's strategy, which is a PlacementDecision specifying the affordance to use.

```
static Solution Solver::getSolution(SolutionRequest request)
{
  Solution solution = new Solution();
  solution.map = MapAnalyzer.getMapAnalysis(request.map);
  foreach (GroupToPlace group in request.groups)
  {
    foreach (Tower t in group.towers)
    {
      foreach (Strategy s in group.strategies)
      {
        List<GridPoint> candidates = s.getPositions(t, map);
        if (candidates. Count > 0)
        {
          GridPoint p = group.tieBreaker.get(candidates);
          solution.add(t, p);
          break;
        }
      }
    }
  }
  return solution;
}
```

one attack tower with the strategy "place the tower at the position where it gets the most usable range." The solver asks the MapAnalyzer for all the affordances on the given map for the specified tower (`getMapAnalysis`), compares the strategies to the affordances and places the tower on the best match (i.e., where the tower's usable range is maximized) then returns where the highest usable range for an attack tower is on the given map and returns a list of positions and the tower to place on each.

For this code to work a few things have to be true. You must be able to explicitly define your strategies (in Listing 15.1, the Maximum Usable Range strategy is an instantiation of the more general `PlaceTowerOnRelativePropertyStrategy`). Second, you must be able to define your affordances. Third, strategies need to be keyed to affordances, or at least, the computer needs to know how to apply a strategy given an affordance (in this case, the tower is placed on the spot where the affordance is detected). Fourth, you need to be able to identify the affordances on the map. We do this through our Spatial Affordance Query System, SAQS. Although the AI and solver code are quite short, SAQS is not and is therefore outside of the scope of this chapter. We believe, however, that by walking through examples, it will be clear how to identify the ones you need.

15.4 Example 2: Spatial Symmetry and the Differential Slowing Strategy

It is often enough to convert a spatio-temporal problem to a spatial one and solve that, but not always. In this example, we consider a situation where we need to think explicitly about time.

15.4.1 The Problem

The map in Figure 15.3 has an interesting property: It is essentially featureless. It has no switchbacks or U-turns or any usable spatial features. The only positions where a tower could reach the creeps on both paths are on the thin strip of wall between the two. The positions on the wall are all essentially identical, with a usable range of 14, less than half that on the U-turn in Example 1 and not nearly enough to stop the invading creeps.

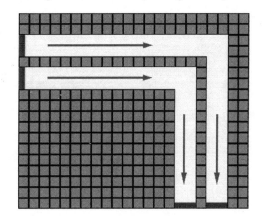

Figure 15.3

The map no left turns.

15.4.2 Discussion: Temporal Asymmetry and the Path Gap Affordance

In Example 1 we said that, although these problems were temporal, not spatial, it did not matter because space is often a good proxy for time. This is a problem where that is not true.

The spatial geometry is mirrored across the diagonal axis. This makes the map symmetric, but only spatially. When it comes to time, the map is strongly asymmetric. We can measure this by measuring where an object is at a given point in time. Pick a position along the path and consider which line of creeps will reach it first. Before the corner, the answer is neither, both lines will arrive at the same time. After the corner, however, the creeps on the inside (lower, left) path will reach a given position before those on the outer one. That is because the outer path is longer, taking longer to go around the corner (Figure 15.4).

We use the term *path gap* to refer to the difference between when a group on one path reaches a position versus when a group on a second path reaches it. Once you know the concept exists, it is easy to see and you will see path gap on every map where you are trying to solve a similar problem (an affordance only exists when it is relevant to one of your goals; if you do not have that goal, the concept stops making sense). If the concept suggests an action, a strategy to exploit it, then it is an affordance. Path gap is certainly an affordance.

We said earlier that our goal is to maximize the amount of time a tower spends firing, which we do by maximizing the amount of time that creeps are in range. Note that this does not refer to the amount of time that a single creep is in range, it is the amount of time that any creep is in range. With that in mind, consider Figure 15.4. A tower placed on the top half of the map will be active for the amount of time it takes a line of creeps to move through it. It does not matter which line since both move through at the same time. A line of creeps is 14 creeps long so the tower is active for as long as it takes for 14 creeps to move through it.

Now consider the same tower placed on the lower part of the map. The outer path is six tiles longer so the second line of creeps does not reach the tower until six tiles worth of creeps has already entered its range. The tower is therefore active for the amount of time it takes the first line of creeps to move through the tower's range, as in the positions along the top of the map, plus the time it takes for the last six tiles worth of creeps from the second line to move through. If we say that a creep is one tile wide, the tower's active

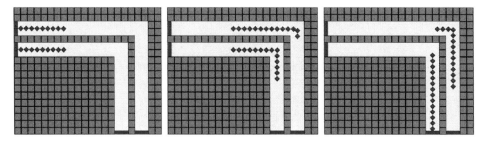

Figure 15.4

As they round the corner, the creeps on the outer path fall behind.

time on the bottom part of the map grows from the amount of time it takes 14 creeps to move through to the amount of time it takes 20 creeps to move through. The physical space in range did not change but the amount of time the tower spends firing did; the map is spatially symmetric but temporally asymmetric and the positions on it are spatially equivalent but temporally different. We have grown time without growing space. We call this the *Exploit Path Gap* strategy.

15.4.3 Discussion: Forcing Affordances and the Differential Slowing Strategy

Path Gap is a spatial affordance in the sense that it is based on the length of a path. As such, it can only be used on maps where the geometry supports it. The key idea, however, is not the length of the paths, it is the difference between when two groups arrive at a location. That gap in arrival times is an affordance we can exploit. Once we know this is valuable property, we not only become more sensitive to other features that can create it, we can consider ways to create it ourselves, even on maps where the geometry does not support it.

In Section 15.2 we mentioned that there are two types of towers, attack and slowing. We did not use the slowing towers in Example 1 because it did not affect the strategy we used (maximizing usable range) or the way we thought about space. Here, where we want to exploit the difference in arrival times, slowing towers give us an interesting option. We could use the slowing towers to slow the creeps while they are in the attack tower's range, a good and straightforward strategy, but we can do better.

In the *Differential Slowing* strategy, slowing towers are placed where they only slow one group, causing it to fall behind the other and effectively creating a path gap. Using our slowing towers, we can slow one line of creeps and not the other, thus causing one group to fall behind the other. In this example, we can combine Differential Slowing with the Exploit Path Gap strategy to create a much larger gap (obviously, both strategies should target the same group).In practice, using both Exploit Path Gap, which exploits a temporal affordance caused by a spatial feature, and Differential Slowing, which creates a temporal affordance, fully separates the two groups, causing them to go through the tower's range at different times (Figure 15.5). This doubles the amount of time the tower spends firing.

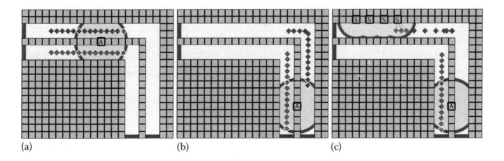

(a)   (b)   (c)

Figure 15.5

Three strategies. (a) *Maximum Usable Range*, tower placed before the corner. (b) *Exploit Path Gap*. (c) *Differential Slowing*.

15.4.4 Implementing the Differential Slowing Strategy

In our study, once players recognized the path gap affordance and figured out the Differential Slowing strategy, they seemed to have little trouble successfully applying it, even on maps they previously struggled on. In contrast, this was the most difficult AI for us to implement. Because of that, we feel it is valuable to spend a little time explaining how we did it.

SAQS keeps an influence map of each affordance it tracks. These maps can be used as filters or weighted and combined. The resulting map is a desirability map. Our AI uses a solver which picks the highest value spot on a desirability map.

For the differential slowing AI we need to combine a few strategies. The attack tower's placement depends on three affordances: usable range, path gap and coverage balance (a ratio of how much of the tower's usable range covers one path versus another; if the spot with the best usable range does not allow the tower to attack both paths, the enemies approaching from the second path will get through). The desirability map is a weighted combination of these three. The slowing towers want to maximize their usable range but only on positions that are *single path overwatch* positions. A single path overwatch is a position that affords the tower the ability to attack one path but not another. The map of single path overwatch positions is a filter. The solver only applies the maximum usable range strategy to those positions returned by the single path overwatch filter.

Creeps must be separated before they are attacked; there is no point in slowing them after they have passed the tower. To achieve this, the map must be divided into two zones, the slowing zone and the kill zone, and the slowing zone must be placed before the kill zone *temporally* (i.e., we do not care where on the map it happens spatially but the creeps must pass through it before they enter the kill zone). In order to determine where *before* is, we need a way to measure the flow of creeps over time through the space. We used a *path* feature (not affordance; the path does not directly or immediately suggest an action and it is an invariant feature of the map rather than being dependent on our goals) with the property *step number*, which is simply how many steps it is from the start of the path.

Dividing the map into zones is not as easy as it might sound. At its most basic we just need a split point—slowing towers go before this point, attack towers after—but determining that split point is not straight forward. The slowing towers want the path-specific single path overwatch positions with the highest usable range. The offense tower wants the position with the highest (weighted) combination of path gap, coverage balance and usable range. If we are lucky, the best kill zone positions are "later" than the best slowing zone positions but we need to handle the situations where they are not. If the best kill zone position is at the start of the map (which it is not here but is on many other maps), you either have to abandon the strategy or pick an inferior kill zone—but not too inferior, or the strategy is not worth it.

To determine whether the strategy makes sense, let us set some minimum requirements (values were chosen after a few iterations of play testing). A slowing zone must have at least four single path overwatch positions (again, overwatching the desired path) with a 45% or greater usable range ration (i.e., at least 45% of the tower's range covers the desired path). The kill zone must have at least one position of some value, say four path gap, 70% usable range ratio, and 60% coverage balance.

We generate a set of candidate split points by using a sliding space-time window. Start at the beginning of time and space (the path start) and move along it, scoring the adjacent positions. In practice, we grab the path of interest, start at the first position on it and ask SAQS for all positions within a slowing tower's range of it. Those that match we store on a map and the count of matches we store on the path. We then move to the next step on the path and repeat. The same process is done for the kill zone but moving backward through time (i.e., start at the end of the path).

Once the sliding window maps are built you can find the split points for the slowing and kill zones where the strategy's minimum needs are met. If the borders cross, the strategy is not going to work and the AI picks a different one (the recognition of affordances on the map triggers strategies that the AI knows; if multiple strategies activate, each can be tested to see which are the most effective). Once found, there are three regions: the minimum areas for the slowing and kill zones, and the unclaimed area between them. Our AI places attack towers first since the quality of attack tower positions often vary greatly, whereas all of the slowing zone positions are guaranteed to let a tower slow one group and not the other. The attack tower placement evaluates positions in the combined kill zone and unclaimed area. Once the towers are placed, the rest of the area is added to the slowing zone and the differential slowing towers are placed.

15.5 Example 3: Quantifying Space-Time and the Attack Window Separation Strategy

Our goal (maximize the amount of time a tower spends firing) is temporal and our action (place an object on a map) is spatial. If space and time are linearly correlated, we can measure everything spatially knowing that when we increase space we also increase time. If space and time can be manipulated independently, as they were with Differential Slowing, we need a way to measure time and a way to convert between space and time. In this section we consider such a metric, as well as its implications for the original U-turn example.

15.5.1 AL: A Metric for Measuring Space-Time

Our work uses a unified space-time metric called *al* (for agent length). It represents the amount of time it takes an agent (in this case, the creep) to cross their body length. It allows us to measure items both spatially and temporally and convert between the two.

We are going to work several examples so we need to set some values:

- A creep is 1 tile wide
- A creep can move 1 tile per second
- An attack tower fires 10 times a second

These are not the exact values from the game but they make the math easier to follow. For the same reason, we are also going to pretend in these examples that all values are whole numbers.

Let us start with a simple example. Suppose we say that a tower has an active time of 6al. We can convert this to a spatial measure and say that the path through the tower's range is six tiles long. We can convert this to a temporal measure and say that the tower is active for six seconds. We can convert this to a nonspatio-temporal measure and say that it fires 60 times and does 60x damage, where x is the amount of damage per shot. If the tower covers four path tiles at a second position, its size at that position is 4al, it will be active for four seconds and fire 40 times doing 40x damage. Placed at the first position, the tower does 50% more damage.

In this case, time and space are linearly correlated and we can find the best spot by just maximizing space, meaning we get no value from the al metric. To see where this is not true, we need to talk about attack windows.

15.5.2 Attack Windows: Spatial and Temporal, Unified and Separated, Agent and Group

In the previous example we said "If the tower covers four path tiles at a second position, *its* size is 4al." We did not say what "it" was. *It* refers to the tower's attack window. An attack window is the opportunity an object has to attack. There are several ways to measure them. A *spatial attack window* is a contiguous block of space where the tower can attack. In Figure 15.2, the tower on the U-turn (C) has one large spatial attack window, whereas the tower in the hallway (D) has two small spatial attack windows. A *temporal attack window* is the period of time the tower has to attack. A tower will have as many temporal attack windows as spatial ones under two conditions. First, the group only crosses through the space once. If a tower has one spatial attack window but a group passes through it multiple times, it is the same as if it had multiple attack windows since the tower gets to attack on multiple occasions. If a group crosses the same space multiple times, the number of temporal windows can be larger than the number of spatial windows. Second, if a tower has two spatial attack windows but a group can be in both at the same time, it is a single temporal window—since, from the tower's point of view, there is no pause between attacks, it is all the same time period. If the group is long enough or the spatial attack windows close enough that a group can be in both at once, the tower can have fewer temporal attack windows than spatial ones. Whether temporal windows are unified or separated is important, as will be shown in the next section.

An attack window's *temporal agent size* is the temporal size of the window for a single agent, meaning it is the amount of time it takes one creep to make it through the attack window. Its *temporal group size* is the size of the window for a group of agents moving through it. This is the one to pay attention to as it is not necessarily correlated with space. The reason for this is that, from a functional perspective (e.g., from the perspective of a tower attacking), groups do not move through time the way individuals do.

Finally, a tower's *active time* is the amount of time the tower spends firing. This is equivalent to the combined temporal group size of all attack windows.

A tower can have multiple temporal group attack windows. The size of each window is the amount of time it takes a group to move through the space. This is equivalent to the time it takes the first member of the group to make it through, the time it takes the last member of the group to make it through and the difference between the first creep exits the range and the last one enters. The time it takes for the first creep to make it through the range plus the time it takes for the last creep to enter the range is just the line length so the temporal group size is:

```
temporalGroupSize = lineLength + temporalAgentSize - 1
```

(the –1 is to avoid counting the last creep twice).

It is worth noting that a tower will fire for as long as there is a creep in range. It does not matter how many there are; the tower does not fire faster with ten enemies than with two. For this reason, the density of enemies does not matter. If two lines of enemies pass through a tower's range at different times, the tower gets two opportunities to attack, but if two lines move through at the same time, the tower only gets one. In the first example we talked about usable range. This turns out to be unimportant. What matters is the path length through the window. To use an example from a different genre, imagine you are in a first-person shooter and have the option of camping over an alleyway or in front of a bank of windows. In the alleyway you can see an enemy running the length of the alley, which takes five seconds. In front of the building you can see five windows. There are five people inside, all of whom cross in front of the window at the exact same, spending one second—the same second—in their respective windows. Even if both positions look over the same amount of space, the amount of time you have to attack (five seconds in the alley, one in front of the windows) is different.

15.5.3 The U-Turn Problem, Revisited

Let us revisit the question asked in Example 1—what is the best position to place an attack tower in Figure 15.2. 58 of 59 people we studied said position C, the U-turn. An attack tower at C has one spatial and one temporal attack window. Its usable range is 30, the length of the inner path is 13 and the outer path 16. Since the temporal agent size is the time it takes one creep to follow the path through the tower, the temporal agent size is the same as the longest path, 16al. There are 28 creeps in two lines of 14. The outer line of creeps takes a longer path, with each corner adding 2 tiles, causing the last four creeps of the outer line to still be in range once the inner line has left (see Figure 15.6). The line length is therefore 18. The data are summarized in Table 15.1. The temporal group size of the U-turn at position C is:

```
temporalGroupSize = lineLength + temporalAgentSize - 1
temporalGroupSize = 18al + 16al - 1al = 33al.
```

An attack tower placed on the U-Turn has an active time of 33al, meaning it has 33 seconds to fire 330 shots to stop 28 creeps.

One of 59 players chose position D, an unremarkable position in a hallway that overlooks two halls. It has two spatial attack windows. They are far enough apart that no creep will still be in the first when the first creeps enters the second. As with the U-turn, because the outer line of creeps passes two corners before entering the second attack window, the line length changes from 14 in the first window to 18 in the second. The data are summarized in Table 15.1. The size of the temporal group attack windows are:

```
Hall AW1 TGS = 14al + 7al - 1al = 20al
Hall AW2 TGS = 18al + 6al - 1al = 23al
Combined Hall TGS            = 43al
```

An attack tower placed in the hallway far enough away from the U-turn that the attack windows are independent (which we call the *Attack Window Separation* strategy) has an active time of 43al, meaning it has 43 seconds to fire 430 shots to stop 28 creeps.

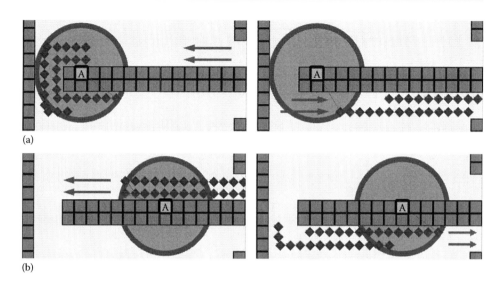

(a)

(b)

Figure 15.6

Two lines of agents moving through across a U-turn. (a) Creeps moving through the range of a tower covering a U-turn. (b) Moving through the range of a tower covering a hallway.

Table 15.1 Spatial data for positions in Figure 15.2

	(C) U-Turn	(D) Hallway
Usable range	30 tiles	26 tiles
Path length	13 inside	AW1: 7 inside/6 outside
	16 outside	AW2: 6 inside/4 outside
AW agent size	16al	AW1: 7al
		AW2: 6al
Line length	18al	AW1: 14al
		AW2: 18al

In most respects, the U-turn is a better position. An attack tower placed there has 15% more usable range, a 23% longer path, a 23% larger attack window temporal agent size (+23%) and 12% longer average line length (+12%). Despite this, the same tower placed in the hallway will active for 30% longer (43 seconds vs. 33) and do 30% more damage.

15.5.4 Attack Window Decay

Because it has a 30% larger combined temporal attack window, it is tempting to say that a hallway tower it is 30% better than a U-turn tower. It is not. In the game, an attack tower placed on the U-turn stops 14 creeps, whereas the same tower in the hall stops 20, 43% more. If the tower only fires 30% more often and therefore only does 30% more damage, why does it achieve a 43% higher score?

We said that the attack window temporal agent size is the amount of time it takes for one agent to walk through a tower's range and is the amount of time the tower has to attack the agent, which can also be phrased as the amount of time the agent is in danger. We need to amend that a little.

The U-turn in the last example had an attack window temporal agent size of 16, meaning it took an agent 16al to move through it and the tower had 16al of space-time to attack it. Suppose the tower kills the agent in 2al. If the enemies are back to back, a second enemy came into range 1al later and has moved another 1al along the path. During this time the tower has been busy with the first enemy, meaning the second enemy has not been attacked or hurt yet. By the time the tower is free to attack it, the second enemy only has 15al it needs to cross, and the tower only has 15al to attack him or her. The temporal attack window has shrunk. By the time the tower stops the second enemy, the third enemy is 2al into the region and the tower only has 14al left to stop him or her. Assuming enough enemies relative to window size and how quickly the tower can dispatch enemies, the tower eventually runs out of time to destroy enemies and can only wound them, which in many applications, from stopping zombies to damaging incoming tanks, earns you no points since the agent still makes it to the area you are defending and is able to do damage.

When an agent is holding a tower's attention, he or she is buffering for the other agents, keeping them from taking damage—in many games, when players do this it is referred to as "tanking." Once the tower finishes with the agent it must play catch up. Since the tower has a fixed rate of fire, catching up is impossible as long as there are enemies in range.

How does a tower catch up? It needs time. It needs to process the queue it has before starting on new work—which it can do if the attack window is divided into parts and it can process each one independently. This is exactly what happens when the tower is placed in the hallway and exactly what goes wrong when it is on the U-turn. It is also why we said earlier that two spatially independent attack windows are a single temporal attack window if enemies can enter the second attack window while the tower is busy with enemies in the first one—the tower does not have a chance to catch up and the temporal attack window continues to decay. The tower needs a breather so that the attack window size can reset.

As a note, we call the strategy we are using here *Attack Window Separation*, and the affordance that triggers it is, of course, *attack window separation*, a numeric measure of the distance between the end of one spatial attack and the start of the next (as before, you need to know how time flows through space, which for us meant path step number). If you know how long the enemy line length is, you could ask the SAQS for all positions where the attack window separation is enough to temporally decouple the windows. As with differential slowing, you can use slowing towers placed between the attack windows to stretch the length as necessary, creating attack window separation affordances that enable an attack window separation strategy on maps where it was not possible before. Because implementing this has no new ideas that were not covered in the previous sections Differential Slowing, we will not walk through the implementation here. We do hope, however, that this and the earlier examples let you appreciate the value of a good spatial affordance query system.

15.6 Conclusion

We know we live in a world of objects moving through space over time and to deal with it we need to do spatio-temporal reasoning, but much of what we do is actually spatial reasoning, allowing space to be a proxy for time. Often our thoughts are spatial, our reasoning is spatial, our strategies are spatial, and the affordances we recognize are spatial. This is not a bad thing and we can often perform quite well this way, but if we can bring ourselves to focus on time—to recognize temporal affordances and craft temporal strategies—we can sometimes do much better.

References

Norman, D. 1988. *The Design of Everyday Things*, New York.
Wetzel, B. 2014. Representation and reasoning for complex spatio-temporal problems: From humans to software agents. PhD diss., University of Minnesota.

16

Pitfalls and Solutions When Using Monte Carlo Tree Search for Strategy and Tactical Games

Gijs-Jan Roelofs

16.1 Introduction

The biggest challenge when building AI for modern strategy games is dealing with their complexity. Utility- or expert-based techniques provide good bang for their buck in the sense that they get the AI to a reasonable, even decent level of play quickly. Problems start to arise, however, when an AI programmer is faced with situations that are not straight-forward or too time-consuming to encode in heuristics. Or when he or she is faced with above average gamers who demand a good opponent and are quick to find any exploits in an AI.

Search techniques seem like an interesting solution to provide adaptable and more dynamic AI. Traditional search techniques, like minimax, iterate over all possible moves, evaluate each resulting state, and then return the best move found. This approach does not work in strategy games because there are simply too many moves to explore.

MCTS (*Monte Carlo Tree Search*) is a new and increasingly popular technique that has shown it is capable of dealing with more complex games. This chapter outlines solutions to common pitfalls when using MCTS and shows how to adapt the algorithm to work with strategy games.

An example of one such pitfall is that implementations of search techniques in game AI tend to work by limiting the search to a subset of moves deemed interesting. This approach can lead to an AI that can easily be exploited because it literally does not see the pruned moves coming. Techniques outlined within this chapter will give MCTS the opportunity to discover these moves while still ensuring a good base level of play in those worst-case situations where it does not find them.

Throughout the chapter we showcase how these techniques were implemented using two vastly different strategy games: *Berlin*, an online Risk-like game in which the player commands hundreds of units in an effort to capture all regions, and *Xenonauts 2*, a tactical game akin to *X-Com* developed by Goldhawk Interactive in which the player commands a squad of 12 soldiers. In *Berlin*, the introduction of the core techniques outlined in this chapter led to a 73% win and a 15% draw rate over the best hierarchical AI based implementation (utility-based driven by behavior tree adjusted weights). The actual gameplay shown by MCTS was adaptive to new player strategies without requiring any input or rebalancing (Roelofs 2015).

This chapter delves into details which assume a basic understanding of MCTS. Those unfamiliar with this technique should start by reading the introduction provided in *Game AI Pro 2* (Sturtevant 2015). For this chapter, we use the most common and battle tested variant of MCTS: *UCT* (*Upper Confidence Bounds Applied to Trees*) (Chaslot 2010).

To ease understanding, the sections of this chapter are grouped into two categories: design principles and implementation tricks. The design principles outline general principles which need to be adapted to each game to which they are applied, and require full understanding to apply correctly. Implementation tricks are general ways to improve any MCTS implementation.

In the next section, we give an overview of the problem. The sections beyond that are structured according to the four major phases of MCTS (shown in Figure 16.1): *Selection*, *Expansion*, *Simulation*, and *Backpropagation*.

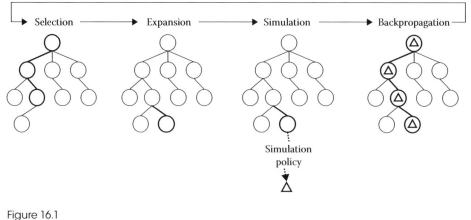

Figure 16.1

The *Monte Carlo Tree Search* algorithm.

16.2 The Problem

The strength of MCTS lies in its ability to cope with large, complex problems in which the long-term ramifications of a move are generally more important than its short-term effects. In other words, in problems where the actual effects only become apparent after executing long sequences of moves, that is, a *deep* search space. It excels in areas where alternative techniques, such as minimax, given ample depth (6–12 ply) still do not return useful strategies.

In general, performance for search techniques starts to falter when the number of choices possible per level of the tree starts to increase, that is, a *wide* search space. Although MCTS tends to cope better with this than many other techniques, increasing the width is still the quickest way to drastically reduce performance (Roelofs 2015).

For strategy games, one common problem is when a single move for a player can be broken down into several actions (e.g., many orders to individual units). If each of these actions affects the outcome of the sequence as a whole, we need to examine all possible combinations of them, resulting in search spaces of often insurmountable width and subsequently, size (Churchill and Buro 2015, Roelofs 2015).

For example, in *Xenonauts 2* a unit can move to upwards of 50 different locations and select between 4 different weapons to attack 1 of 16 different targets, not to mention additional unit abilities. Even after pruning those locations, weapons, and targets which are not interesting we are still left with about 12 options per unit. Given 16 different units, this results in 12^{16} different combinations of actions to search through per turn. No amount of calculation time will ensure that the search returns with good results if we try to look at all combinations of actions.

Luckily, more often than not these actions do not influence each other that much, or if they do, there are specific actions which have large ramifications and thus stand out. Often, the AI programmer might not know which particular action would work well, but he or she has an understanding that certain types of actions have the potential to perform far better than others. This is better explained with some concrete examples:

In *Xenonauts 2*, some units had the ability to mind control an enemy unit. This ability tended to have a far bigger effect on the outcome of a mission than other actions. By creating a heuristic function based on the worth (objectives or worth of the units to the player) and potential for the AI (weapons, abilities, and position) we were quickly able to get the AI to function at a decent level of play. However, throughout development we kept discovering that the AI missed crucial moves which were extremely situational and nightmarish to encode through heuristics. Moves which were the result of combinations of abilities or weaknesses on units in both the player and AI squad, objectives which invalidated or revalidated certain tactics, or moves which resulted in wins further in the future through sacrifice of units.

In *Berlin*, an example of such an action would be the capture of a region that would not be deemed valuable using common heuristics, but would provide a crucial vector of attack in subsequent turns giving the AI an advantage in the long run.

These are actions that if done correctly would have given the player pause but if done incorrectly would be glaring mistakes. In short, actions that are not easily found through the use of heuristics or for which the actual effects several turns from now need to be simulated to see their actual worth. The essence of the solution we propose is to enable

MCTS to discover and subsequently exploit these actions—that is, actions that have a large impact on the overall outcome of a move—in an effort to exploit those moves that contain them.

Before delving into the details and actual approach, we reiterate and define the key terms used throughout the chapter:

- *Move*: A sequence of independent actions constituting a full player turn.
- For example: All units have received orders for the turn.
- *Action*: An independent part of a move.
- For example: The orders to be sent to a single unit, attack enemy X, or move to location A.
- *Action set*: All of the possible values for a particular action.
- For example: A unit can attack {X, Y, or Z}, move to {A, B, or C}, or use special ability {J, K, or L}.

16.3 Expansion

This section outlines how to restructure the search such that MCTS will be able to identify good actions and subsequently use exploitation to ensure it can spend more time on moves that contain them and less on moves that do not. The key to this is to first expand into those actions which we expect to perform well. This provides good early estimates that later help the exploitation process of MCTS. Which actions we expand into can be specified through heuristics, learned using entropy learning or by restructuring the expansion such that MCTS learns it during search (Roelofs 2015). Furthermore, splitting up the move also allows us to prune actions or options in an action set which are not of interest, or simply select without search those for which we know a good solution exists through heuristics.

16.3.1 Restructuring Your Search Space (Design Principle)

By default, at each expansion step MCTS expands into all possible moves from the current node. The problem with this type of expansion is that there is no transfer of information between moves at the same level. MCTS simply cannot exploit information gained from one move to prefer one over another and needs to inspect each move individually.

By dividing the move into actions we can enable MCTS to understand that move B, which is a minor variation of a good move A that it explored earlier, might be a good move as well. Instead of expanding over all possible moves at each expansion step, we select a specific action within the current move and expand into the actions defined in its action set. We can further enhance performance by carefully pruning or ordering the action set of an action before the start of the search, or during it based on the actions already explored in the current move. To distinguish from the default expansion strategy, we term *hierarchical expansion* as expanding into actions as opposed to moves.

In *Xenonauts 2*, we carved up a move into the orders per unit, each action being a single order assigned to a unit. Each unit could have multiple orders assigned to it until a move consisted of actions in which it had spent all of its time units or was put on overwatch. The reasoning behind this was that often the outcome of a mission could be swayed by the actions of a single unit, and thus the selection between individual actions was crucial.

This was helped by the fact that we limited the search to those units in engagement with the player and let overall positioning of nonengaging squads be done by simple heuristics.

In *Berlin*, the move was carved up into a single action per region, in which we decided how soldiers would attack or reinforce adjacent regions. The reasoning behind this was that we only needed to hone in on the decisions of specific regions. Looking at the soldier level would result an in excessive increase in size of the search space.

Figure 16.2 gives a graphical example of hierarchical expansion given three action sets, each with two actions ({A, B}, {C, D}, {E, F}). In this example, as the search starts MCTS will explore the actions A or B and subsequently all moves which contain those actions. As it becomes apparent that one action results in significantly better results, it will avoid the other action, and subsequently all moves that contain it. The core idea being that if action A or B is truly better than the other, it will show through the simulations, regardless of which move it was played in.

Herein lies the drawback of this approach. If we start with an action set which has no apparent good move, or if a good move happens further down the line, we may lose crucial calculation time. MCTS will keep switching between the nodes as it is unapparent which sequence of actions is good, and the quality of the result suffers. Another issue is that this technique works only when the search space starts becoming large. If it is not, we are simply wasting time by adding in extra nodes and splitting the tree. As a general rule, once we start dealing with games in which a single move can be broken down into actions, and a combinatorial number of moves exist, the technique can be applied (Roelofs 2015).

16.3.2 Expansion Order of Actions (Design Principle)

The key understanding in all this is that we stimulate MCTS to exploit the value found for an action, and thus avoid those moves which do not contain any interesting actions.

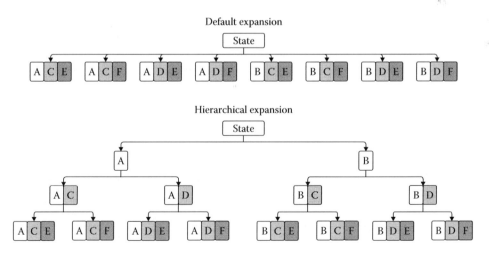

Figure 16.2

Hierarchical expansion for three action sets, each with two actions, resulting in one level for normal expansion, and three levels for hierarchical. (*Note:* As MCTS is a best-first search algorithm, more interesting lines of the tree will be explored in favor of others. The above figure of a balanced tree is to illustrate how expansion happens in a fully explored tree.)

If we can ensure that action sets with apparent good choices are explored first, MCTS will quickly converge and exploit the moves which contain them, avoiding large swathes of uninteresting search space. This basic understanding is why the algorithm performs well while we are counterintuitively increasing the number of nodes in the tree. This approach also has the added benefit of ensuring that most time is spent on those actions which are important as they are simply considered first.

Per example, in *Xenonauts 2* we first expand into orders for enemy units nearer to the player under the assumption that they would provide good opportunities of attack. The action set itself was ordered to prefer attack and ability actions, followed by movement. This ensured that the algorithm was unlikely to miss any crucial attacks on player units. The AI played stronger, and players were quick to label the AI as "stupid" if it missed obvious strong ways to attack thus necessitating the focus on attacks.

In *Berlin* we expanded into regions closer to enemy regions first, under the assumption that crucial troop movement would occur there.

Even if the value of an action is not apparent it is often relatively intuitive to provide an ordering on which actions to explore first. From our earlier example: We might not know the heuristic value of the mind control ability, but we know it tends to be more valuable than any other action. Even if it is not effective in the current situation it allows us to exclude those moves that do not contain it.

To test the overall strength of a given ordering, or find out an ordering if no heuristic is known, we can use two alternative strategies to provide one:

1. *Entropy-based*: The *entropy* of an action set represents the ease with which MCTS can make a decision between the actions in it. If the entropy is low, and thus all values are nearly equal to each other, MCTS will often find it hard to converge on a specific action. If the entropy is high, values of actions differ wildly and MCTS will be quicker to converge. We can simply calculate the entropy of an action set by using the ratio of the number of times MCTS has visited an action compared to its parent as $P(x)$ in *Shannon Entropy*: $-\sum_{i=1}^{n} P(x_i) \log P(x_i)$

2. This technique is mostly used to either discover an ordering we can use as a heuristic or to check whether the heuristic ordering you have defined is good enough.

3. *Dynamic ordering*: Normally, we select a specific ordering to the actions at the start of the search, and which action is expanded is determined by the layer of the tree we are in. Looking at Figure 16.2 we can see that we first expand into {A, B}, followed by {C, D} and finally {E, F}. If we select a random action set to expand into for *each expansion of an action*, we essentially allow MCTS to exploit the ordering itself during the search. To better explain this concept using Figure 16.2: After action A we could expand into {E, F}; after action B we could expand into {C, D}. This strategy works best if actions are truly without sequence. It works because if an action set truly has an important choice, the search will gravitate toward where this action set exists nearest to the root. This strategy tends to give far better results than just choosing an arbitrary ordering as there we can have the bad luck that the action sets with interesting choices exist too deep in the tree, with the search never reaching them (Roelofs 2015).

16.3.3 Dealing with Partial Results (Design Principle)

Using default expansion, only complete moves are explored in MCTS. The end result of a search is simply the best node at the root of the tree: a move that can be applied immediately. However, if we split up the move, the actions at the root are just part of the answer. We need to reconstruct the complete action by iteratively applying the *final node selection* strategy up the tree gathering the resulting actions and reconstructing the move.

When using the above approach, MCTS will not always be able to return a move if the actions in the tree are not sufficient to create a complete move. We used two different strategies to complete a so-called partial move, in order of performance:

1. *Estimated values*: During the backpropagation phase of MCTS, maintain an average value of the actions used in the playout. When completing a partial move, we simply select the action that scored the best on average through all playouts. This technique worked well when the playout itself was guided by heuristics as well, or even better, a portfolio of heuristics. The actions which returned then would always be at least actions we approved by heuristics, but evaluated in context. This would allow us to reclaim information lost due to MCTS switching between branches of actions.
2. *Heuristics*: Apply the strategies used in the playouts to complete the action, assuming they are using heuristics. This tends to lead to better performance than just randomly completing the action as we can then ensure at least a base level of play.

16.3.4 Pruning Action Sets (Design Principle)

The key concept is that we only explore those actions in MCTS which we think actually need exploration. If a solution is apparent for a certain action set, then there is no reason to add these to the search. By pruning those action sets from expansion all together and letting them be resolved through heuristics we can improve on the quality of the search as it can spend more time on action sets which actually require it.

For example, in *Xenonauts* any unit far away from the area of conflict would either just go to the nearest applicable cover, or move toward the conflict if so requested by any unit in it. We do not need to explore the actions of these units as the choice is rather apparent.

For *Berlin* we determined that regions some distance away from the front should move their units toward the front, as this was the decision returned often by the search.

When applying MCTS to multiplayer games with more than two players, this concept can be applied by only focusing on the strongest player. At expansion into the moves of other players, simply determine the strongest opponent and ignore moves from others (Schadd and Winands 2011).

16.3.5 Iterator-Based Expansion (Implementation)

The default implementation of the expansion phase is to create all actions, adding them as child actions as shown in Figure 16.1. However, if there are many possible moves this tends to be quite wasteful as MCTS might decide that the parent action is no longer interesting after a single iteration. By using an *iterator pattern* and only adding a single action per expansion we can avoid a lot of resource waste resulting in a significant performance boost.

The order in which actions are created by this pattern affects the performance of the algorithm. If the sequence is always the same, the first actions returned will be explored far more often in the overall search. When the first action returned is a badly performing action the node will be undervalued in its first iteration and it might take the algorithm a while before revisiting it, if at all. Returning a random ordering of actions, or providing the best actions according to some heuristic first thus tends to improve the quality of the result.

16.4 Simulation

Complexity rears its ugly head again in the simulation phase of MCTS. In the following sections we will explore how judiciously applying heuristics to guide the playout can increase its value and how abstracting over the simulation can lead to more and better iterations, and thus a better result.

16.4.1 Better Information (Design Principle)

For strategy games the traditional approach, in which we simulate the move chosen by the search by playing random moves until the game ends, tends to give little useful information. Due to the enormous size of the search space, playing random moves rarely gives any interesting results or represents good play. Using heuristic-based strategies tends to increase performance of the algorithm as the information provided by a single playout increases. However, this does come at an expense: It will ensure that certain actions are overlooked in the simulation and that the AI works with partial information. This in turn can result in exploitable behavior as the AI becomes blind to certain actions, or even lower performance if the AI misses crucial actions.

Heuristics strategies can further decrease performance if they are expensive to compute. Increasing the time in simulation reduces the number of iterations of MCTS, in turn reducing performance. On the other hand, heuristic strategies can actually speed up the simulation by ensuring that a game ends quickly in the simulation phase. A game played randomly can take quite a lot longer before it ends as opposed to a game played with a valid strategy.

The best of both worlds is to use a mixed strategy approach, often called an epsilon-greedy playout, resulting in far stronger play than a pure random or heuristic strategy. This can be achieved by constructing a weighted portfolio of strategies to use in the play-out, including the default random playout, and selecting an action from this portfolio (Roelofs 2015).

16.4.2 Abstract Your Simulation (Design Principle)

Most often the simulation phase uses the actual game rules as they are readily available and correct. However due to the fact that by their very nature strategy games tend to be complex problems, it is advisable to use an abstraction in the simulation phase. Instead of actually calculating the results of sending your units and simulating the full conflict using game logic, build an abstraction of the conflict and define a function that given a setup quickly calculates whether the conflict is a loss or victory. The key to this approach is that the actions explored within the tree are still legal moves in your game.

In *Xenonauts* using the actual game logic was infeasible as it was tied to too many systems outside the AI and performance-wise was never intended to be used in simulations. We therefore created a model in which soldiers were represented solely by their computed strength (based on their health, inventory, and abilities), and position (to calculate cover and LOS). The outcome of confrontations then became a simple computation that could be iterated over much more quickly. Actions executed during the expansion and selection phases, and thus not in simulation, would be executed using actual logic to ensure they would be correct. The moment the search entered simulation, the current values of the state would be transferred to the constructed model.

16.5 Backpropagation

Game AI programmers have ample experience in constructing evaluation functions in order to enact specific behavior on a character. Modeling an evaluation function for a search technique has some minor, albeit very important, distinctions. The primary difference is that how we structure our evaluation function influences not only the results found (and thus the behavior of the character), but also influences the *behavior of the search* as it executes.

MCTS has a poor track record for tactical decision-making. More accurately, it struggles with problems that have a very narrow path of victory or success. The game Tic Tac Toe is a prime example of this: Making a single mistake will lead to a loss. A simple evaluation function that returns –1 for losses and that returns +1 for wins will take quite a while to converge on the proper set of moves. However, if we severely punish the AI for losses with –100, MCTS displays a very paranoid behavior in which it will only select nodes that give the enemy no chance of a win. The end result is a search that converges to the correct move far sooner.

Adjusting the evaluation function in this way causes MCTS to quickly move away from nodes that lead to negative reinforcement, or alternatively make it so that it is eager to explore nodes that have not encountered any losses.

Proper evaluation functions, such as evaluating the margin of victory, that give continuous values are preferred. However, these functions run the risk of diluting which actions are better from the perspective of the algorithm. We would rather have that the search explores one action deeper than keep switching between two actions of similar value. Changing the range of your function to make the differences in actions more apparent often leads to better results.

16.6 Selection

The goal of the selection phase is to determine the "best" node according to some strategy, often *UCT*. The optimization in this section is based on the fact that only a single node per layer gets its value updated during backpropagation. Also, as MCTS starts to converge, most nodes do not, or barely, change their position in this order. So, instead of repeatedly recomputing the rank of each node during selection, an optimized variation of insertion sort can be used to cache the rank of each node and store which node should be selected next. This becomes particularly important when the number of moves or actions increases. A code example of this is provided in Listing 16.1. In a single thread environment, or in *playout* parallelization, this solution will be sufficient. If a *root* parallelization technique is chosen, the update of this order should be moved to the backpropagation phase, in order to more easily lock the node in question (Chaslot et al. 2008).

Listing 16.1 also showcases an often overlooked requirement: The *selection* phase of MCTS should ensure that all child nodes have received some minimum number of visits T (often $T = 20$) before actively selecting the best child. This ensures that the value of the node is somewhat reliable, and not just the result of a single lucky playout.

Listing 16.1. Returns the next node to visit, after all children have been visited a minimum number of times.

```
public Node selectNextNode(Node node, int minVisits)
{
    Array<TreeSearchNode> children = node.getChildren();
    int childrenNo = children.size;
    int minVisitsOnParent = minVisits * childrenNo;

    // If the parent node hasn't been visited a minimum
    // number of times, select the next appropriate child.
    if(minVisitsOnParent > node.visits) {
        return children.get(node.visits % childrenNo);
    }
    else if(minVisitsOnParent == node.visits) {
        // Sort all children once, the sorted state
        // which we'll keep updated afterwards with
        // minimal effort
        children.sort(nodeComparator);
    }
    else {
        // The first child is always the one updated;
        // so it is the only node we need to sort to
        // a new location.
        Node frontChild = children.first();

        // Determine its new location, often very near
        // to it's previous location.
        int i = 1;
        for ( ; i < children.size; i++){
            if(frontChild.score >= children.get(i).score)
                break;
        }

        i--;

        // Move everyone by one, and set the child
        // at its newest index.
        if(i > 0) {
            if(i == 1) {
```

(Continued)

```
                        // Special case where we optimize for
                        // when we are just better than the
                        // second item. (often)
                        Object[] items = children.items;
                        items[0] = items[1];
                        items[1] = frontChild;
                    }
                    else {
                        Object[] items = children.items;
                        System.arraycopy(items, 1, items, 0, i);
                        items[i] = frontChild;
                    }
                }
                else {
                    return frontChild;
                }
            }

    return children.first();
}
```

16.7 Conclusion

This chapter introduced new insights and optimizations to tackle large and complex problems using MCTS. Any reader implementing MCTS is recommended to skim through the sections marked as implementation to find optimizations to the algorithm that can be used in any situation.

The main technique explored to deal with complexity is to break up a move into smaller actions, and provide these in order of apparent importance such that the strengths of MCTS may be used to explore and exploit the search space, judicially applying heuristics to various aspects of the algorithm to make it feasible.

Readers interested in the details of hierarchical expansion and concrete results on the comparison of the various techniques outlined in this chapter are referred to (Roelofs 2015), where a complete analysis is presented using the game of *Berlin*.

References

Chaslot, G. Monte-Carlo Tree Search. Maastricht University, 2010.

Chaslot, G. M. J.-B., M. H. M. Winands, and H. J. van den Herik. Parallel Monte-Carlo Tree Search. In *Computers and Games*, eds. H. Jaap van den Herik, X. Xu, Z. Ma, and M. H. M. Winands. Berlin, Germany: Springer, pp. 60–71, 2008.

Churchill, D., and M. Buro. 2015. Hierarchical Portfolio Search: Prismata's Robust AI Architecture for Games with Large Search Spaces. *Proceedings of the Artificial Intelligence in Interactive Digital Entertainment Conference*. University of California, Santa Cruz, 2015.

Roelofs, G. Action space representation in combinatorial multi-armed bandits. Maastricht University, 2015.

Schadd, M. P. D., and M. H. M. Winands. Best reply search for multiplayer games. *IEEE Transactions on Computational Intelligence and AI in Games* 3(1): 57–66, 2011

Sturtevant, N. R. Monte Carlo tree search and related algorithms for games. In *Game AI Pro 2: Collected Wisdom of Game AI Professionals*, ed. S. Rabin. Boca Raton, FL: CRC Press, 2015, pp. 265–281.

17

Petri Nets and AI Arbitration

Sergio Ocio Barriales

17.1 Introduction

A Petri net is an abstract, formal model of information flow in systems, particularly in those in which events can occur concurrently and where some form of synchronization or ordering is required.

In a video game, there are a variety of situations that require some sort of coordination or arbitration to decide what a group of agents should be doing and make sure their actions do not invalidate their peers'. Deciding who gets to use a special resource (e.g., a mounted gun) or how roles are selected in a combat scenario are examples of problems Petri nets can help resolve. Also, since these nets are represented as graphs and, at a first glance, can look similar to FSMs, they are easy for AI developers who are familiar with that approach to understand.

In this chapter, we will talk about Petri nets and how they can be used for arbitration in multiagent scenarios.

17.2 Petri Net Basics

Petri nets are a graphical and mathematical modeling language used to describe how information flows in a distributed system. They were developed by Carl Adam Petri in 1962 (Petri 1962). A Petri net is a graph built using two different types of nodes: *places* and *transitions*. Places are connected to transitions via directed *arcs* and vice versa, but nodes of the same type can never be connected directly. A *place* represents a condition and a *transition* is a gate between places. There is a fourth element involved, a *token*. Tokens are found inside places, and a single place can hold multiple tokens; when a token is present in a place, it means that the condition associated with that place is met.

In a Petri net, execution is controlled by the position and movement of the tokens. For example, in Figure 17.1a we have a single token in $p1$, which means that this node is the only one that is currently active.

Transitions have a number of preconditions, or input places. A token in an input place is interpreted to mean that the precondition is true. Transitions are fired when they are enabled; a transition is enabled when it has tokens in each of its input places. For example, in Figure 17.1a, $t1$ is enabled and can fire. Figure 17.1b shows the state of the net after the first transition is triggered. When a transition fires, it consumes the tokens in its input places and generates a new token for each of its output places. This new state—also known as a *marking*—of the net enables $t2$; $t3$ is not yet enabled, since it is missing a token in $p3$. The execution continues in Figure 17.1c. Finally, $t3$ is enabled, since both $p3$ and $p4$ have tokens. The net keeps running and $p5$ receives a token, as shown in Figure 17.1d.

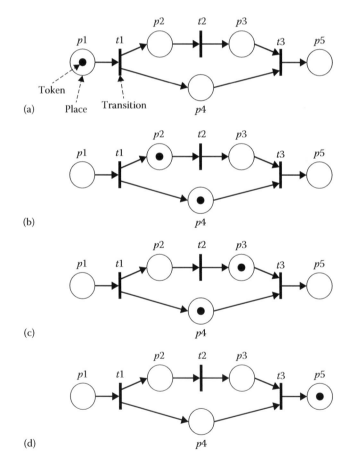

Figure 17.1

An example Petri net with five places and three transitions.

Running a Petri net becomes more complicated if multiple transitions are connected to a single place. In this case, the evolution of the network is no longer deterministic; if we have one token in the place, every transition will be enabled. If we fire any of the transitions, the token will be consumed, invalidating the remaining, previously enabled transitions. In this case, we say the transitions are *in conflict*. Depending on which one we choose to trigger, we will have different resulting markings, as shown in Figure 17.2.

Arcs can be labeled with the number of tokens a transition requires in a particular input place before it can be enabled. After the transition fires, it will consume that number of tokens from the input place. Likewise, a transition can generate multiple tokens if the arc to the output place shows the label. This is depicted in Figure 17.3.

We can also have transitions without any input place—*source* transitions—that are unconditionally enabled and whose sole purpose is generating tokens, and transitions with no output place—*sink* transitions—that only consume tokens.

This section has only presented a few examples and key concepts, but a vast amount of work has been done with Petri nets over the past 50 years. Many resources are available on them; the articles by Peterson (Peterson 1977) and by Murata (Murata 1989) are good places to start.

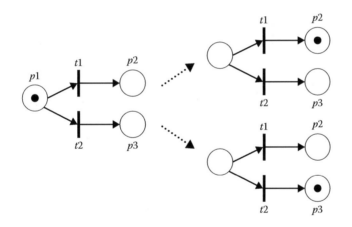

Figure 17.2

Both *t1* and *t2* are enabled in this markings; if either fires, the other will be invalidated.

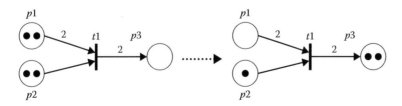

Figure 17.3

Transitions can consume and generate multiple tokens as required.

17.3 An Example Arbitration Scenario

Now that we know the basics, let us discuss how we can use Petri nets to coordinate multiple characters in a setup where they must utilize a finite number of nonshareable resources (i.e., resources that can only be used by a single agent) to accomplish their goal. To do so, we will choose an example and analyze how we would model it with Petri nets.

Let us depict a scenario where a group of agents that were unaware of enemy presence are suddenly attacked by the player. After an initial reaction, the agents must decide how to deal with the attacker. A quick analysis of the surroundings reveals there is a mounted gun nearby, and the AI decides controlling that weapon is the key, but only one character can use the special weapon at a time. So how do we decide who goes first?

One option is to use a first-in, first-out solution, so the first agent that gets updated by the system selects and locks the gun, whereas the others select other actions. However, this could lead to the AI that is farthest from the weapon being chosen, making the characters look stupid and inefficient. We could also modify this approach and have each AI ask the rest of the group "is there anyone closer than me to the gun?" and skip the assignment until the closest agent is updated and selected. This method generates a better looking result, but the behaviors and decision-making logic of our agents gets polluted by these interagent communication requirements.

Trying to resolve every potential scenario by having individual behaviors take into account every other possible AI and their desires and intentions can be problematic. Having a higher level AI entity—that we will call *arbiter*—help agents resolve these resource management disputes can help simplify the system. It is the arbiter's job to track and manage resources and assign them to the appropriate actors.

Going back to our example, a Petri net controls the arbiter. For simplicity, we will just focus on assigning the mounted gun, and will not model how other points are chosen for the NPCs, so the net will just queue AI agents' requests and put them on hold until the special weapon is available. In a more complete solution, our agents would not really directly know about the mounted gun—they would be running a behavior that would try to use the best possible point to attack the enemy, and this point would be returned by the arbiter. Agents would not be reserving this point directly, but just registering to be assigned the best possible one.

Initially, this net's marking is as shown in Figure 17.4a, a single token in the "gun available" place, which indicates nobody has requested using the gun and thus it is still unused. When the agents in the group start reacting to discovering the enemy, they register with the system. For each registered actor, we get a new in the "ready to assign" place. Once the "n" agents in the group are registered, the "start assignment" transition is enabled and run, getting our "n" tokens transferred to the "ready to use gun" place. This is shown in Figure 17.4b and c.

In order for the "assign gun" transition to run, we need the gun to be available and at least one actor to be ready to use it. When both conditions are met, the transition runs some logic to select the best agent to fill the role—based on factors such as proximity to the gun, archetype and capabilities (e.g., an AI agent with better accuracy would be preferred)—and a token will be transferred to "gun busy," while the "gun available" and one of the tokens "ready to use" are consumed. We show this in Figure 17.4d.

If at any point the agent manning the gun is incapacitated, the "agent incapacitated" transition will trigger, moving the token to "gun available," as shown in Figure 17.4e. As long as we have other agents to reassign, the process will continue, just as depicted in Figure 17.4f.

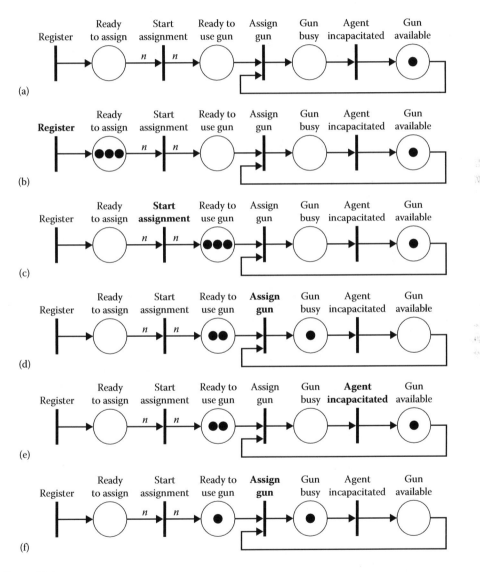

Figure 17.4

The arbiter runs a simple Petri net that controls the status of the mounted gun, allowing other agents to register and get their turn as the weapon becomes available.

17.4 Conclusion

Petri nets are powerful tools that offer a simple way to describe processes where actions need to be synchronized or depend on one another. They have been applied to a broad set of problems, from manufacturing to chemistry and beyond.

In this chapter, we have presented the basics of what the Petri net model offers and how to apply them to model resource arbitration for multiagent scenarios. By using a Petri net, we can separate group coordination to use shared resources from individual behaviors, leaving the high-level decision-making and agent synchronization in the hands of the net. This greatly simplifies the complexity of our single agent behaviors.

References

Murata, T. 1989. Petri nets: Properties, analysis and applications. *Proceedings of the IEEE*, 77(4), 541.

Peterson, J. L. 1977. Petri nets. *ACM Computing Surveys (CSUR)*, 9(3), 223–252.

Petri, C. A. 1962. *Kommunikation mit Automaten*. Bonn, Germany: Institut für Instrumentelle Mathematik, Schriften des IIM Nr. 2, 1962, Second Edition, New York: Griffiss Air Force Base, Technical Report RADC-TR-65-377, Vol. 1, 1966, Suppl. 1, English translation.

18

Hierarchical Portfolio Search in *Prismata*

David Churchill and Michael Buro

18.1 Introduction

Many unique challenges are faced when trying to write an AI system for a modern online strategy game. Players can control groups of tens or even hundreds of units, each with their own unique properties and strategies, making for a gigantic number of possible actions to consider at any given state of the game. Even state-of-the-art search algorithms such as Monte Carlo Tree Search (MCTS) are unable to cope with such large action spaces, as they typically require the exploration of all possible actions from a given state in a search tree. In addition to the difficulty of dealing with large state and action spaces, other design features must be considered such as varying difficulty settings, robustness to game changes, and single player replay value.

In this chapter we will discuss the AI system designed for *Prismata*, the online strategy game developed by Lunarch Studios. For the *Prismata* AI, a new algorithm called Hierarchical Portfolio Search (HPS) was created which reduces the action space for complex strategy games, which helps deal with all of the challenges listed above. This results in a powerful search-based system capable of producing intelligent actions while using a modular design which is robust to changes in game properties.

18.2 AI Design Goals

In addition to creating an intelligent AI system for strategy games, other design decisions should also be considered in order to ensure an enjoyable user experience. When designing *Prismata*, the following design goals were laid out for the AI system:

- *New player tutorial*: Strategy games often have complex rules, many different unit types, and a variety of scenarios that the player must adjust to. All of this leads to a steep learning curve. Our primary goal with the *Prismata* AI was to aid new players as they learned to play the game, so that they would eventually become ready to face other players on the online ladder. This required the creation of several different difficulty settings so that players could continue to be challenged from beginner all the way up to expert play.
- *Single player replay value*: Single player missions in video games are sometimes designed as rule-based sequences of events that players must navigate to achieve some goal. In *Prismata*, that goal is to destroy all of the enemy units, which can become quite boring if the AI does the same thing every time it encounters similar situations. Our goal was to build a dynamic AI system capable of using a variety of strategies so that it does not employ the exact same tactics each time.
- *Robust to change*: Unlike games in the past which were finalized, shipped, and forgotten about, modern online strategy games are subject to constant design and balance changes. Due to their competitive nature, designers often tweak unit properties and game rules as players find strategies that are too powerful, too weak, or simply not fun to play against. We required an AI system that is able to cope with these changes and not rely on handcrafted solutions that rely on specific unit properties which would be costly to update and maintain as units continue to change.
- *Intuitive/modular design*: Often times when creating a game, the behavior of the AI system, although intelligent, may not fit with the designer's views of how the AI should act. By designing the AI in such a way that its structure is modular and intuitive, designers are better able to understand the capabilities of the AI system and thus can more easily make suggestions on how behaviors should be modified. This leads to a much smoother overall design process than if the AI system was simply viewed as a magic black box by designers.

18.3 *Prismata* Gameplay Overview

Before diving into the details of the AI system, we need to understand the characteristics of the game it is playing. Here we will briefly describe the high-level game rules for *Prismata*.

Prismata is a two-player online strategy game, best described as a hybrid between a real-time strategy (RTS) game and a collectible card game. Players take turns building resources, using unit abilities, purchasing new units, and attempting to destroy the units of their opponents. Unlike many strategy/card games, there is no hidden information in *Prismata*—no hands of cards or decks to draw from. Units that players control are globally visible and players can purchase additional units from a shared pool of available units which changes randomly at the start of each game (similar to the board game Dominion [Vaccarino 2009]). The rules of *Prismata* are also deterministic, meaning that there is no possible way for the AI to cheat by magically drawing the right card from the top of the deck, or by getting some good "luck" when most needed. In game theoretic terms, this makes *Prismata* a two-player, perfect information, zero-sum, alternating move game. This means that the AI does not need any move history in order to pick its next move—it can act strictly on the visible game state at any time.

Due to these properties, the *Prismata* AI was designed as a module that is separate from the rest of the game engine, accepts a current game state as input, and as output produces an ordered sequence of actions for the current player to perform. This architecture also gives the developer an option of where to run the AI calculations—a game state could be sent over a network to be calculated (if the game is being run on a platform with limited computational power), or run locally on a user's hardware (as they are in *Prismata*).

18.4 Hierarchical Portfolio Search

The algorithm that was used to form the basis of the *Prismata* AI is hierarchical portfolio search (Churchill and Buro 2015). HPS was designed to make decisions in games with extremely large state and action spaces, such as strategy games. It is an extension of the portfolio greedy search algorithm, which is a hill climbing algorithm that has been used to guide combat in RTS games (Churchill and Buro 2013). The main idea behind these "portfolio-based" search systems is to reduce the branching factor of the game tree by using a portfolio of algorithms to generate a much smaller, yet hopefully intelligent set of actions. These algorithms can range from simple hand-coded heuristics to complex search algorithms. This method is useful in games where a player's decision space can be decomposed into many individual actions. For example, in an RTS game in which a player controls an army of units, or in a card game where a player can play a sequence of cards. These decompositions are typically done *tactically*, so that each grouping in the portfolio contains similar actions, such as attacking, defending, and so on.

HPS is a bottom-up, two-level hierarchical search system which was originally inspired by historical military command structures. The bottom layer consists of the portfolio of algorithms described above, which generate multiple suggestions for each tactical area of the game. At the top layer, all possible combinations of those actions sequences generated by the portfolio are then iterated over by a high-level game tree search technique (such as alpha–beta or MCTS) which makes the final decision on which action sequence to perform. While this method will not produce the truly optimal move on a given turn it does quite well (as we will show in Section 18.5). Furthermore, the original problem may have contained so many action possibilities that deciding among them was intractable.

18.4.1 Components of HPS

HPS consists of several individual components that are used to form the search system. We define these components as follows:

- **State** s containing all relevant game information
- **Move** m = <a_1, a_2, …, a_k>, a sequence of Actions a_i
- **Player** function p [m = p(s)]

- Takes as input a State s
- Performs the Move decision logic
- Returns Move m generated by p at state s
- **Game** function g [s' = g(s, p_1, p_2)]
  - Takes as input state s and Player functions p_1, p_2
  - Performs game rules/logic
  - Implements Moves generated by p_1, p_2 until game is over
  - Returns resulting game State s'

These components are the same as those needed for most AI systems which work on abstract games.

In order to fully implement HPS, we will need to define two more key components. The first is a *Partial Player* function. This function is similar to a Player function, but instead of computing a complete turn Move for a player in the game, it computes a partial move associated with a tactical decomposition. For example, in a RTS game if a player controls multiple types of units, a Partial Player may compute moves for only a specific type of unit, or for units on a specific part of the map.

- **Partial Player** function pp [m = pp(s)]
  - Takes as input State s
  - Performs decision logic for a subset of the turn
  - Returns partial Move m to perform at state S

The final component of HPS is the portfolio itself, which is simply a collection of Partial Player functions:

- **Portfolio** P = <pp_1, pp_2, ..., pp_n>

The internal structure of the portfolio will depend on the type of game being played, however it is most useful if the Partial Players are grouped by tactical category or game phase. Iterating over all moves produced by combinations of Partial Players in the portfolio is done by the `GenerateChildren` procedure in Listing 18.1. Once we have created a portfolio, we can then apply any high-level game tree search algorithm to search over all legal move combinations produced by the portfolio.

18.4.2 Portfolio Creation

An important factor in the success of HPS is the creation of the Portfolio itself, since only actions generated by partial players within the portfolio will be considered by the top-level search. Two factors are important when designing the portfolio: The tactical decomposition used to partition the portfolio and the variety of Partial Players contained within each partition.

In Table 18.1, we can see an example tactical decomposition for the portfolio of partial players in *Prismata*, which is broken down by game phase. The Defense is the "blocking" phase of the game, and contains partial players that decide in which order to assign blocking units. The ability phase involves players using the abilities of units to do things such as gather resources or attack the opponent. The buy phase involves purchasing additional

Table 18.1 A Sample Portfolio Used in *Prismata*

Defense	Ability	Buy	Breach
Min cost loss	Attack all	Buy attack	Breach cost
Save attackers	Leave block	Buy defense	Breach attack
	Do not attack	Buy econ	

Note: Organized by tactical game phase.

units to grow the player's army. Finally, the breach phase involves assigning damage to enemy units in order to kill them. Each of these partial players only compute actions which are legal in that phase of the game—so in order to generate a sequence of actions which comprises the entire turn we must concatenate actions produced by one of the Partial Players from each phase.

This "game phase" decomposition works well for games that can be broken down temporally, however not all games have such abstract notions. Depending on the game you are writing AI for, your decomposition may be different. For example, in a RTS game setting categories may involve different types of units, or a geometric decomposition of units placed in different locations of the map. In strategy card games these categories could be separated by different mechanics such as card drawing, card vs. card combat, or spell casting. It is vital that you include a wide variety of tactical Partial Players so that the high-level search algorithm is able to search a wide strategy space, hopefully finding an overall strong move for the turn.

18.4.3 State Evaluation

Even with the aid of an action space reducing method such as HPS, games that go on for many turns produce very large game trees which we cannot hope to search to completion. We therefore must employ a heuristic evaluation on the game states at leaf nodes in the search. Evaluation functions vary dramatically from game to game, and usually depend on some domain-specific knowledge. For example, early heuristic evaluations for Chess involved assigning points to pieces, such as 1 point for a Pawn and 9 points for a Queen, with a simple player sum difference used as the state evaluation.

These formula-based evaluations have had some success, but they are outperformed by a method known as a *symmetric game playout* (Churchill and Buro 2015). The concept behind a symmetric game playout is to assign a simple deterministic rule-based policy to both players in the game, and then play the game out to the end using that policy. Even if the policy is not optimal, the idea is that if both players are following the same policy then the winner of the game is likely to have had an advantage at the original evaluated state. The Game function is used to perform this playout for evaluation in HPS. We can see a full example of the HPS system using Negamax as the top-level search in Listing 18.1.

18.4.4 HPS Algorithm

Now that we have discussed all of the components of HPS, we can see a sample implementation of HPS in Listing 18.1, which uses the Negamax algorithm as the high-level search algorithm. Negamax is used here for brevity, but could be replaced by any high-level search algorithm or learning technique (such as MCTS, alpha–beta, or evolutionary

```
procedure HPS(State s, Portfolio p)
    return NegaMax(s, p, maxDepth)

procedure GenerateChildren(State s, Portfolio p)
    m[] = empty set
    for all move phases f in s
        m[f] = empty set
        for PartialPlayers pp in p[f]
            m[f].add(pp(s))
    moves[] = crossProduct(m[f]: move phase f)
    return ApplyMovesToState(moves, s)

procedure NegaMax(State s, Portfolio p, Depth d)
    if (d == 0) or s.isTerminal()
        Player e = playout player for evaluation
        return Game(s, e, e).eval()
    children[] = GenerateChildren(s, p)
    bestVal = -infty
    for all c in children
        val = -NegaMax(c, p, d-1)
        bestVal = max(bestVal, val)
    return bestVal
```

algorithms). The core idea of HPS is not in the specific high-level search algorithm that you use choose, but rather in limiting the large action space that is passed in to the search by first generating a reasonable-sized set of candidate moves to consider.

18.4.5 Creating Multiple Difficulty Settings

In most games, it is desirable to have multiple difficulty settings for the AI that players can choose from so that they can learn the game rules and face an opponent of appropriate skill. One of the strengths of HPS is the ease with which different difficulty settings can be created simply by modifying the Partial Players contained in the portfolio, or by modifying the parameters of the high-level search. There are many difficulty settings in *Prismata*, which were all created in this way, they are as follows:

- *Master Bot*: Uses a Portfolio of 12 Partial Players and does a 3000 ms MCTS search within HPS, chosen as a balance between search strength and player wait time
- *Expert Bot*: Uses the same Portfolio as Master Bot, with a 2-ply Alpha–Beta search, typical execution times are under 100 ms.
- *Medium Bot*: Picks a random move from Master Bot's Portfolio
- *Easy Bot*: Same as Medium, but with weaker defensive purchasing
- *Pacifist Bot*: Same as Medium, but never attacks
- *Random Bot*: All actions taken are randomly

An experiment was performed, which played 10,000 games between each difficulty setting pairing, the results of which can be seen in Table 18.2. The final column shows

Table 18.2 Results of 10,000 Rounds of Round Robin between Each Difficulty Setting

	UCT100	AB100	Expert	Medium	Easy	Random	AVG
UCT100	—	52.1	67.3	96.4	99.7	99.9	83.1
AB100	47.9	—	68.0	94.7	99.5	99.9	82.0
Expert	32.7	32.0	—	90.7	98.9	99.8	70.8
Medium	3.6	5.3	9.3	—	85.9	97.4	40.3
Easy	0.3	0.5	1.1	14.1	—	86.3	20.5
Random	0.1	0.1	0.2	2.6	13.7	—	3.3

Note: Score = win% + (draw%/2) for row difficulty versus column difficulty. UCT100 and AB100 refer to UCT (MCTS with UCB-1 action selection) and Alpha–Beta each with 100 ms think times. Pacifist Bot was omitted, since it is designed not to attack and therefore cannot win.

the average scores of each difficulty setting (100 meaning unbeatable, 0 meaning never wins), from which we can see that the difficulty settings perform in line with their intuitive descriptions. The modular design of HPS allowed us to make slight changes to the portfolio and search settings to create multiple difficulty settings, which satisfied our design goals of creating both a new player tutorial for beginners, and strong opponents for expert players.

18.5 Evaluation of HPS Playing Strength

To test the strength of the AI system in *Prismata* in an unbiased fashion, an experiment was run in which the AI secretly played against human players on the ranked *Prismata* ladder. *Prismata*'s main competitive form of play is the "Ranked" play mode, where players queue for games and are auto-matched with players of similar ranking. Player skill is determined via a ranking system that starts at Tier 1 and progresses by winning games up until Tier 10. Once players reach Tier 10, they then ranked using a numerical system similar to those used in chess.

To test against humans, a custom build of the client was created in which the AI queued for a ranked play match, played the game against whichever human it matched against, and then requeued once the match was finished. The AI system was given randomized clicking timers in order to minimize the chances that the human players would suspect that they were playing against an AI. The AI used was the hardest difficulty setting, "Master Bot," which used MCTS as its top-level search with a think time of 3 seconds. After 48 hours and just over 200 games played, the AI had achieved a rank of Tier 6 with 48% progression toward Tier 7, and stayed at that rank for several hours. This placed the AI's skill level within the top 25% of human players on the *Prismata* rank ladder, the distribution of which can be seen in Figure 18.1.

Since this experiment was performed, many improvements have been made to the AI, such as improved tactical decision-making in the blocking and breaching phase, an improved playout player, and fixing some obvious blunders that the bot made in its attack phase. Master Bot is estimated to now be at Tier 8 skill level, which is stronger than all but the top 10%–15% of human players.

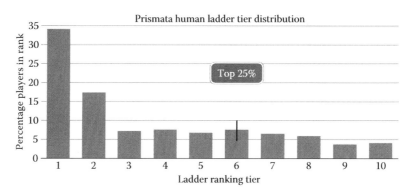

Figure 18.1

Distribution of player rankings in "Ranked" play mode in *Prismata*. After 48 hours of testing, Master Bot had achieved a rank of Tier 6 with 48% progress toward Rank 7, which placed its skill level in the top 25% of human players.

18.6 Conclusion

In this chapter, we have introduced HPS, a new algorithm which was designed to make strong decisions in games with large state and action spaces. HPS has been in use for over two years as the basis of the *Prismata* AI system, with nearly a million games played versus human opponents. Because of its modular design, search-based decision-making, and intuitive architecture, it has been robust to over 20 game balance patches, producing intelligent actions even with major changes to many of units in *Prismata*.

The search-based nature of the AI has yielded a system which has high replay value, in which the bot will have different styles of play depending on the given state of the game. Creating different difficulty settings using HPS was merely a matter of changing the algorithms in the underlying portfolio, which resulted in a total of seven different difficulties—from pacifist punching bag to the clever Master Bot. These difficulty settings have proved to be a valuable tool for teaching players the rules of the game as they progress to new skill levels. The hardest difficulty of the *Prismata* AI, Master Bot, was played in secret on the human ranked ladder and achieved a skill within the top 25% of human players, showing that HPS is capable of producing strong moves in a real-world competitive video game.

References

Churchill, D., Buro, M. 2013. Portfolio greedy search and simulation for large-scale combat in starcraft. *CIG*, Niagara Falls, ON, Canada, 2013.

Churchill, D., Buro, M. 2015. Hierarchical portfolio search: Prismata's robust AI architecture for games with large search spaces. *AIIDE*, Santa Cruz, CA, 2015.

Vaccarino, D. X. 2009. Dominion. Rio Grande Games.